"... towns without houses..."

A History of Kay County, Oklahoma

Written and Researched
by Darlene Platt

Edited by Keith Barley

All Photos are in the Public Domain

".. the Devil and the Deity are in the details .."

Bold Ideas Publishing
Ponca City, Oklahoma 74604

ISBN-13: 978-0986162411
ISBN-10: 0986162418

Printed in the United States of America

Cover Illustration: © Keith Barley

Table of Contents

Introduction

History is not static. It is not formed from trees, rocks, rivers or mountains. It is the action of people who imagine and then do. For millennia Kay County was static until the primitives of prehistory made their appearance. Their actions had to be discovered much later from archaeological digs. There will be a supplement to this Volume which will put faces to the names and context to events on a more personal level. It will also introduce Preston and Margaret George, amateur archaeologists of professional stature, who will offer their account of life in the Kay County wilderness.

The ancestors of these migrates from Asia became the indigenous peoples that ranged over the North American continent. Those preferring the open spaces of the Great Plains roamed through Kay County hunting the bison that numbered in the millions across the tall grass lands from the Dakotas to the Red River at the southern border of what is today Oklahoma. Those with a bent to growing their food were attracted to the rivers, streams and wooded areas of north central and eastern Oklahoma. At first, having no written language, their history was written in the memory of the people. It would take those willing the listen to preserve it for us.

As the rest of the world developed technologies to travel great distances and seek out new lands to discover and conquer, if need be, it was inevitable that their impact would be felt in north America and Kay County. These were the Empire builders. Predominately, Spain, France and England would compete for control over the continent for centuries. England began on the East coast. Spain in the Caribbean, Florida and later up the Mississippi River and its tributaries to Oklahoma. Spain would claim all they saw for their homeland. France would follow a similar path but were more interested in trade goods and less in converting the locals than the Spanish. Spain would build missions and forts while the French would learn the ways of the natives to gain their cooperation for trade.

European conflicts put pressure on both countries to relinquish and regain control. The area of Kay County would pass back and forth between Spain and France a number of times. At a time when France claimed the area, the United States, after gaining independence from England, offered to buy the Louisiana claim. Napoleon needed the money for his European campaigns. The Louisiana Purchase as it came to be called put Oklahoma and Kay County in the hands of the United States.

Since no one was sure what constituted the purchase, the United States commissioned military and civilian explorers to map the area to settle property claims in dispute with Spain, Mexico, and or England. The Americans were able to enlist the help of the less belligerent indigenous peoples (Indians) in this effort. Unlike the Europeans, the Americans were a more energetic, ambitious, independent and productive people. As a nation, growth and progress was in their DNA. Those uncomfortable with the urbanization of the East set out for the West to make their own way. It was difficult for most of them to see potential and not exploit it. Fortunately, or unfortunately, this often meant pushing those less ambitious out of the way, i.e., the Indians. It was not meant to be malicious but simply a clash of cultures. Fight back as they may, the Indians would lose unless they adopted a new mindset. Today many tribes retain their traditions while utilizing American industry. In the meantime, the Indians were forced to sell or more often give up ancestral hunting grounds to be herded into Indian lands not of their choosing.

For a time the Indian Territories were places to be left alone, but not for long. Cattlemen in Texas realized a market for their beef cattle in the East. However, the new railroad lines were north of Indian Territory in Kansas and Missouri Territories. Shipping the cattle east meant huge detours around Oklahoma. Across the northern part of Oklahoma was the area assigned to the Cherokee Indians. Because of it's sparse use by the Cherokee, cattlemen began driving their cattle across this Outlet to Kansas. A number of well worn trails were established such as the Chisholm Trail. When the cattlemen began to stop along the trail to allow their cattle to graze, the Cherokee saw an opportunity to enrich themselves and started charging a head tax for the privilege. The cattlemen were willing to do this as long as it stayed reasonable and amiable. However, others thought if the cattlemen can use the land for cattle why can't we use it for farming? Soon pressure would be brought to bear on the U.S. Government to open these lands to settlers.

Those who spoke loudly and vociferously (the Boomers) for settlement started to take action and intrude into the Indian Territories in violation of treaties between the government and the tribes. Under those Presidents unconcerned with the fate of the Indians, tribal areas were assumed and made available for settlement. Since no way of systematically allotting land was feasible, the government decided a 'first come first served' method would be the best. They would arrange a Land Run. All who were interested would register then race to the platted land and literally stake a claim. The first of these was the Land Run of 1889, in the area of Oklahoma City and south of the Cherokee Outlet. Later, the Land Run of 1893 would begin the settlement of the area that included Kay County.

Only the heartiest and most determined survived living on an open undeveloped plain with nothing but buffalo grass and severe weather to contend with. The land was fertile and the successful grew crops that would eventually feed the world. Soon communities were established. Some were planned while others cropped up on their own. In any case, these pioneers brought with them commerce, culture and the independent character of America.

Multiple economic set backs brought on by unbridled market speculation resulting in depressions and World War drove the prices of wheat and corn so low many farms began to fail. Droughts and unpredictable weather contributed to the hardship. It looked like subsistence farming was the future.

From time to time a farmer would drill a water well only to hit a pocket of natural gas. For those with the resources it could be piped off for light and heat, but for the most part it was a nuisance. Somewhere in the East they were refining oil into kerosene which Oklahoman's, like everyone else, used for their lamps. If an Oklahoman was unlucky enough to strike oil, it was a mess that spoiled crop land and fouled equipment. Until …!

Early in the twentieth century E.W. Marland came to Oklahoma. His vision was not for farming but oil. He meant to find it and sell it in the East. Later, he took it a step further and refined it on the spot shipping the products all over the world. He wound up employing the unemployed who were then fed by the area farmers. The wealth he was able to create enriched the entire area, bringing the railroad, roads, services jobs and all the businesses that communities require.

This overview is what you can expect in the following pages but in comprehensive detail. The events and the people who made the history you will experience maintained the notion that there are in the minds of the men of action, **"... towns without houses...".**

CHAPTER ONE:
Crossroads on the Prairie

No one can say just when, why, or from where mankind first came to the area that would become Kay County, Oklahoma. What can be said of Oklahoma is that it is one of the oldest areas of human occupation on the North American Continent. Man arrived 10-25,000 years ago, drawn by the abundance of game. Central and western Oklahoma offered good grazing and water holes which were able to support herds of prehistoric bison and mammoths. Hunters followed game along streams and river valleys, taking shelter in caves and under rock ledges.[1]

By the latter part of the prehistoric period 2000 B.C. to 1500 A.D., they began to live in villages located in river valleys.[2] Two of these cultures were the Clovis and Folsom. Clovis spearheads prove these hunters were here around 11,000 years ago.[3] Signs of hunting camps and prehistoric villages are scattered along creeks and rivers in the state.[4]

The Golden Age of Oklahoma's prehistory was the era of the Spiro culture, between 500-1300 A.D.[5] Drawn to Oklahoma by the abundance of game, they appeared along with their man-made mounds, in eastern Oklahoma. This culture, located along navigable waterways, played an important role in controlling trade, monitoring traders, travelers, and potential enemies. The Spiro civilization was very well developed---a complex society, highly skilled and intelligent.[6] This can be seen in artifacts found at the Spiro mounds located six miles east of Spiro, Oklahoma in La Flore County.[7] Though they lived in the pre-Columbian period classified as the "Stone Age", it is significant to note their used of metal goods.[8] The culture began to decline sometime after 1200 A.D. Meanwhile, in Europe the stage was being set for the discovery of Oklahoma.[9] By the time Europeans first encountered the Caddo, Pawnee and Wichita,[10] considered to be ancestors of the Caddoan Indians, these natives were bison hunters and part-time farmers.

Life was never completely static on the North American continent. Even before the Europeans arrived, various native tribes split, merged, warred on each other, and made truces. They migrated from one region to another to such a degree that modern Americans might find it difficult to imagine. Climatic changes, drought, famine, and threats from more powerful tribes set off successive waves of migration. This caused some tribes to drift hundreds of miles away from their places of origin. When Europeans came, they introduced natives to horses, guns, new technologies and unknown diseases (especially deadly to the American natives), causing the increasing instability to continue.[11]

Spanish explorer, Francisco Vasquez de Coronado, entered the North America from the southwest in the 1500's and Spaniard, Hernando De Soto, entered from the southeast. Each party had the same objective in mind, to find a rich empire, both failed. It is believed the two parties came within 200 miles of each other, unaware of the others' existence.[12] They were the first non-Indian people to view this region. On Castle Rock, at the Cimarron River north of Boise City, Oklahoma, is the inscription "Coronado 1541". This is the first historical record in Oklahoma.[13] Coronado was the first explorer to keep records of his adventures in the Oklahoma region. He gave us our first knowledge of the natives occupying Oklahoma at that time. He wrote that because wood was scarce except near rivers, his men were forced to cook over cow-dung fires and go for days without water. He wrote in his journal of an "...ocean of short grass..." and where the buffalo roamed as being"...so level and bare...", noticing the absence of trees on the plains.[14] His adventures took him through Oklahoma, where he found Indians who would fight for their food supplies. Coronado did not notice the agricultural potential of the land beneath his horse's hooves. He claimed the area for Spain, including the western half of the Mississippi Valley. In 1539, De Soto discovered the "Father of Waters", the Mississippi River, Claiming the lower Mississippi River for Spain. The Spanish could see no further reason to return to Oklahoma, but Kay County was now under the Spanish flag.

Spain had laid claim to a vast territory. Monarchs attempted to hold these claims by spreading their influence among the natives. The problem of holding onto the empire was especially acute in colonies north of Mexico. Spanish authorities created a line of settlements along the far northern frontier in New Mexico, Texas, and Louisiana in an attempt to keep foreign intruders out and create a buffer zone for Mexico. The Spanish worked diligently through missionary efforts, military expeditions and trade to win and hold the friendship and loyalty of such Indian tribes as the Wichita and Pawnee. They became frequent visitors in the grass-thatched lodges of the Wichita villages and earthen lodges of the Pawnee.[15]

In 1682, Robert Cavalier Sieur de la Salle claimed all lands drained by the Mississippi and its tributaries for France.[16] French explorers in the late 1600's and early 1700's traveled the streams of the Mississippi River Valley looking for Indians with whom to barter. The Osage and Kansa Indians were more closely allied with the French, as seen in the number of French surnames among them to this day. Unlike the English and Spanish, the French were more interested in the fur trade than settling the land. There was a ready market in France and its colonies for such American products as furs, skins, meat, lard and tallow. Whenever the intermittent European wars of the seventeenth and eighteenth centuries permitted safe sea transportation, French colonial merchants would ship these products abroad for a profit.

The natives of the Great Plains found themselves involved in European politics. European desires for native loyalties sometimes created these situations for the tribes. When French traders began to by-pass the Osage to trade directly with the Wichita in Kansas, the Osage were annoyed. They did not want the Wichita to have the guns the French were willing to trade for Wichita goods. Eventually, trouble between the Osage and Wichita Indians led to the Wichita moving south down the Arkansas River, where they formed a settlement in Kay County at the point where Deer Creek empties into the Arkansas River east of present day Newkirk. Many historians argue that "settlement" is too grand a term for what was, in all probability, two Wichita villages of 1500 to 2500 people living in 75 to 125 thatched lodges.[17] These villages have been referred to as "Ferdinandina", "Fernandino", but contemporaries refer to them simply as the twin villages.[18]

What made them unique was the cooperative nature of the business conducted between French hunters and the Wichita. There was a good market in France and its colonies for the furs and meat products abundantly available on the Great Plains. In the early 1700's French hunters began coming up the Arkansas River from Arkansas Post, near the mouth of the river to trade with the Wichita of the twin villages. They found the villages well located, easily reached by canoe, near prairies that were abundant with game, and near the Great Salt Plain salt deposits just to the west of what is now Alfalfa County. The prairies abounded with bison, deer and mule deer with black bear and grizzly bear in the western two-thirds of Kansas. These animals provided furs, skins, tallow and lard that fetched a good price in France. Thus, between 1716 and 1758, many French hunters came up the Arkansas River to spend a season, or even live year-round, among the friendly Wichita in the twin villages.[19]

This situation was not welcomed by the Spanish in New Mexico and Texas. The French presence on the Arkansas River was a threat to their security south of the Red River. At the same time this presented an even greater danger. The French not only brought the Wichita dyes, cloth, iron implements and other trade goods, but guns and ammunition as well. Spanish colonial authorities became alarmed when these last items began appearing among the Comanche Indians who lived west of the Wichita. Comanches were implacable enemies that habitually raided Spanish settlements deep into Mexico. No wonder the Spanish were concerned about what went on at the twin villages and among the Wichita Indians. The Spanish were so concerned that they questioned every traveler who appeared in New Mexico from the east. This procedure furnished them a good description of life in the twin villages on Deer Creek in Kay County.

In the year 1750, when the French–Wichita activity in these villages was at a peak, a Spaniard, Felipe de Sandoval, passed through on his way to Santa Fe. Sandoval had been captured by the English more than two years before and imprisoned at hard labor in Jamaica. He escaped to a French colony, then made his way back to Spanish territory. Traveling up the Mississippi to the Arkansas River, he joined six other travelers going west. Sandoval recalled that, "... after fifty days we arrived at two towns of Indians, very friendly to the Frenchmen, which were situated on the banks of this river, and called Panipiquees. All are lined [tattooed]... We were well received by them, and we stayed twenty days in these towns, during which time I observed with care the two towns. They are near each other. The houses are (made) of poles and grass, all fortified with poles and earth, with openings. They are pagans, without social graces, but are good-natured. They live there the year round. They plant corn, beans, and squash. There are about 500 men in the two towns. All use firearms, although they are not very accomplished in their use. They have powder and bullets supplied by the French. They are at war with various nations, among them the Pananas [Pawnees] (who are) also pagans and devoted to the French... ."

He continued to say, "They are very friendly with the French and trade with them, and in my short time there, the

17

commandant or French general, in the name of his sovereign, had given them various things: vermilion, beads, knives, guns, ammunition, hats, cloth, and other supplies, and the French flag which is there. I saw it. They keep it in their town, caring for it with diligence and affection. They have some horses that another nation, their comrades, had given them who in this region are called Comanches. Although I came here by boat, I observed it is good flat land, without mountains, having some woods, and a few gullies. The rivers that join the Napestle [Arkansas] come down from the north. These are the river of San Andres, that of Febre [i.e. Fabry; the Canadian River], the small one [the Cimarron?], and the salty one [Salt fork rather than Salt Creek?], and along all these banks there are many bison. From these towns I left in the company of the aforementioned Frenchmen, and twenty Panipiquees or Jumanes, for the Comanches..."[20]

Sandoval's account shows that it was a busy place and that the Wichita were used to the presence of Frenchmen. Very likely those conditions continued until European warfare put a damper on trade about 1758. The twin villages disappeared when the Wichita moved south toward the Red River, under pressure from the Osage.[21] by the time the French and Indian, or Seven Years' War, ended in 1763, the French, who traded with the twin villages, found themselves ousted from North America. As a part of the settlement of the war they had to give up their claims to North America. They awarded their colony of Louisiana (by which they claimed Oklahoma) to Spain, as agreed to in the "Family Compact Agreement".[22]

Even as one European power departed Kay County, a new power began to emerge to the east: the United States. The land was claimed by the Spanish while English colonists laid claim to broad strips of America from the Carolinas and Virginia to the Pacific, labeling the western land their land as well. Though very weak at first, the same war that removed the French from the twin villages pushed English colonists on the Atlantic seaboard deeper into discontent with their mother country. This discontentment became the American Revolution in 1775. The revolution was a success for the colonies and the United States was born. The survival of this struggling new country was by no means assured. England and Spain watched, waiting, ready to take advantage of any weakness. In the case of Spain, it was an apprehensive regard. Americans showed an avariciousness for land that made Spanish authorities on the western frontier nervous. When Napoleon took control of most of Europe at the turn of the nineteenth century, he appropriated Spain's colony of Louisiana, placing Oklahoma once again under French rule. But that rule was short-lived for Napoleon sold the colony for $15 million dollars to the United States in 1803.

Once again Spain found itself uneasily facing aggressive Americans across the Mississippi River. In 1803 President Thomas Jefferson decided to send the first of several expeditions westward to determine the extent of the Louisiana Purchase. Meriwether Lewis and William Clark traveled in a northwest directions, up the Mississippi River, across the Rocky Mountains to the Pacific Ocean on the most famous of these explorations. In October, 1804, William Dunbar and George Hunter started up the Red and Arkansas Rivers.[23] This expedition hoped to reach the headwaters of the rivers and determine the exact boundaries of the United States with respect to Spanish territory to the southwest, but did not succeed. In 1805 Lieutenant Zebulon Montgomery Pike led a similar trip northward to find the headwaters of the Mississippi River. Within months of his return from this trip, he was ordered out again, this time up the Arkansas River to find its headwaters.

In each of these expeditions, one of President Jefferson's motivations was to learn more about the lands and the people brought into the United States by the Louisiana Purchase. But Jefferson, fascinated by natural history, had an even more important and immediate reason for these expeditions. There was a need for accurate information about the American-Spanish boundaries in the southwest. The French government was not specific about what it was selling in the Louisiana Purchase and simply passed territory to the United States as it was received from Spain. Spain claimed its eastern boundary lay just west of the Arroyo Hondo in western Louisiana, but the United States claimed it lay farther west along the Rio Grande.[24] In fact, as Pike was leaving St. Louis for the west, American and Spanish armies were facing each other belligerently across the Arroyo Hondo.[25] Information gained by the Pike Expedition about Louisiana Territory would help resolve the boundary question and help avert possible conflict between Spain and the United States.

Accompanying Pike was First Lieutenant James Biddle Wilkinson, the son of General James Wilkinson of the Aaron Burr conspiracy. Young Wilkinson was ordered to leave the main body of the expedition in central Kansas and turn south to explore the lower reaches of the Arkansas River. The expedition, as ordered, left St. Louis on July 15, 1806 and headed westward up the Missouri River. Their route took them up the Osage River along the Neosho, Verdigris, Smoky Hill and Republican Rivers into central Kansas. Near Larned, Kansas, on the Arkansas River, Wilkinson and five others, along with two Osage scouts, turned southward. They expected to have an easy time just float down river and return to the Mississippi within two to three weeks. They carried enough supplies for 21 days in their two canoes and all were capable hunters in an area teeming with game. However, they were plagued by bad luck almost from the beginning taking 73 days to reach the Mississippi.[26]

It was late October and cold weather came early that year, the river was already icy. The party had gone less than 100 yards when they had to get out of their canoes and tow them through the shallow water and ice, making only five miles before dark. Progress was so slow that two days later they abandoned their canoes and set off walking along the riverbanks. Each man carried with him a gun, buffalo robe, and a few cups of corn. At the mouth of the Little Arkansas they found deeper water, constructed two piroques (dugout canoes), and were once again water borne. But luck was not with them as they found more shallow water. They had to tow their canoes while wading ankle-deep in the icy river. The canoe carrying their ammunition and fresh supply of meat capsized, leaving them hungry with no means to hunt. To add to their woe, they found themselves in the hunting grounds of the unfriendly Pawnee.

The Wilkinson party pressed on. Just north of the present-day Kansas-Oklahoma border their luck finally changed. They encountered a winter hunting party of Osage Indians who welcomed Wilkinson as a friend. The Osage killed a supply of fresh meat for the party of hungry explorers. Wilkinson was recognized as the man who once befriended a group of Osage chiefs on a visit to Washington. Now, hundreds of miles away on the prairie, these Osage Indians helped him. They asked him to accompany them to see one of the chiefs, Tuttasuggy, who was ill. Wilkinson agreed and on November 30, 1806, traveled by mule to an Osage village located near present day Ponca City, Oklahoma.[27] They were the first official American explorers to enter Kay County, Oklahoma.

Wilkinson's party spent several days in the Kay County area. Resupplied, they hoped to move on down the Arkansas, but the ice-choked river made travel by canoe difficult. On December 3 they halted once again for three days near the mouth of the Salt Fork, hoping the ice would clear. Wilkinson used the time to explore the surrounding country.

When the party embarked again, travel was little better. The river was still icy and the temperature had dropped. The men were forced to hack a path for their canoes with axes in the frigid water. A snow storm overtook them before they reached the junction of the Arkansas and Cimarron Rivers, capsizing one of the canoes, again leaving them exhausted, frostbitten and hungry. They finally made it down the Arkansas River to the Three Forks area. Late in December they reached the Arkansas-Oklahoma line and ended their journey at the Arkansas Post on January 9, 1807. They had accomplished their assignment, to explore and map the Arkansas and take geographical and topographical notes of the area. They noted camps and village sites of the Osage that would be useful information in case of a war with Spain. They had also met, befriended and made treaties with Osages in the Three Forks area. Though the work of the Wilkinson party was overshadowed by the more spectacular and dramatic adventures of the Pike party, it contributed to the American government's knowledge of the Louisiana Territory and the area that would one day be Kay County and Oklahoma.[28]

By the time the next American Party reached Kay County, conditions were somewhat different. The year was 1811 and relations between the United States and Spain were sometimes strained, especially when American traders attempted to take goods into New Mexico, or tried to appropriate Spanish territory along the frontier.[29] There was also a possibility that in the event of a war between France and England, (which broke out the next year), Spain might be dragged into the hostilities as an English ally. Americans were interested in the vast Louisiana Territory and keeping peace with the powerful native tribes living there. George Champlin Sibley was sent to visit the Plains tribes, under orders from the Superintendent of Indian Affairs for Missouri, William Clark. The primary and official reason for Sibley, a 29 year old Indian agent from Fort Osage in Missouri Territory, was to win the tribes over to the side of the United States.[30] Sibley had a strong interest in the future of the American West. Unofficially, he hoped to visit the great salt deposits that he heard existed in the area now known as the Great Salt Plains near Cherokee, Oklahoma.[31] His motive may have been merely curiosity or that he hoped to engage in salt mining as a business venture, since salt was an important commodity on the frontier.

Sibley left Fort Osage on May 11, 1811, with a servant, a French interpreter, the Osage war chief San Oreille, and four other Osages. By early June he had accomplished his mission of visiting and making peace with the Kansa and Pawnee tribes. He then turned south toward the rumored salt deposits.

Unlike Wilkinson's' expedition, Sibley's was a pleasurable adventure. The season was summer, the company congenial, and the plains abounded with game to hunt. On the Arkansas River where it crosses the Kansas-Oklahoma border, his party came upon a Little Osage hunting camp (a band of the Osage tribe), one of several in the vicinity. It consisted of the whole tribe, men, women, children, horses and dogs. Another hunting camp was that of Chief Clermont, of the Great Osage (another band of the Osage tribe), who had expressed a wish for better relations with the United States Government. Sibley decided to visit Chief Clermont and traveled with the Little Osage band he met on the Arkansas River. Regarding them as old friends, he enjoyed every minute of the 10 days trip south to Clermont's camp.

Sometime on the 21st or 22nd of June, Sibley and the Little Osage Band crossed the future state line of Oklahoma and entered what would become Kay County, Oklahoma. Near the vicinity of Blackwell, they found Clermont's camp. Sibley described the area as "...abounding in game...", the climate as "...salubrious and pleasant..." and the soil as being "...fertile and fruitful...".[32]

Before Sibley turned west, succeeding in his quest for the Great Salt Plains, he presented Clermont with a American flag. Though Sibley's expedition was as much a pleasure trip as official mission, he helped secure the friendship of the powerful Osage people for the United States, and extended American influence into Oklahoma by way of Kay County.[33]

Through the early years of the 1800's all of Oklahoma, including Kay County, lay at the center of a struggle for control of the vast heartland of North America. While Europeans and later Americans bid for loyalties of the perplexed native tribes, they made the best of the situation. The Indians adopted new ways that appealed to them, otherwise carrying on with traditional ways of life. The new country to the east, no longer weak after defeating England twice, was now spilling its population across the Mississippi River. The "long knives"*, as the natives called them, carved out farms and set traps on Oklahoma streams, with little regard for the Indians that laid claim to the land.[24] By the early 1820's the politics and priorities of the United States would change the face of things west of the Mississippi forever.

23

Oklahoma and Kay County would have to change with them.

* A term referring to the military by the Iroquois of the northeast but used generally to describe aggressive non-native people.

CHAPTER TWO:
Indian Territory

Through the early 1800's the region, one day to be known as Oklahoma, followed a course similar to other frontiers in the United States. Backwoodsmen filtered into the area, followed by families intent on establishing farms. Settlements formed, soon to become permanent towns similar to those their founders left back in states such as Mississippi, Tennessee and Kentucky. This was especially true in eastern Oklahoma, where early settlers, such as Nathaniel Pryor, arrived soon after the War of 1812 to congregate along the Grand, Illinois and Verdigris Rivers.[1] American traders and trappers, working out of the Three Forks area, may have ventured up the Arkansas or Salt Fork Rivers finding them just as inviting as the French had nearly a century before.

They would not, however, find the twin villages at Deer Creek still inhabited by the Wichita. They had moved southward to the Red River Valley where, deserted by their former French allies and decimated by European diseases (1778 and 1801 epidemics of smallpox), they lived in poverty.[2] Instead, Americans found, as did young Lieutenant Wilkinson and Agent Sibley, transient parties of Pawnees, Kiowas and Osages.

Late in the 1700's while the Spanish were still in possession of Louisiana, provincial authorities denied the powerful French fur trader Pierre Chouteau of St. Louis, trading privileges with the Osages; giving them instead to a Spaniard, Manuel Lisa.[3] Chouteau moved his trading enterprise south from Salina into the Three Forks area of eastern Oklahoma to the junction of the Arkansas, Verdigris and Grand (Neosho) rivers. He persuaded around 50 percent of the Osage tribe, under chiefs Big Track and Clermont (Claremore), to move south as well.[4] It was these clients of Chouteau's that Wilkinson met on the Arkansas River in 1806. The region to be known as Kay County was still vacant of permanent Indian or American settlements, even though it was a popular seasonal hunting ground for the

Osage.

Tribal Migration and The U.S. Government

The nature of settlement in eastern Oklahoma, in the early 1800's determined the unique destiny of Kay County. Some Cherokee living in the newly formed southeastern states of Tennessee, Kentucky, Georgia and Alabama were intent on establishing new homes on the far western frontier in Arkansas Territory. Cherokee desiring to go west received permission to begin their journey, guaranteed by a treaty with the United States, signed on July 8, 1817. It stated that the Cherokee would receive as much land in the west as they were giving up in the east. Two thousand Cherokee left for new homes in northeast Arkansas, becoming known as the 'Western Cherokee" and later as the "Old Settlers".[5] Along with the Cherokee came white Americans pouring across the Mississippi River into Arkansas, Missouri, and Louisiana territories. As more and more white settlers crowded into Arkansas, it looked as if this frontier would follow the pattern of similar areas. The land would fill up with settlers, a territory would be organized, and eventually a new state would be formed. It would just be a matter of time.

Another factor encouraging the influx of pioneers was the settlement of the long-standing boundary dispute between the United States and Spain in 1819. The Adams-Onis Treaty defined boundary lines between the United States and Spanish territories. These boundaries followed the Red River and the 100th meridian, dividing Texas and Oklahoma, Kay County now lay within the United States. With this barrier to settlement removed, more settlers began to pour into the area. Two years later, in 1821, Mexico won its independence from Spain.[6] As a result of their victory, Mexico took over Spanish provinces in the west. Traders were optimistic when they heard Mexico was going to lift trade and expeditions began originating in eastern Oklahoma near the Three Forks settlements and the newly established Fort Gibson.[7] Lands west of Arkansas seemed to face a bright future.

The federal government however envisioned their own

out- come for Oklahoma. Though eager pioneers saw the lands west of Arkansas as a future state, the government saw the lands as the solution to a long-standing problem, what to do with Native Americans. In 1803, President Thomas Jefferson had visions of turning Louisiana Territory into a giant Indian reservation when he purchased it from France. It was his thought that an "Indian Territory" could be created to receive all the eastern tribes where they could live in protected isolation, out of the path of white settlement. White settlers were already diminishing the land available for his proposed Indian Territory. Yet, as more and more Americans were suggesting, in fact demanding, that Indians east of the Mississippi River be expelled, the federal government began to look upon present day Oklahoma, the region just southwest of Missouri, as a diminished "Indian Territory". What a better place for them than the wild, arid, sparsely populated land west of Arkansas known as the "Great American Desert", a description made by Major Stephen H. Long. Long was to explore the Red River, but he actually explored the Canadian River, and his description kept many frontier Americans from moving into the Oklahoma area. Some believed the "Great American Desert" was a natural, God-given barrier to American expansion, designed to prevent too much dispersal of the small American population.[9] Surely, politicians reasoned, no one else would want to settle such a wasteland. Therefore, it could be set aside for the Indians. Eastern tribes could be resettled there, along with those who moved into Arkansas and eastern Oklahoma earlier. The idea was not a new one, for the British tried it in 1763 after the French and Indian War in hopes of preventing further problems by separating the settlers and Indians.[10]

Time and again throughout the infancy of the United States, the government forced different tribes to give up portions of their lands and move onto smaller "reservations". The dual purpose was for preventing further conflict and freeing Indian land for cultivation by white farmers. Members of the Five Civilized Tribes tried to cooperate with the United States government hoping to protect their lands. They also tried to accept the white man's ways in the hope they would be accepted by their white neighbors.[11] However, avaricious frontier farmers saw that forcing Indians on to reservations meant freeing little-used land for them to have for settlement and exploitation. Voices calling for the complete removal of tribes east of the Mississippi grew louder and stronger than those calling for fair and honorable treatment of Indians.

The Osages claimed much of this part of the Plains. They resented the presence of the Western Cherokee who migrated across the Mississippi into Arkansas and Missouri. It became necessary for an agreement to be reached with the Osage tribe. Steps to reach such and agreement were undertaken in 1817 when Cherokee agent, William Lovely, bought a 7,000,000 acre tract of land from the Osages. This land was north of the Arkansas River and east of the Verdigris River in northeastern Oklahoma. It was just west of Cherokee lands in Arkansas and was to be their hunting grounds. The hope was that this would help prevent further bloodshed between the Cherokee and Osages.[12] Conflict continued over the hunting grounds and led to frequent raids and bloodshed on both sides as Osage war parties would attack Cherokee hunting parties. In October, 1817, near Claremore Mound, the Cherokee launched a retaliatory attack on the Osage. This attack has been considered one of the bloodiest Indian battles in Oklahoma history.[13] The attack merely angered the Osage, who took their vengeance out on everyone, including whites. In 1824, a major from Ft. Gibson was killed by the Osage. As a result, the United States government exacted a treaty with the Osage, who ceded all their land in Oklahoma. The Osages were moved into Kansas, leaving the northeastern section of Oklahoma, known as Indian Territory, vacant and available for the resettlement of the Cherokee and other tribes. On May 6, 1828, the Western Cherokee agreed to move further west, out of Arkansas, due to white settlers.

Soon other Indian tribes from eastern states began moving into "Indian Territory" on land specifically set aside for them. The diminished Indian Territory would include western portions of

Arkansas after new boundaries were established. The United States government moved all whites out of the area, giving them land in Arkansas. They would forfeit the land if they did not leave Indian Territory by December 28, 1828.[14] Indian treaties, along with the Intercourse Act of March 30, 1802, forbade white settlement and regulated trade with the Indians beyond Fort Smith, Arkansas. This idea did not set well with settlers who had already created farms, towns and counties in western Arkansas. The United States Army stood by to enforce these treaties, forming an "Indian Line" which would force settlers to travel north into Iowa or south to Texas. As long as other land was available, it was easy for the government to keep white settlers out of Indian Territory.[15] Oklahoma was on a unique course, the result of being set aside for the resettlement of immigrant Indian tribes.

A faction of the Cherokee tribe, still living in Georgia, agreed to move to Indian Territory through the Treaty of New Echota, signed December 29, 1835. This treaty, which sharply divided the tribe, provided the Cherokee with a "perpetual outlet west, and free and unmolested use of all the country west " of their northeastern Oklahoma land.[16] It would allow them access to the buffalo ranges for hunting purposes and since it bordered on Spanish territory, the outlet guaranteed the Cherokee would never be surrounded by American settlers. This was the birth of the "Cherokee Outlet", a 57-mile wide strip across the northern border of Oklahoma from the 96th meridian west to the 100th meridian.

Just north of the Outlet, in what is now the state of Kansas, lay a narrow ribbon of land less than three miles wide. It stretched from the Missouri line to the 100th meridian due to a discrepancy between two surveys to determine the north boundary of the Outlet and became known as the "Cherokee Strip". The first survey was conducted by the Reverend Isaac McCoy. His starting point was the southeast corner of the Osage Reservation in Kansas as defined by the Osage treaty of 1825. The second survey was made by General Joseph E. Johnson in accordance with the Kansas-Nebraska Bill of 1854. This bill fixed the south line of Kansas at the 37th parallel of north latitude. The two and 46/100th miles between the two survey lines was claimed by both the Cherokee and the state of Kansas.[17] (Common usage of the terms "strip" and "outlet" have become interchangeable, but in fact there is a distinct difference.)

The Five Civilized Tribes

Surrounding territories including Arkansas, Missouri, Kansas and the Republic of Texas, soon filled with enough white settlers and black slaves to achieve statehood. Well before the Civil War era, Indian Territory became the new home of the "Five Civilized Tribes": the Cherokee, Creek, Chickasaw, Choctaw, and Seminole nations, along with several smaller tribes, who purchased land east of the 96th meridian or in the Outlet. The Outlet itself, little used by its Cherokee owners except to hunt buffalo and grazing livestock on the eastern edge, lay nearly vacant. Most Cherokee preferred to live east of the Outlet in the Cherokee Nation proper, where timbered hills felt more like the homes they left east of the Mississippi. The same was true of other tribes: the Senecas, Shawnees and Quapaws, to whom the Cherokee sold land for reservations. They too, preferred to create new homes in the far northeastern corner of Indian Territory.

The years 1830 – 1861 were considered the Golden Years for the Five Civilized Tribes, but this was not to continue.[18] The Civil War started the beginning of the end of Indian Territory. The tribes of Indian territory attempted to remain neutral, but when the Federal government withdrew its troops ending their enforcement of the Indian Line, it was an admission they could no longer protect the Indians from white intrusion. Several tribes within Indian Territory signed agreements with Union forces, but when Confederate forces arrived from Texas, the remaining tribes felt forced to side with the south.[19]

After the fall of Fort Smith it became obvious that a southern victory was not to be. Northerners wanted to do away with tribal governments and their land ownership. Senators

Samuel Pomeroy and James Lane of Kansas managed to put an end to Indian Reservations in Kansas by 1863, forcing tribes living in Kansas to move to Indian Territory. All government treaties with the Five Civilized Tribes in Indian Territory were voided by 1865.[20] The government felt they had forfeited all their rights when they agreed to fight for the Confederacy. In May, 1865, Indian Territory leaders met to decide whether they should continue to fight with the south or surrender. Threats from Union forces caused them to choose not to fight.

While not all of the tribes fought for the Confederacy, they all would suffer as a result of the war, an interruption from which tribal governments never completely recovered. Indian Territory suffered more than any other Confederate state. The winter of 1865-1866 was one of extreme suffering for the Indians. Their lands were stripped of livestock, fences were torn down, homes burned, and former productive fields were a mass of grass and weeds. Short supplies of food and medicine resulted in much hunger, malnutrition and cholera. The Indians of Indian Territory had to rebuild homes, plow the land, plant fields, and heal the wounds inflicted by the war, including quarrels within the tribes between north/south supporters. The Five Civilized Tribes diminished 25% due to disease, malnutrition and war.[21]

A new treaty, the Reconstruction Treaty of 1866, considered the "Seeds of Destruction", was forced upon the tribes. The Cherokee agreed to cede all their lands in Kansas to the United States. This included the three mile wide "Cherokee Strip". By an Act of Congress May 11, 1872, it was provided that the lands of the Strip would be sold and "... the amounts received for the sale be invested in registered five per cent bonds of the United States for the benefit of the Indians."[22] Though the Cherokee Nation retained title to the Cherokee Outlet, they also agreed to allow the federal government to colonize other tribes in the Outlet itself. The federal government began to exercise this option in 1867 with the settlement of several small tribes east of the 96th meridian. They were followed by tribes settling in the Cherokee Outlet itself.

Cherokee Outlet Tribes

Among the tribes that would be settled in the Cherokee Outlet were the Osage, Kansa and Ponca. Soon to be neighbors and a vital part of the Kay County area, they also shared a history. The Osage, Kansa and Ponca tribes were part of a Siouan group that contained around 50 tribes, families and sub tribes, known as the Middle-Mississippi culture. Tribal warfare, disease and population displacement hastened the fall of the culture that seemed to disappear before the arrival of the white man. Their only link with the Sioux family was the Dhegiha language.[23]

Their travels took them to the Ohio River and its junction with the Mississippi. Here the tribes of the Mississippi Siouan Family split into two groups before 1540. The two groups derived their names from the direction they took: the Quapaw (downstream) and the Omaha (upstream). The Omaha Tribe consisted of the Omaha, Osage, Kansa and Ponca. They traveled the area of Osage and Gasconade counties in Missouri where the Osage and Kansa tribes settled along the Osage River east of Jefferson, Missouri. The Omaha tribes continued through Missouri, Iowa, and Minnesota, following the Des Moines River to an area near Pipestone, Minnesota. Later, they journeyed to the Big Sioux River, built a fort and village north of Sioux City, Iowa, around 1700 to 1702.[24] Battles with the Dakota (also know as the Sioux) caused the Omaha group to abandon the village and leave the area.

Traveling west to the area of Lake Andes in South Dakota, they turned north along the Missouri River to the mouth of the White River, where the Omaha remained. Around 1715, the Ponca tribe journeyed on to the Black Hills in search of a better place to live, eventually rejoining the Omaha. After venturing south along the Missouri River, a separation took place between the Omaha and Ponca at Bow Creek near Wynot, Nebraska.[25] The Ponca remained in the vicinity of Niobrara, Nebraska and the Omaha settled in Nebraska to the Northeast. The Osage, Kansa and Ponca would eventually be neighbors in the Cherokee Outlet, surrounding Kay County, Oklahoma.

The Osage

The first tribe to resettle in the Cherokee Outlet was its old claimant, the Osage Indians. Marquettes' autographed map of 1673 provides the first record of the Osage on the Osage River in Missouri.[26] Referred to as "The children of the middle water", the Osages were feared, due to their readiness to fight and their skill and courage during battle.[27] On November 10, 1808, the Osage ceded to the United States all their land running due south from Ft. Clark, Kansas to the Arkansas River and lands west of the Missouri River, which eventually became the Western Cherokee's homeland. The Osage warred with the Cherokee and many neighboring tribes. Due to continuing conflicts, a treaty was drawn up in 1825 in which the Osage ceded all their lands north of the Canadian and Arkansas Rivers, as well as northwest Arkansas, western Missouri and nearly half of Kansas to the United States. In 1829, the Osage, numbering 5000, moved out of Indian Territory to the vicinity of what is now Neosho County, in southeast Kansas.[28]

Like the Cherokee, they were divided by the Civil War. The Great Osage joined the Confederacy, and the Little Osage furnished troops for the Second Indian Brigade of the Union Army.[29] Their reservation was overrun and devastated by guerrillas during the war.[30] Afterwards, they faced increasing pressure from white settlers, who wanted their land in Kansas. In compliance with an Act of Congress on July 15, 1870, their Kansas lands were sold and new lands in the Cherokee Outlet were purchased with the proceeds.[31] This move south into the Cherokee Outlet began the arrival of those Osage who would be most closely associated with the future Kay County, Oklahoma.

The new Osage reservation stretched from the 96th meridian west to the Arkansas River. It consisted of present day Osage County and northeastern Kay County. The tribe attempted to establish small farms but this was some of the poorest land in Indian Territory. Life in the Outlet was no easier then it had been

33

in Kansas.[32] The Osage people, weakened by difficulties of the last few years, now faced a scarcity of food, clothing, and medical supplies.

Agent Isaac Gibson established a new Osage agency at Pawhuska in 1872. Missionaries of the Society of Friends worked to set up day schools and tried to improve living conditions.[33] Catholic missionaries founded the St. Louis Mission at Pawhuska, a school for girls, and St. John's Mission, a school for boys at Hominy. In the 1880's, with the guidance of Agent Laban J. Miles, the Osage Nation formally organized.[34] A constitution was written and a National Council chosen with James Bigheart elected as principal chief. By 1877 the Osage population had diminished to 3001, and by 1886 they numbered 1582, approximately half of what it had been.[35] Disease and dislocation accomplished what enemies had never been able to do: diminish the once proud and powerful Osage. Slowly, the Osage began to recover from the troubles of the past two decades.

The Kansa (Kaw)

The next tribe to move into the Cherokee Outlet was the Kansa (Kaw) who, like the Osage, was part of the Siouan tribe. The Kansa, according to tradition, lived along the Wabash, far up the Ohio River many hundreds of years ago. Tradition says that "---their home at one time was near the shores of 'the sea of the rising sun,' from whence came the mysterious sacred shells of the tribe."[36] When they reached the Missouri River, they followed it upstream, settling within the forks of the Missouri and Kansas Rivers. Subsequently, they moved up the Missouri where their northern most settlement was located at the mouth of Independence Creek, in the northeast corner of Kansas.

The Kansa name went through many variations of spelling through the years. There were at least 125 different versions, some of which were Kanzan, Canzan, Kanzon, Canzon, Kan, Kaw, Can Caw, Kantha, Kansies, Kancez, Canceas, Canses, Quans, Kensier, Curgh and Escansaques.[37] In the Siouan language, the word Kansa refers to "winds", giving reference to them as the "wind people". It is suggested that Kansa meant "those who come like the winds sweeping across the prairies" since the wind was a disturbing element on the plains in the early days. "Kansa" is derived from the Spanish noun, meaning "a troublesome people, those who continually disturb and harass others." It also comes from the verb, cansar, "to molest, to stir up, to harass" and the noun, cansado, "a troublesome fellow, a disturber."[38] The Kansa name was adopted by the Bureau of American Ethnology, but the tribe is most often referred to as the Kaw.

The Osage claimed that the name Kaw, or Kah-sah, meant coward.[39] The Osage, who disliked the Cherokee when they migrated into Arkansas, asked the Kansa to join them in war against the Cherokee in the early nineteenth century. The Kansa refused and eventually the Cherokee came into eastern Oklahoma, depriving the Osage of certain lands. This resulted in the Osage harboring many hard feelings toward the Kansa and warring with them for many years. Even though the term Kah-sah, applied to them by the Osages, meant coward, it does not explain the older and more general word, Cansa or Kansa, used by the Spanish and Father Marquette in 1673.[40]

In 1601, the Spanish explorer, Onate, first met the marauding Kansa.[41] He learned that the Kansa, a wild and powerful tribe, annually pillaged and made war upon the Quivirans (Pawnees) living close to cultivated fields on the Smoky Hill and Kansas Rivers. A great enmity existed between the two tribes with the Kansa bent upon destroying the Pawnee. The Spanish decided to teach the Escansaques or Kansa a lesson---not to make further raids upon the more docile Quivirans. A battle ensued in which many Kansa were killed by the Spanish with their superior weapons. The Kansa mistrusted and disliked the Spanish, but were friendly with the French, whether they were explorers, traders, trappers or missionaries.[42]

The Kansa nation was highly respected for the skill and bravery of its warriors. Their war chiefs were selected through bravery. Zebulon Pike said of them, "In war they are yet more courageous than their Osage brethren; being, although not more than one-third of their number, their most dreaded enemies and frequently making the Pawnees tremble."[43] In his writings he often placed the Kansa nation at the head of the list when enumerating Indian tribes. In later years the Kansa nation seldom initiated war just for the love of fighting but were not slow to defend themselves when attacked. When small parties of their braves were assailed by larger forces on their annual hunting trips, it was frequently said "a handful of the Kansa on the plains, by their skillful defensive maneuvers, could put to flight several times their number of enemies."[44]

Pike visited the Osage villages and recruited Osage guides to lead his expedition to the Pawnee village in northern Kansas. The guides took him fully 100 miles further than necessary, due to their fear of the "Kans". After reaching the Pawnee village, a dozen Kansa came into the camp. Pike induced two of them to accompany his expedition and to enter a treaty council with him and the Osages of his party. The following day Pike met with the Pawnees. An agreement of peace and friendship was entered on September 28, 1806, which lasted through the years between the Kansa, Osage and the United States. Kansa representatives helped with the ceremonies as they removed the Spanish colors and raised the stars and stripes. Highly pleased when the American flag was raised, the Kansa openly professed their pleasure at being under American protection.[45]

The Kansa, masters of a great part of the present state of Kansas, had villages along the Missouri, Kansas and Neosho Rivers and their branches. The earliest know capital was called the "Grand village des Cansez" or "Grand village des Quans" located at the mouth of Independence Creek.[46] M.Etienne Venyard de Bourgmount visited the Kansa there in the summer of 1724. The French wanted to establish friendly relations with border tribes to help prevent further advancement of the Spanish from the Santa Fe region toward the Missouri Valley. A compact of friendship was formed and existed between the Kansa and French for years to come.[47] A second village was located about twenty miles down the Missouri from the Grand village at present-day Oak Mills in Atchison County. "It was probably the first governmental center in Kansas where white men lived in a permanent community, erected buildings and transacted business."[48] It became an important French fort and trading-post.

In 1815 the first formal recorded treaty was made between the Kansa and the United States. It was a treaty of peace, friendship, and forgiveness for the Kansa leaning towards the British during the War of 1812.[49] White Plume, one of the signers, was just coming into prominence and later became one of the great chiefs of the tribe.[50] The Kansa were located at the mouth of the Blue Earth River, two miles east of the present city of Manhattan. Their village consisted of 160 lodge sites, 10 to 50 feet in diameter and served as their capital. In the treaty of June 3, 1825, the Kansa bartered away almost one-half of the state of Kansas, for which they received $4000 in merchandise, horses, cattle, hogs, chickens, an annual tribal annuity of $3500 for twenty years and a limited reservation along the Kansas River. Twenty-three half-breed Kansa children each received a section of land fronting on the north side of the Kansas River. The village became quite a settlement by 1830 with their chief White Plume. The government built him a substantial stone house, but he preferred his wigwam lodge erected in front of the house.[51]

By 1827, a village sprang up on the far eastern allotment. It was composed of agency officers, their families, Indians and some half-breed families. Later, it was learned that the village was on land reserved for the Delaware Indians by their treaty of September 24, 1829. The village, at the site of the present Union Pacific station site in Williamstown, 20 miles east of Topeka, was abandoned. The tribe centered around the Mission Creek Villages. Frederick Chouteau's trading-post, across the river from the settlement, moved to Mission Creek in 1830, followed by Daniel Morgan Boone in 1835.[52]

Entering into another treaty with the government, they

gave up their lands on the Kansas River and were assigned to a twenty square mile reservation in the Neosho valley, near Council Grove. Three new villages were established, each one governed by a chief who obtained the position through birthright.[53] The largest village, located on Cahola Creek south of the present town of Dunlap, was ruled by Hard Chief, (Kah-he-ga-wah-che-cha) until his death in the 1860's. He was succeeded by Al-le-ga-wa-hu, who became one of the greatest chiefs of the Kansa. The second village, that of Fool Chief, (Kah-he-gah-wa-ti-an-gah), was located in the valley near the present town of Dunlap and the third was located near Big John Creek, less than a mile southeast of Council Grove. Peg-gah-hosh-he ruled there until his death in 1870, succeeded by his nephew.[54]

Efforts to improve conditions of the Kansa were made when an impressive Methodist Episcopal Mission was built in 1850. The conservative Kansa were convinced that white civilization would ruin their children, refusing to allow them to join the church or attend the school.[55] The Methodist Indian Mission built them homes but most refused them in favor of their earth lodges. They believed houses breed disease and were not as healthy as wigwams and lodges, but they did stable their ponies in the houses when the weather was bad.[56] Kansa men were instructed in farming and stock-raising, but they considered it to be woman's work; men were raised to be warriors and hunters. A few members of the tribe began to conform to the white way of living, but the Kansa tribe, as a whole, was not influenced enough to change their old ways.[57]

Smallpox was an enemy the Kansa were unable to defend themselves against. Epidemics hit the Kansa tribe in 1827, 1831, 1839, and the winter of 1852-1853. In 1855 another epidemic hit, killing over four hundred. Scattered along the Neosho Valley and on the neighboring slopes were their burial grounds.[58] In succeeding years, many others died from epidemics and hardships they were subjected to by white settles: the killing of game and the introduction of whiskey.

The Kansa reservation reduced in size again after the treaty of 1859. They were moved on to what was referred to as a "diminished reserve", located about four miles southeast of Council Grove. The government constructed substantial buildings, an agency house, stables, store house, council-house, two large frame school buildings and 150 small stone cottages. The plan was to civilize them through education, which included teaching them to farm. Quakers were in charge of teaching them.[59] The mighty Kansa numbered about 1700 in 1846 but continued to decrease as John Delashmitt came from Iowa and enlisted 80 men in the Union Army. Their population of 741 in 1863 decreased the following year to 701.[60]

The Kansa surrendered their happy homes, far-reaching hunting-grounds occupied by the tribe for ages and were driven from one diminished reserve to another. With the coming of the railroad, white settlers were putting great pressure on Washington to open the Indian lands for settlement. In 1872 Columbus Delano, Secretary of the Interior, came to the agency to discuss the removal of the Kansa to Indian Territory. Arriving in a special railroad car, he summoned the chiefs and head men in to council with him. He told them the advantages of going to where they could have a good reservation, be near their kinsmen the Osage, be near other tribes and from the sale of their lands could have enough surplus to improve homes, buy farming supplies and live better than they had ever lived before, all of this in a land teeming with wild game. When he finished, Al-le-ga-wa-hu arose, deliberately folding his blanket beneath his arms. As he recounted the Kansa history, he spoke in slow, measured terms, weighing each word. Stretching to his full six feet, six inches, he looked down into Delano's eyes and vehemently declared: "Be-che-go, great father, you treat my people like a flock of turkeys. You come into our dwelling places and scare us out. We fly over and alight on another stream, but no sooner do we get well settled than again you come along and drive us farther. Ere long we shall find ourselves across the Bah-do-Tunga (mountains) landing in the Ne-sah-tunga (ocean)."[61]

The chief continued protesting against giving up their land, where they had fields and homes and where their dead were sleeping on the hill tops, but to no avail. In the end Delano replied, "It is the policy of the President, to give to the Red Men a country to themselves, where you can meet and mingle together free from the interruption of the whites and it is my duty to say too that you must sell your land here and select a new reservation in Indian Territory."[62] The government took about half of the richest part of Kansas from the Kansa tribe for a mere pittance.

To help with their removal, the Kansa Indian Agent, Mahlon Stubbs, hired 40 men with teams to help with the poorer families. He instructed the others to pack their ponies as if they were going to or from buffalo country.[64] Arriving in Indian Territory 17 days later, in the summer of 1873, they found no buildings for their use. Families of the government employees were cooking meals under the trees and sleeping in tents. Only a small portion of the $25,000 appropriated had been used; the remainder was to revert to the United States treasury at the end of the fiscal year. Agent Stubbs went to Lawrence, Kansas, meeting with the Commissioner of Indian Affairs. He told him of their situation and with winter coming on, that the matter was serious. He received the backing of the commissioner to use the remainder of the appropriated money to build the needed buildings.[65]

The Kansa agency was established among the great oak trees at the junction of Big Beaver Creek and the Arkansas River. Before winter set in a collection of frame buildings was completed. These included an office, commissary, log cabins for the physician and blacksmith, grist mill, saw mill, and a residence for the superintendent. The full-bloods continued to live in tepees and dugouts, but the half-breeds occupied the log cabins built by the government.[66] In 1885 a large four-story stone boarding school was built flanked by the infirmary, barn, and other well constructed buildings.

Conditions continued to be perilous and many Kansa perished. Of the 533 Kansa who arrived in 1873, they saw 339 perish by 1889.[67]   Chief Al-le-ga-wa-hu died shortly after the Kansa reached Oklahoma, and Wa-shun-gah, the last of the blood chiefs, ruled until his death in 1908.[68]   The Kansa village of Washunga was named in his honor.

The Osage and Kansa accepted their removal to Indian Territory peaceably but this did not reflect the general nature of the relations between Native Americans and white Americans. The continuing westward movement of the American frontier caused increasing conflict from the late 1860's into the 1880's. In 1867, councils at Laramie, Wyoming, and Medicine Lodge, Kansas, attempted to alleviate trouble by moving all of the Plains tribes onto reservations in hopes of preventing further bloodshed.[69]   However, Washington found that setting a policy was far easier than implementing it. Even though some tribes would go peaceably, others were prepared to fight to the death to retain their homelands.   The government's reservation policy created sporadic warfare on the Plains and mountains of the West for nearly three decades. The Ponca and Nez Perce were the next two tribes to be assigned reservations in the Cherokee Outlet. Their removals demonstrated the worst of government policies in action.

The Ponca

The Ponca were part of the Siouan tribe which had crossed the Mississippi River centuries earlier. They moved far up the Mississippi River into Minnesota, the Black Hills of South Dakota, and then to Nebraska. There is no known meaning for the name Ponca.[70]   The Osage referred to the Ponca as the "Paw-Hunkah" or "Pah-Hah'n", meaning "gentle leaders".[71] The Omaha, Kansa, Quapaw, Iowa, Otoe and Missouri referred to them as "Ponka".   Other tribes referred to them as "La Pong", "Panka" and "Punka".[72]

When the Ponca were contacted by European explorers, they were considered a typical prairie tribe. The Ponca began trapping for furs in return for trade items they could get from European traders. Explorers, Captain Merriwether Lewis and

Captain William Clark, met the Ponca on September 4, 1804 in the area of the Niobrara River, in northern Nebraska. The Ponca were so friendly that Lewis and Clark stayed with them while exploring the area.[73]

Seven clans of the Ponca tribe were noted for their chieftainship. Ponca were often in conflict with the powerful Sioux. According to tradition, Little Bear went to war with the reigning Ponca chiefs against their enemies, the Sioux. He distinguished himself as a warrior in battle and when the reigning chief's son was slain, he was chosen chief, although his clan was not in power at the time. After his death, his grandson, White Eagle, was chosen chief of the Ponca. White Eagle, a man of rare ability, keen judgment and insight, had the ability as an orator to rouse the spirits of the warriors and spur them on to victory in battle.[74] In another treaty between the United States and the Ponca on March 12, 1858, the Ponca ceded away what was considered the richest and best part of their reservation in Nebraska, retaining land that bordered the Sioux tribe.[75] The United States government promised to protect the tribe's possession of this domain as their permanent home, securing them in their persons and property. This diminished reservation was near the mouth of the Niobrara River in northern Nebraska and southeastern South Dakota. Eventually the federal government forced them to cede one-third of this land in 1865. The government, in return, guaranteed them certain tracts of land and protection from the marauding Sioux.[76]

In 1863, at the hands of the United States government, a crucial blunder was made in their negotiations with the Sioux.[77] In these negotiations, the government ceded to the Sioux all of the Ponca land, both ceded and unceded. The Sioux took advantage of the fact that the Ponca were now considered intruders on Sioux land. The attacks on the Ponca became worse, continuing for eight years with what seemed to be the consent of the United States government. The Ponca repeatedly called upon the government for help but it seemed they were being sacrificed along with their rights. The Ponca tribe had never made war upon the United States. No attempt was made by the United States government to correct the error or protect the Ponca against the Sioux as promised in the 1858 treaty.[78]

The Ponca showed their strength as warriors on June 14, 1872. White Eagle and the Ponca, armed with old-fashioned weapons, were attacked by the deadly Sioux tribe who were armed with modern weapons furnished by the government. The Ponca pushed the Sioux back 20 miles until the Sioux took refuge in the woods. "This was the hardest fought battle between these deadly foes recorded in history and lasted two days. Many Indians were killed and wounded before the battle ended in victory for the Ponca."[79]

This battle did not stop the Sioux attacks. By 1876, conditions had become so bad that one-fourth of the Ponca tribe had lost their lives.[80] The government finally had to take a stand, but it was not one the Ponca expected.

A provision was inserted into the Indian Appropriation Bill authorizing the Secretary of the Interior the sum of $25,000 to remove the Ponca to Indian Territory if they consented to go. A 58 year old Ponca headsman name Standing Bear emerged in this time of crisis as a spokesman for the Ponca.[81] He told the government representatives, "We do not wish to sell our land, and we think no man has the right to take it from us. Here we will live and here we will die."[82] Surprised by the possibility of removal, eight chiefs, including White Eagle, Standing Bear and Little Dance, accompanied an agent to Indian Territory to select a site for a new reservation. The agent tried to get the Ponca chiefs to select an area in northeastern Oklahoma but the chiefs refused and asked to go back to Nebraska. He was so provoked at them that he deserted them with only a few dollars and one blanket each. The chiefs started their journey home by foot, in winter, walking the 500 miles. Fifty cold and hungry days later they reached the Otoe Agency in southern Nebraska. The Otoe agent gave them horses and provisions to make their way as far as the Omaha reservation. There, a sympathetic missionary convinced Standing Bear he should take his protest to the Great Father himself, President Rutherford B. Hayes."[83]

Arriving at Sioux City, Iowa, Standing Bear paused to tell his story to the *Sioux City Journal* and sent an explanatory telegram to the President. A few days later officials from the Indian Bureau arrived at the Ponca Agency in Dakota Territory to speak with Standing Bear. He told them, "This is my land. The Great Father did not give it to me. My people were here and owned this land before there was any Great Father. We sold him some land, but we never sold this. This is mine. God gave it to me. When I want to sell it I will let you know."[84] Standing Bear's defiance caused his arrest the next morning, but he was soon released. Nevertheless, the government refused to give up plans to remove the Ponca to Indian Territory.

The Ponca appealed to the Secretary of the Interior and Commissioner of Indian Affairs, stating they did not consent to being removed and were opposed to leaving their homes. With their appeals disregarded and their refusal to leave of their own free will an order was issued on April 12, 1877 that would force the Ponca's removal. E.A. Howard, of Hillsdale, Michigan, was appointed to effect the removal, with the aid of Army troops if needed.[85] Not only was the removal a violation of the cession agreement of 1865, it was also a violation of Ponca tradition. Unlike many of the Plains tribes, the Ponca were not primarily hunters but farmers. Land tenure for them was important both materially and culturally. Even though they were under constant harassment from the Sioux, the Ponca did not want to give up their lands in Nebraska.

Most of the tribe refused to leave, saying that they would rather die in defense of their homes. On April 30, 1877, E.C. Kemble, United States Indian Inspector, arrived and arranged for the movement of those who were willing to leave.[86] Howard was then ordered to forcefully remove the rest of the tribe. The Ponca were awakened by the Army standing outside their doors with bayonets. They were told they would be leaving for Indian Territory. Although White Eagle did not want to leave the Ponca lands in Nebraska, he saw that his people, like the buffalo, would become extinct and fade into the setting sun if they did not go.[87] The Ponca were only allowed to take what they could carry on their ponies or in wagons. On May 16, 1877, escorted by a detachment of 25 U.S. Troops, the second group left their beloved home in Nebraska for Indian Territory. White Eagle led his tribe to their new home, a journey that became known as the Ponca' "Trail of Tears".[88]

Hampered by heavy rains and high water, the Ponca's journey became an ordeal. Many died along the way. A tornado struck their camp near Milford, Nebraska (20 miles west of Lincoln, Nebraska), and the deaths continued. "An indian became hostile and made a desperate attempt to kill White Eagle, head chief of the tribe, for having allowed the tribe to be brought into this trouble."[89] "Out of approximately 900 people, 200 perished on the trip."[90]

Upon their arrival in Indian Territory, they found their Trail of Tears did not end. It was summer, very hot and still raining. There was little housing, poor food, and inadequate medical supplies at the Quapaw agency, near Baxter Springs, Kansas. Many Ponca were struck down by dysentery, tuberculosis, and malaria. A disease these northern Indians had not encountered before.[91] In addition, no definite provisions had

been made for their permanent settlement. Originally the government planned for them to occupy the Quapaw reservation. The Quapaws were to move further west to the Osage lands, but the

Quapaws refused to leave.[92] The government had also not kept its promise to resupply the Ponca with the farming tools they had left behind in Dakota Territory. With no way to grow their own food, they were dependent on the government for their subsistence. These conditions continued through most of 1877.

In November of 1877, Standing Bear and some companions received permission to go to Washington to visit President Hayes personally. Though Hayes refused their request to be allowed to return to their traditional home on the northern plains, which he felt would set a bad precedent as far as the government was concerned, he did promise that they could choose better lands in Indian Territory for a permanent home.[93]

Late in 1877, with the personal guarantee of President Hayes, three Ponca Chiefs searched out a new reservation in the Cherokee Outlet. This location was west of the Kansa reservation. The Commissioner of Indian Affairs did not want them near the influence of the conservative Kansa. The Ponca agreed on lands further south, that now lay in Kay and Noble counties of Oklahoma.[94] Their new reservation consisted of 101.894 acres astride the Salt Fork river. It was bounded on the north by the south boundary of Range 26 North (Hartford Avenue in Ponca City), on the east by the Arkansas River, on the south by the south boundary of Range 24 North (Noble County, Oklahoma line), and on the west by the Indian Meridian.[95] On July 21, 1878, a large party of Ponca left the Quapaw lands for the area on the Salt Fork. They arrived to take possession July 29, 1878, after a trip of 185 miles in the heat of summer.[96] Once again, it was too late to plant crops, even if they had received the tools and livestock the government had previously promised. Since their annuities had not been paid, there was no money to make purchases or build shelters.[97] Sickness caused by the conditions continued to debilitate the people and kill the weakest. Since leaving their Nebraska home, nearly one-third of the tribe had died and the remainder were sick.[98]

Conditions the Ponca were enduring received national

publicity. There was sympathy among many white Americans, and many Eastern reformers, who were dedicated intellectually to the improvement of conditions for distant Native Americans. Even frontier Americans, who usually saw Indians as potential enemies or obstacles to settling the land, were of the opinion that the Ponca had been treated badly by the government and were deserving of reparations. Former neighbors of the Ponca in Dakota Territory, in fact, asked the government to allow them to return to their old northern homes. These white settlers preferred to have the peaceful Ponca between them and the fierce Sioux.[99] In 1878 the case of the Ponca received even greater national publicity, forcing the government to make fundamental changes in its treatment of Indian tribes and Indians as individuals. The main actors in the drama were two Ponca Indians, Standing Bear and Big Snake.

Standing Bear was the spokesman for the tribe when the Ponca were first ordered to move to Indian Territory. He had never really resigned himself to the removal and agitated continually to be allowed to go home to Dakota Territory. His name was known both on the northern plains from his newspaper releases, and in Washington, D.C., where he appeared before President Hayes to plead the cause of the Ponca. In the early months of 1879, his name and cause became even more famous all over the nation.

Late in the dark days of December, 1878, while disease was still ravaging the Ponca on their Salt Fork reservation, Standing Bear watched as his son died of malaria. On his deathbed, he asked his father not to bury him in the foreign land called Indian Territory, away from his ancestors. Standing Bear had lost a daughter on the trek to the Quapaw Agency, and another child after the tribe's arrival. He also saw his mother-in-law and grandmother die while the Ponca were waiting for a permanent settlement in the Cherokee Outlet.[100] The death of his son was the final blow for Standing Bear. Bowed down with grief, homesick, and wanting to grant his son his final request, Standing Bear put his son's bones in a wagon drawn by two worn-out horses. Standing Bear and a party of 30 followers started home to Dakota Territory and the tribal burying grounds, slipping away from their camp near the mouth of the Chikaskia River, in January, 1879.[101]

The camp on the Chikaskia was eight miles from the agency headquarters. Ponca agent, William H. Whiteman, did not notice the group missing for six days. Upon discovering their absence he notified the army to be on the lookout for them.[102] As a result, of their disappearance the government forbade any Ponca Indian from leaving Indian Territory or taking any property with him. Anyone who did would be arrested for stealing. The action was taken to deter others from trying to return to Nebraska.[103]

Word was sent to the Otoe and Omaha agencies in Kansas and Nebraska of Standing Bear's departure. If seen or asked for any help from the agencies, they were to be arrested. On March 4, the half-starved band arrived at the Omaha Agency where they received a warm welcome from their Omaha friends. General George Crook was ordered to arrest Standing Bear's group and return them to Indian Territory. After Standing Bear was arrested, he was brought before General Crook at a military tribunal. At the tribunal, Standing Bear stood proud, dressed as a proud Ponca chief, wearing leather, draped in a red and blue blanket, with a beaded belt and bear claw necklace. His followers were dressed in white men's clothing. Addressing General Crook, Standing Bear spoke in his own defense saying, "I was to go back to my old place north. I want to save myself and my tribe. My brothers, it seems to me as if I stood in front of a great prairie fire. I would take up my babies and run to save their lives; or as if I stood on the bank of an overflowing river, and I would take my people and fly to higher ground. If a white man had land, and some one should swindle him, that man would try to get it back, and you would not blame him. Look on me. Take pity on me, and help me to save the lives of the women and children. My brothers, a power, which I cannot resist, crowds me down to the ground, I need help."[104]

Standing Bear's plea reached far beyond general Crook. Upon their arrival at the Omaha reservation, they had been the topic of much discussion in the Omaha, Nebraska newspapers. Word of their return had also reached Yankton, Dakota Territory, where petitions for the Ponca to be able to return to their northern homes were circulated. When the petition reached the United States Senate, Senator Paddock of Nebraska and the influential Senator Henry M. Teller of Colorado united to support it. Teller stated that the government's treatment of the Ponca had been "a shame and disgrace to the nation."[105] The Omaha Committee, including a number of prominent citizens and attorneys, seconded the petition and brought suit on behalf of Standing Bear before Judge Elmer Dundy of the United States District Court. Demanding a writ of habeas corpus, they challenged the government's right to remove any Indian anywhere in violation of a treaty. On May 19, 1879, Judge Dundy ruled that an Indian, although not a citizen, was a person within the meaning of the habeas corpus act and entitled to sue the courts for a writ. He further stated, "In time of peace no authority, civil or military, exists for transporting Indians from one section of the country to another, without the consent of the Indians, nor to confine them to any particular reservation against their will, and where officers of the government attempt to do this, and arrest and hold Indians who are at peace with the government, for the purpose of removing them to, and confining them on a reservation in the Indian Territory, they will be released on habeas corpus."[106]

Judge Dundy's decision dealt a severe blow to the United States government's reservation policy in favor of Indian rights. Washington bureaucracy was quick to strike back by appealing his decision to the Federal Circuit Court. While the appeal was working its way through the federal judicial system, Standing Bear and his followers camped on an island in the Niobrara River. The island was an area that had been overlooked in the Treaty of 1868. No longer considered wards of the government, they were not allowed to stay on any other Indian reservation. They lacked time to plant and harvest crops that year and without annuities from the government to buy supplies, they were dependent on the charity of the Omaha Committee through the fall and winter.[107]

The Omaha Committee continued to publicize the difficulties of the Ponca tribe. The Reverend Thomas H. Tibbles, assistant editor of the *Omaha Daily Herald*, went on a tour of the East coast to rally political and financial support for the Ponca. Tibbles and the committee hoped to bring a suit on behalf of the Ponca before the Supreme Court. They hoped the court would return the Ponca northern reservation to them, allowing them to go home and rule on the legal and civil status of all Indians.[108] Tibbles began his tour in June, 1879, spending several months addressing interested citizens in the East. Boston was receptive to his cause. Edward Everett Hale and Wendell Phillips led Boston philanthropists who encouraged Tibbles in his campaign. Late that summer Tibbles returned to Omaha, preparing for a second lecture tour with Standing Bear by his side.[109]

While Standing Bear's cause stirred up public opinion in the rest of the nation, conditions improved somewhat on the reservation in the Cherokee Outlet. Several buildings were under construction by the end of 1878; agency structures, a school and Indian homes now marked the beginning of the village known as the Ponca Agency. Later, this agency was to be renamed White Eagle. By spring of 1879, promised farm implements began arriving, making it possible for the Ponca to break 450 acres of tough prairie sod. They worked hard to plant their crops but the weather that year was uncooperative. Agent Whiteman wrote to the Commissioner of Indian Affairs. E.A. Hays, "...the rain which goeth around he just and the unjust, the red man as well as the white man, left their crops to dry up and wither." For the third year in a row, the Ponca were unable to harvest a crop of their own and were forced to subsist on government rations.[110]

In spite of the improvements, there was still considerable discontent among the Ponca on the Šalt Fork reservation. A ringleader of this discontented element was Big Snake, the younger brother of Standing Bear, Big Snake stood six feet four inches tall, was in his prime of life, and very proud of his great physical strength. He was not averse to using his size and strength to intimidate the soldiers who patrolled the Ponca reservation. After Judge Dundy's ruling that supported Standing Bear, Big Snake was heard to boast that he would leave if he chose to go. In late spring, 1879, Big Snake made good on his boast. The Ponca were in need of riding stock and Big Snake thought it would be a good idea to go visit the Cheyenne on their reservation in western Indian Territory. Visiting other tribes was a popular custom among many Indian tribes. On such visits, friendships were renewed and gifts exchanged. It was Big Snake's hope that the Cheyenne might be generous, giving the Ponca the ponies they needed. Another Ponca leader, The Chief, and several others seconded Big Snake's idea. However, when White Eagle asked the agent for a pass for the visit, his request was denied. Big Snake decided to go anyway. Early in May, 61 Ponca men and five women slipped away from the reservation to visit the Cheyenne. Among those who accompanied Big Snake were The Chief, Standing Buffalo, Little Picker, Cheyenne, No Heart, Packs The Horse, Little Shooter, Buffalo Head, Yellow Bird, Sick Bull, Little Water, Little Soldier, Harry King, Child Chief, Foretop, Shines White, Spirit, Bear's Ear, Blue Black, Not Afraid, No Ear, Pretty Hawk, Louis Primeaux, Stand Black, Little Walker, Poison Hunter, Walking Sky, Little Voice, Antoine Roy, McDonald, White Buffalo, Bull Pawnee Chief, and Makes Noise.[111]

Agent Whiteman immediately notified Fort Reno at the Cheyenne-Arapaho reservation when he learned of Big Snake's expedition. At his request, Major J.K. Mizner, commander of the post, sent troops to intercept and arrest Big Snake and The Chief. On May 29 the two ringleaders were brought in and imprisoned while soldiers escorted the rest of the Ponca back to the reservation. Big Snake and The Chief were kept in the post guardhouse through June and July. Accustomed to freedom, Big Snake hated confinement. He was homesick, missed his wife's native cooking, and as the days dragged on, he became more and more depressed. For entertainment, he performed feats of strength during his exercise periods in view of nervous guards.[112]

Big Snake and The Chief were released and returned to the Ponca Reservation in early August; but Big Snake was still not inclined to comply with agency restrictions. His attitude remained sullen and he was making vague threats toward Agent Whiteman and refusing to speak to him when they met. On two occasions Big Snake defied agency rules by leaving without a pass to visit the Pawnees to the southeast. He returned each time with ponies, gifts of his hosts, making him the subject of envy and admiration among his friends.[112]

Reaching his limit of tolerance, Agent Whiteman sent a letter to his superiors in Washington detailing his grievances against Big Snake. The Poncan, he stated, flouted the agency's pass system as well as its other rules. He was a bully and a bad influence not only on the Ponca but other Indian tribes in the vicinity. According to Whiteman, Big Snake was a hindrance to the entire reservation system and its goals of civilizing the Indians. His letter eventually reached Carl Schurz, Secretary of the Interior. Schurz ordered the military to arrest and imprison Big Snake. These orders went down the army chain of command from the Secretary of War through General William T Sherman, Lt. General Philip Sheridan to Major General John Pope. Pope passed the order along to Major Mizner at Fort Reno, who sent Lieutenant Mason and a detail of 13 men from Company H, Fourth Cavalry to the Ponca Agency. Their orders were to arrest Big Snake and bring him back to the fort.[114]

Unaware that the federal government was after him, Big Snake continued his unruly ways. He only went to the agency to draw his weekly rations of sugar, salt, beef, beans, and coffee or to get his pay for occasionally bringing in agency freight from Arkansas City, Kansas. On October 31, Big Snake made a periodic visit to the agency, unaware that Agent Whiteman and Lieutenant Mason were waiting for him. It had been decided not to try to arrest Big Snake outside in the open but to wait until he came into the agency office. This 15 foot square room would limit the use of his great physical strength and isolate him from possible defenders. Even with these preparations, the soldiers and their officers were nervous. Had Big Snake been warned of their presence? Would he make good on his often-repeated boast in the Fort Reno guardhouse that he could take up any three of them and throw them away dead? Along with the persistent rumors that the Nez Perce and the White River Utes in Colorado were planning an uprising caused even the peaceful Ponca to look suspiciously fearsome to the troopers. How would the overly hostile Big Snake react to arrest?"[115]

It was mid-afternoon when the unsuspecting Big Snake arrived at the agency. In the small agency office he saw two Indians, trader J.S. Sherburne, Clerk A.R. Satterthwaite, Whiteman, a Pawnee interpreter named Joseph Esau, and the agency carpenter, George Frisbie, all tending to their usual agency business. Besides them were Lieutenant Mason, Corporal William Dobbins, Private James Casey, and two enlisted men. As Big Snake stepped into the room, Mason approached him and informed him that he was under arrest. Big Snake did not understand. He had not killed or injured anyone, nor had he stolen anything. How could he be under arrest? Ignoring his protests, Agent Whiteman told him he must go with Mason to Fort Reno. Big Snake agreed on the condition that his wife could accompany him, but his request was denied. Big Snake asked that an interpreter go with him. Again, his request was denied. Big Snake stood, spread the folds of his blanket wide to show that he was unarmed and sat down, he would not go. Impatiently Mason called six more soldiers into the room.[116] A carpenter, George Frisbie, later told what happened: "The six soldiers took hold of him. He hung back. The officer then ordered his men to handcuff him. As Big Snake began to make use of his wonderful strength. He threw the soldiers from him like chaff. A soldier struck him over the head with the butt of his gun, a blow that would have brought an ox to the ground, but still Big Snake kept his feet and would not be taken."[117] Blood was pouring down Big

Snake's face as he staggered back against the wall. Dobbins put the muzzle of his gun against Big Snake's head and fired.

The reverberations of the shot that killed Big Snake echoed around the nation. The dead Poncan's brother, Standing Bear, was in Boston, having accompanied the Reverend Tibbles there on his second lecture tour of the East, Joseph Cook, minister of Boston's Clarendon Street Baptist Church, spread the news in his published Monday lecture series about Big Snake. Many Eastern newspapers carried Cook's charge that "the brother of Standing Bear has been shot like a dog for asserting the rights maintained on this platform by our revolutionary heroes."[118] Sympathetic Bostonians quickly rallied to demand a congressional investigation into the situation at the Ponca Agency, Senator Henry L. Dawes, of Massachusetts, led the agitation in Congress itself. A committee of five men, including the governor of Massachusetts and the mayor of Boston passed resolutions insisting that the Ponca and all other Indians were persons under the law and should be guaranteed all rights and protection of the Constitution.[119]

Much of the outrage over the treatment of Standing Bear and the death of Big Snake fell on the head of Secretary of the Interior Carl Schurz, the "darling" of the liberals and reformers in Washington. Pro-Ponca Easterners were quick to blame Schurz and his department, including the Bureau of Indian Affairs, for all the wrongs done to the Ponca. A few muttered about the "Prussianization" of Schurz's department (a reference to the immigrant secretary's nationality) as others accused his department of having conspired to assassinate Big Snake. Novelist, Helen Hunt Jackson, who, a short time later, published *A Century of Dishonor* her famous attack on the Indian policy of the federal government, engaged in a public argument with Schurz through a series of letters in the *New York Tribune*. Schurz admitted wrongs had been committed against the Ponca, attempting to shift the blame elsewhere, a maneuver President Hayes sternly said was beside the point, stating that the real issue was how to right the wrongs already done.[120]

Schurz soon took some positive steps to make the Ponca reservation in Indian Territory more attractive to them. He changed the agency personnel, provided new frame houses, furniture for each family head, saw that each family had a milk cow, horses, farming implements, and brought in cattle for an agency herd. The original agency school was replaced with a large, square, three-story brick structure, one of the most imposing in the entire Indian service. While under construction, it provided jobs for 50 Ponca and was completed in 1880. Other Ponca were able to earn wages as agency herdsmen, Indian police and freight haulers. In 1881, Congress appropriated $20,000 to be used as a per capita payment to the Ponca for past suffering during the tribe's removal from its home in Nebraska.[121]

A committee of four, including General George Crook and General Nelson A. Miles, visited both the Ponca Agency, in Indian Territory, and Standing Bear's exiled band, on the Niobrara River, to determine the real situation. Their reports led to important changes in the government's treatment of the Ponca. First, the agency did away with the pass system for visiting neighboring tribes and gave the Ponca one year in which they might travel freely back to Dakota Territory, allowing them to decide whether to stay with Standing Bear in the north or settle permanently on the Cherokee Outlet reservation. Standing Bear's followers became known as the "Cold-country Ponca" or "Nebraska Ponca", also known as the "Osni-Ponka". Most decided to stay in Indian Territory under the leadership of Chief White Eagle, becoming know as the "Hot-country Ponca" or "Maste'-Ponka"[122]

Some Easterners believed the decision to stay in Indian Territory was because they feared being killed if they left even for a visit to the north. White supporters felt they won a victory when the government appropriated another $165,000 reparations for the Ponca's removal to the Cherokee Outlet and the Sioux return of the Dakota lands to Standing Bear. Though the Standing Bear case never went before the Supreme Court, it set precedents in lower courts insofar as the rights of Indians were concerned.[123]

No one was ever charged with the death of Big Snake. This fact continued to convince some that Schurz and his department had ordered the Indian's assassination. There was never any proof of the allegation.

Improved conditions on the reservation during the early 1880's caused to Ponca to become more reconciled to their new location. They were guided by White Eagle, hereditary chief of the tribe, a quiet, forceful leader who made many trips to Washington on their behalf.[124]

He condemned the use of intoxicating liquor and endeavored to have the tribe lift itself morally to a higher level. Frequently, while in Council, he spoke at great length on the necessity of the younger generations attending various Indian schools to learn a trade, enabling them to earn a living in the competitive field with the white man.

Chief White Eagle

He had the vision and foresight to see that eventually the Government would relinquish the care of its wards. He knew they must make their own way in the world the same as their white neighbors. As a friend of officials he secured many favors for the tribe that otherwise they would not have received from the White Father in Washington. In later years, he was assisted in the council by his son, Horse Chief Eagle.[125]

About the time the Ponca were arriving in Indian Territory, another tribe of Indians was taking their first steps down the long road toward Kay County. This tribe, the Nez Perce, would be exiles, as well as prisoners of war.

The Nez Perce

The story of the Nez Perce was like that of the Ponca Indians. It consisted of tragedy and deceit by the United States government. The Nez Perce in 1805 numbered around 6000 to 7000 and were well known as breeders of the famous Appaloosa horses. These people, proud, honest, tolerant and friendly, occupied the Salmon and Snake River Valleys in the Pacific Northwest. Life on the Columbia Plateau between the Cascade Mountains and the Bitterroot Range of the Rocky Mountains was pleasant and prosperous.[126] Their relations with the growing number of white Americans, who came in search of gold, was always a peaceful one until the mid-1870's. But on January 6, 1877, the federal government coerced the Nez Perce to give up 1,000,000 acres of their land in exchange for 1,200 acres on the Lapwai reservation in Idaho. (This was about the same time the Ponca tribe learned of the governments removal plan for them.) Since 1876, the life of the Nez Perce had been so drastically changed by pressures from the government and military, that they agreed to the treaty.

Before they could leave their homeland for the Lapwai reservation, trouble broke out. A Nez Perce was killed by whites. Three young Nez Perce revenged the death, killing four white men and wounding a fifth. This lead to war between the Nez Perce, led by Chief Joseph, and United States Army. From June 17, 1877 to September 30, 1877, the Nez Perce fought a continual battle under the leadership of Chief Joseph.[127] ZigZagging over the course of several hundred miles across Idaho, Wyoming, Montana and through the Rocky Mountains, the Nez Perce attempted to escape the pursuing army. The army was in awe of the military and tactical strategies Chief Joseph used.[128] Thirty miles short of their haven, the border of Canada, they were surrounded. The Nez Perce surrendered on October 5, 1877 to Brigadier General Nelson A. Miles.[129] The terms of their surrender were they would spend a short time in custody, then be allowed to go on to the Lapwai reservation. However, the government repudiated the terms of the agreement as soon as the Nez Perce were in custody. Plans had already been made for their ultimate disposition. The 418 Nez Perce were to be sent to Fort Leavenworth, Kansas, then be moved permanently to a reservation in Indian Territory.[130] Thus begins the story of the Nez Perce "Trail of Tears".

The winter of 1877 was spent at a dreary campsite located in the Missouri River bottom. It provided poor sanitation conditions and by summer, malaria and other illnesses reduced the number of Nez Perce from 431 to 410. Word went up the chain of command from the local Bureau of Indian Affairs officials to the Secretary of the Interior that something must be done

Chief Joseph of the Nez Perce

about the Nez Perce in the name of humanity.[131] After eight months at Fort Leavenworth, they were escorted to the Quapaw Agency near Baxter Springs, Kansas.

This move was anything but an improvement. The Quapaw Agency was under the control of Agent Hiram Jones, cousin of Central Superintendent of Indian Affairs, Enoch Hoag. Both men practiced unabashed nepotism with 11 out of 12 employees at the agency being related to one man or the other. All six tribes of Indians quartered at the Quapaw Agency, including the Nez Perce, suffered from neglect, poverty, inadequate food, housing, and lack of medicine at the hands of Jones. There were frequent complaints that Jones bought far fewer heads of beef to feed his Indian wards than was reported to his superiors. So evil was the reputation of Jones and Hoag at the Quapaw Agency that white neighbors from Seneca, Missouri, in a position to know what was going on, felt it was scandalous. A local farmer named H.H. Gregg was moved to write indignantly to the Bureau of Indian Affairs, September 28, 1878, "Sir, My home is the nearest of any white man's to the present camp of the Nez Perce Indians (being but a little more that a mile away). I have a family and cannot therefore, be indifferent to what is happening with these Indians. Since moving here about two (2) months ago, forty-three (43) from a total of four hundred and five (405) of these people have died."[132]

The Nez Perce waited for the government to make good on its promise to provide them with a reservation in Indian Territory. They arrived at the Quapaw Agency with optimism, thinking they might soon be able to settle down again. Now, however, it seemed that the government had forgotten them and left them helpless and homeless in an alien land. The Nez Perce waited patiently for an improvement in their circumstances. Chief Joseph sent a series of letters to Washington asking for help. In them he said, "Since our surrender I have tried to influence my people to be orderly and peaceable, and to avoid intoxications and live right."[133] In January 1879, Chief Joseph, Yellow Bull and interpreter, A.L. Chapman, appeared in Washington to plead for a permanent home. They proposed to give up all their lands in Idaho in return for "A body of land equal in area to four full townships [which] shall be set apart in the Indian Territory as a permanent home for said band, the sight [sic] to be selected for them by the Secretary of the Interior, out of the best agricultural lands which may be available and suitable for that purpose, to be purchased for them by the United States Government out of their own funds."[134]   He also asked for $250,000 in moving expenses for his people.

In the meantime, the "corrupt" Hiram Jones was replaced by J.M. Haworth. Chief Joseph and others met with Haworth on April 23 and 24, 1879. Though some Nez Perce still insisted on returning to Idaho, Chief Joseph and the majority were prepared to settle in Indian Territory. Haworth convinced those wanting to return to Idaho to settle in Oklahoma. Land was chosen for the tribe near present-day Tonkawa, Oklahoma consisting of the four full townships that Chief Joseph asked for. It was located at Townships 25 and 26 North Ranges 1 and 2 West.[135]   The reservation lay in the southwest corner of present day Kay County With its south boundary along the Kay-Noble county line, west boundary along the Kay-Grant county line, its southeast corner contiguous with the northwest corner of the Ponca reservation. It was bisected west to east by the Salt Fork of the Arkansas River and the east boundary lay roughly along the lower reaches of the Chikaskia River. The 90,710 acre tract, known as the Oakland Reserve, did, as Chief Joseph had asked, comprise some of the richest agricultural land in Indian Territory.

Agent Haworth was notified of the agreement with the Nez Perce and began assembling the wagons and mules needed to transport the tribe 180 miles to the west. With the best interests of the Indians in mind, Haworth wanted to make the trip between the high water season of early spring and the intense heat of summer. The party of 370 Nez Perce and their escorts got under way June 6, 1879. The first day, due to adjustments of loads, they only made eight miles before stopping to camp. The second day they made 30 miles and continued good progress as they traveled along the west bank of the Neosho River toward Chetopa and on to Coffeyville, Caineyville, Cedarvale and Arkansas City, Kansas.[136] From Arkansas City, Haworth sent a telegram to Agent William H. Whiteman at the Ponca Agency. He advised him of their imminent arrival, asking that food and supplies be prepared. The message took the harried Whiteman by surprise; he had no instructions as to what to do with the Nez Perce party. They arrived at the Ponca Agency in good spirits, having made the trip with only two deaths, both victims of sickness contracted at the Quapaw Agency.[137] The Ponca, led by Chief White Eagle, turned out to welcome them. Leaving the Ponca reservation, the Nez Perce arrived at the junction of the Salt Fork and Chikaskia Rivers. They made camp on their own land at last on June 14.[138]

The Nez Perce occupied the Oakland Reserve for the next six years. Cattle allotments and farming implements received from the government made it possible for them to establish farms and plant crops. Their crops failed due to drought and cattle that tromped them down.[139] New homes were built while both adults and children attended a day school at the Oakland Agency, near present day Tonkawa. Some economic recovery was made by leasing out lands to ranchers for grazing.

The Nez Perce never overcame their homesickness for the mountains and plains of the Pacific Northwest. They never became adjusted to the climate, as did the Ponca. Their death rate continued to be high, especially among the children. In 1884, an inspector went to the Nez Perce cemetery, counting 100 graves--- mostly children, including Chief Joseph's daughter.[140] The elderly also seemed to take the climate badly. One of those buried near Tonkawa was a elderly man named Halahtookit, the natural son of William Clark of the Lewis and Clark expedition. They seemed to be "dying as much from broken hearts as from disease".[141]

Chief Joseph constantly lobbied in Washington and wrote letters to Congress asking that his people be allowed to go to Idaho as had been agreed to when they surrendered to the army. A number of white sympathizers, including General Nelson A. Miles, who officiated their surrender in 1877, joined Joseph in his suit to receive permission to return to the northwest. General William T. Sherman, who also took part in the surrender, was in charge of the Northwest area. He was considered to be the one who coined the phrase, "The only good Indian is a dead one." He blocked the Nez Perce return every chance he had.[142] Finally, an act of Congress on July 4, 1884, allowed them to leave Indian Territory. On May 21, 1885, the surviving Nez Perce collected their belongings, retrieved their children in the Chilocco Indian School and boarded a train at Arkansas City, Kansas. One hundred eighteen arrived at Lapwai on June 1, 1885, eight years after they departed. Chief Joseph never saw the Nez Perce homelands, for 150 Nez Perce, including Chief Joseph, were sent to the Colville reserve, located in Washington state, near the Grand Coulee Dam. Chief Joseph died there in 1904, after having paid the ultimate price of burying all nine of his children. "According to the agency physician, Joseph died of a broken heart, while sitting before his tepee fire."[143]

The reservation that the Nez Perce vacated in Indian Territory did not remain empty for long. Far to the south, in Texas, were two other bands of Indians who looked at the Oakland Reservation, not as a place of exile but as a place of refuge. The last two groups of Native Americans to inhabit Kay County were the Tonkawa and Lipan tribes. Together they settled in Indian Territory.

The Lipan and Tonkawa

The Lipan were an industrious and clannish tribe that called themselves Tcichi, "people of the forest". Members of the Athapascan linguistic family, they were originally located in the north and west, part of the Jicarilla Apache. About 1600 they separated from the Apache and later became enemies. Gradually they migrated eastward to the plains of Texas and Oklahoma, becoming one of the far eastern sub-tribes of the Apache. They were well known for their raiding expeditions during their struggle for existence in Texas. French commandant La Harpe met them in 1719 in the vicinity of present day Wilburton in Latimer County, Oklahoma. He called them "Cancy", the French form of the Caddo name, "Kantsi" for Apache. The Lipan remained in the area until Comanches and other enemies pushed them south to the Gulf of Mexico and eventually into Old Mexico.[144]

The San Saba Mission was built near the present town of Menard, Texas, in 1757. Father Santa Ana, a Roman Catholic, hoped to establish a mission among the Apache to help pave the way for the conversion of them and other tribes of the area, including the Lipan. But the Comanche, jealous of Apache strength that might be gained, destroyed the mission within a year.[145]

Spanish officials negotiated a treaty in 1787 providing a settlement for Apache sub-tribes near Santa Rosa on the Sabinas River in Old Mexico. On March 6, 1788, Juan de Ugalde, the governor of Coahuila, appointed Picax-Ande, the great chief of the Lipan, to be head chief of the tribes near Santa Rosa. Picax-Ande was noted for his soldierly bearing, character, truthfulness and prestige among the Apache sub-tribes. In a meeting with the governor, he once said, "There are only three great chieftains, The Great One above, you, and I. The first one is looking down upon us and listening to what we say so that we shall see who is lacking in truth."[146]

Due to animosity that erupted between Indian tribes and

Texas settlers, the United States commissioners made a treaty on May 15, 1846. At Council Springs, the chiefs and leaders of ten tribes the Penateka Comanche, Hainai, Anadarko, Caddo, Lipan, Tonkawa, Kichai, Tawakoni, Wichita and Waco, acknowledged the United States as their protector. The treaty brought about the promotion of peaceful relations with the Texas tribes. Thirteen years later, efforts on the part of government agents to set aside a reserve for the tribes who signed the treaty brought about the selection of a 37,152 acre reservation about 12 miles south of Fort Belknap, in Young County, Texas. The Anadarko, Caddo, Waco, Tawakoni, Kichai, Tonkawa, Lipan and some Delaware and Shawnee settled here, on what was known as the "Lower Reserve". They grouped in tribal villages--- the Lipan and Tonkawa closely associated from this time forward.[147]

Tonkawa were first recorded when they lived on the Trinity River in Texas. Luis de Moscoso, the governor who succeeded De Soto, met them in 1542. French commandant La Harpe, in 1719, called them "one of the roving nations" of the upper Red River region. Their territory included central Texas, western Oklahoma and eastern New Mexico. Until the close of the eighteenth century, hostilities existed between them and the Texas-Oklahoma Lipan and Apache tribes. Tonkawa warriors aided the Comanche in the destruction of the San Saba Mission. The Tonkawa tribe consisted of a large numbers of warriors feared by their native neighbors, the Kiowa, Comanche and Caddo people. They became even more feared when the Spanish introduced them to horses. Their reputation was so terrible that they were considered man-eaters by other tribes. There was never any proof that this story was true.

The Tonkawa were industrious people, producing weapons, saddles, bridles, ropes, shields, tepees, blankets, moccasins, clothing, ornaments, cups, spoons, thread and glue. Spanish traders competed for their large quantities of hides, tallow, buffalo robes and buffalo tongues.[148] From around 1800 the Tonkawa were allies of the Lipan and friendly to Texans and other southern divisions. The Tonkawa drifted toward the southwestern frontier of Texas and were among the tribes identified in the Mexican territory by 1837.

The tribe settled on the Lower Reserve on the Brazos River in Texas around 1855, beginning a long association with the United States Army in 1858. Several served as scouts for Captain (Brevet Major) Earl Van Dorn on an expedition against the Comanches in southwest Oklahoma. Their part in the engagement at Rush Creek in Grady County, caused them to be hated by the Comanches, Wichita and Caddo tribes.[149]

In December of 1858, peaceful conditions abruptly ended between the whites and Indians in Texas. As hatred spread through Texas, United States agents pushed plans to move the tribes to Indian Territory. On July 1, 1859, the chiefs and leaders of the nine tribes met with officers at Fort Arbuckle. Word was suddenly received at the Brazos Agency that Texans planned to massacre all the Lower Reserve Indians. Superintendent Neighbors immediately hastened preparations for the removal. Texas troops were on guard, preventing the Indians from gathering up horses and livestock on the open range. Four thousand four hundred and thirty men, women and children, many on foot, began their journey on the evening of August 1, 1859, to their new location. They made the 170 mile trip to the Washita River in the "Leased District" in Indian Territory in 15 days. Exhausted and sick from the stress of traveling during the August heat, they were impoverished, having left personal belongings, household goods and most of their livestock at the Brazos Reserve.[150]

Barely recovering from the recent removal, they began building homes and breaking land for their new settlement when they were drawn into the Civil War. The Tonkawa, like many other tribes, chose to ally themselves with the Confederacy, eventually to suffer for that choice. On October 23, 1862, the Wichita Agency was attacked by the Federal supported forces of Delaware and Shawnee Indians. The Tonkawa, armed only with bows and arrows, set out for Confederate held Fort Arbuckle, seeking safety. On October 24, 1862, four miles south of Anadarko, a force of Shawnees, Delaware, Caddos and Wichita attacked the Tonkawa party, killing 167 men, women and children. If it had not been for a group of the Tonkawa tribe on a buffalo hunt, the entire tribe could have been annihilated. Survivors were allowed to locate in the Chickasaw Nation for the remainder of the war. Remnants of Tonkawa drifted about the Oklahoma and Texas plains after the war. In 1879 they were gathered together at Fort Griffin, Texas, generally starving and considered outcasts. Captain J.B. Irvine, who was given charge of them, pleaded with the government for aid. They had, he said, always been friendly to the whites, and served well as guides and scouts. Congress responded in 1884, including them in the Indian Appropriation Act.[151]

On June 30, 1885, 92 Tonkawa and 17 Lipan arrived in Indian Territory at the reservation vacated by the Nez Perce. Fording one river after another, they came at last to the Chikaskia, which they crossed exhausted and destitute. They set about establishing homes and farms. The report from their agent in 1886 stated that they had produced excellent crops on 35 acres of rich soil using four old horses, two or three plows and some hoes. They were happy to have a home at last. The area was rich with deer, wild turkey, prairie chicken, and other game. One agent for the Tonkawa was G.C. Brewer. He was removed as agent in 1893 and returned in 1898, serving until 1909.[152] His wife, Martha Brewer, was the first white woman to live on the Oakland reservation and she conducted a school for the children there. Mr. Brewer showed the Tonkawa how to plant and harvest wheat in 1889 after the government purchased them a horse-powered thresher.[153] They planted 160 acres of wheat, yielding 30 bushels.[154] A Methodist mission was established and nearby a cemetery was dedicated. However, life was not good for the Tonkawa, even after their resettlement. Though some of their culture had survived, their population continued to decrease as tuberculosis took its toll.[155] Notations were made on the gravestones of the descendants of those fierce Tonkawa warriors who had served the army as scouts. They included Standing Buffalo, Buck Bill, Lolla Collins, Jesse, Sergeant Johnson, John Kaise, George Miles, Sherman Miles, Grant Richards, Lamar Richards, Jack Rush, Tanasta, Joseph Toco and John Williams.[156]

Thus, by 1886 the once-vacant Cherokee Outlet was home to a number of tribes of Native Americans, three tribes in Kay County alone. For the time being, this was "Indian Country", but the day was coming, in fact, had already arrived, when the Ponca, Kansa and Tonkawa, all of whom had received their lands in perpetuity, would have to share them with white settlers. The vanguard of that new invasion was already poised along the Kansas border. Before they flooded into Indian Territory, it would undergo yet one more transformation and become "Cow Country".

CHAPTER THREE:
Indian Country Becomes Cow Country

The Cherokee Outlet underwent a considerable amount of activity between the Civil War and when it was opened for homesteading in 1893. This "unsettled frontier" saw the resettlement of Osage, Kansa, Ponca, Nez Perce, Tonkawa and Lipan tribe onto reservations in the Kay County area. It also saw the United States Army patrol the Outlet while white men conducted business in the Outlet, sometimes legitimate, and sometimes not.

Legitimate businesses included freighting supplies to various Indian agencies and new forts constructed in western Indian Territory. Unlike the Ponca, Kansa, Tonkawa and Lipan tribes, the Kiowa, Comanche, Cheyenne, and Arapaho actively resisted being placed on reservations. This resulted in Indian wars that kept the cavalry busy throughout most of the 1870's and into the 1880's. Supplies for the cavalry and Indians on the Cheyenne-Arapaho, Wichita-Caddo, and Kiowa-Comanche reservations began to roll southwest over rough wagon roads from the Kansas border towns of Arkansas City, Hunnewell and Caldwell.

In 1879, one of these roads, the Arkansas City-Reno Road, cut diagonally across Kay County. Beginning at Arkansas City, it ran about one mile west of the Chilocco School buildings, southwest across Bitter Creek, continued to the Chikaskia River, went three miles northwest of Blackwell, and traveled toward Thompson Creek, skirting the northwest corner of the Nez Perce reservation. Crossing the Salt Fork River southeast of Lamont and the headwaters of Red Rock Creek, it moved down across Skeleton Creek, joining the Abilene Cattle (Chisholm) Trail at Hackberry Creek, near Waukomis. The trail then turned south across the North Canadian River toward Fort Reno, Fort Reno was located on the North Canadian River. Along with Fort Sill in the southwestern quadrant of the territory and Fort Supply, Fort Reno was built in an effort to control the Plains tribes upstream from Reno in the Cherokee Outlet.

L.F. Carroll, in 1938, recollected how the government, in the early 1880's, desired a more direct route to Fort Reno and Fort Sill. Cattlemen plowed a furrow west of Chilocco in an almost straight line to Fort Reno. Grass was burned about ten rods (55 yards) on either side of the trail to make a fire guard in case of prairie fires. The furrow marking the trail was said to be the longest ever plowed---about 125 miles. The trail crossed the Chikaskia River at Black Dog Ford, east of present-day Blackwell (one block south of the east bridge), and the Salt Fork River at Yellow Bull Ford, near present-day Tonkawa. Later, stagecoach and mail services ran over this Arkansas City-Reno Road.[1]

Trails that crisscrossed Kay County were created by Indians, buffalo, cattlemen, the military and Boomers. Among the trails were the Ponca Trail, running south of Arkansas City through the Ponca reservation to the Salt Fork river. This trail ran parallel to present day Highway 77.[2] Black Dog Trail was an Indian trail that followed the north side of the Salt Fork river. Another less used trail ran up the north side of Red Rock Creek.[3] A trail east of Ponca City branched off into three buffalo trails. They were the Pawhuska Trail, the Hominy Trail and the Grey Horse Trail.[4] Located at Rock Falls was the Old Taylor Trail that crossed the Chikaskia at Rock Falls ford.[5] Boomers, David Payne and William Couch, also cut trails through Kay County. The Couch Trail extended from the Ponca Trail south towards Oklahoma City. Payne founded a new trail by leaving the Arkansas City-Reno Trail just west of the Nez Perce reservation, going south and intersecting the Couch Trail. This trail became known as the Payne Trail.[6] Another road across Kay County led from Hunnewell, Kansas, southeastward toward the Kaw Agency and Osage lands. It intersected the Arkansas City-Reno Road at Bitter Creek ford, about four miles west of Braman. Freighters hauled supplies to Indian Agencies over these roads, often employing Indians as teamsters. Shipments of freight sent out of the agencies consisted of hides and fence posts used by cattlemen. Less legitimate operations included hunting, timber cutting along stream beds, and grazing livestock.[7] All were illegal but happened frequently, in spite of attempts by the cavalry to keep intruders out of Indian lands.[8] A more daring, colorful breed of lawbreakers were the numerous outlaws who made the Cherokee Outlet their stomping grounds. Aware that Cherokee Nation was unable to enforce the law and cavalry patrols were too few to keep an eye on all thirteen million acres, outlaw gangs such as the Daltons and Doolins preyed on victims in both the Cherokee Outlet and the adjoining Unassigned Lands. Their kind helped enhance Indian Territory's reputation best typified by the slogan, "There is no Sunday west of St. Louis, no God west of Ft. Smith."

A less colorful, yet important breed of men were cattlemen. They made great use of the Outlet and inadvertently demonstrated how valuable its land really was. Cattle-raising was an industry started centuries earlier in the Southwest by Spanish missionaries who introduced livestock to their converts. The Five Civilized Tribes began raising "wohaws" or cattle and horses, long before they were forced into Indian Territory.[9] Before the Civil War, a few enterprising cattlemen from Texas began to drive herds north. Crossing Indian Territory to Fort Gibson through Missouri to one of the river towns like St. Louis, St. Joseph or Kansas City, these markets thrived until the war. The Indian Nation was stripped of livestock by both sides during the conflict, causing their cattle business to suffer a real depression until about 1866. The cattle industry's future was changing.

Railroads furnished cheap, fast transportation to an eastern market enlarged by industrialization and urbanization, leaving Easterners hungry for meat. Since they were city-dwellers and factory-workers, they could not produce their own meat. Commercial hunting of buffalo became profitable with the arrival of the railroads in Kansas. Although Indians would only kill enough buffalo for their winter supply, as commercial hunters began to decimate buffalo herds for their hides, tongues and hindquarters, the animals were nearly annihilated on the Great Plains. In 1877, a head of 40,000 buffalo was reported to be grazing near Fort Supply, In 1885, only one small buffalo herd could be found far out in the Oklahoma Panhandle.[10] This created a swift and drastic change in a market that had been opened for commercial buffalo hunters. The annihilation of the buffalo left an open, favorable environment for cattle. Cattlemen now had a market for their herds even though the nearest railroad lay several hundred miles to the north in Kansas. The problem could be overcome by driving herds across Indian Territory to one of several terminals.

Immediately after the Civil War, a few Texas cattlemen rounded up cattle, driving them to Kansas using a prewar trail, the East Shawnee Trail. It crossed the Red River at Colbert's Ferry, cut northeast to Fort Gibson, and paralleled the Grand River toward Seneca, Missouri. An alternate route went to Baxter Springs, Kansas. Cattlemen found they could get as much as $35 dollars per head for animals that were practically worthless in Texas, making up for the difficulties of driving cattle through the rugged western Ozarks and the Cross Timbers, which runs north and south through central Oklahoma. Some cattlemen began looking for easier routes, finding them to the west of the East Shawnee Trail. One cut northwestward at Fort Gibson and followed the east bank of the Arkansas River through Kay County to Wichita, Kansas. Another variation, called the West Shawnee Trail, left the East Shawnee Trail at Boggy Depot in southern Oklahoma and running more or less north, passed through Kay County on the west bank of the Arkansas River, traveling through the present-day town of Ponca City. The "Shawnee Trails" were abandoned by 1869 for the more popular (and famous) Chisholm Trail, also known as the Abilene Cattle Trail.[11] (See, Cattle Trail Map)

The Chisholm Trail was originally a trade route blazed by mixed-blood Cherokee, Jesse Chisholm. It crossed the Red River west of the Shawnee trails at Fleetwood Store and ran north toward Caldwell, Kansas. This trail had the advantage of crossing relatively flat, open country which aided in avoiding Indians, both civilized and uncivilized. What really made the Chisholm Trail popular was the work of Illinois cattle buyer, Joseph G. McCoy, who persuaded the Kansas Pacific Railroad to build loading pens and stockyards at Abilene, Kansas. McCoy began his campaign in 1867 and was so successful that most herds were being driven up the new trail within two years.[12]

The use of these trails, as well as those blazed later, saw more than five million head of cattle pass through the Outlet between 1866-1884.[13] Texans herding cattle in the late 1860's and early 1870's had ample opportunities to analyze the value of the Outlet land for grazing. They took their time moving herds across the Indian Nations. Kansas farmers allowed herds to drift south across the border to fatten up on the prairies of the Outlet.[14] Cattlemen recognized that the flat, open prairie was a fine place for cattle. In the eastern Outlet, grass types included the big bluestem, Indian grass and switchgrass, while further west buffalo grass, blue grama and sideoats offered good pasturage.[15]

Each year increasing numbers of cattlemen turned their herds loose in the Outlet. The only problem was that in 1867, the Cherokee Nation began levying a tax of 10 cents per head on transient cattle.[16] The Cherokee were given this right by the Indian Act of 1834, reaffirmed in Washington in 1878. The Cherokee Nation appointed tax collector, L.B. Bell, to assess cattlemen who had herds in the Outlet in 1879 and cattlemen protested. The tax collector and his assistant were unable to locate all of the owners, consequently taxing only 25 owners for 20,000 head of cattle, while failing to tax another thirty owners for cattle being fattened on Cherokee grass. Both the cattlemen that were taxed and those who were not resented the presence of the tax collector.[17]

As a result, the Cherokee raised the grazing tax to 50 cents per head but were still unable to collect it. In 1881 they took a tougher stance by opening a tax collector's branch office in Caldwell, Kansas. Collecting the names of delinquent taxpayers, they sent them to the agent of the Five Civilized Tribes in Muskogee. With the backing of the United States government, the

Cherokee then prepared to evict the delinquents. This alarming development caused cattlemen to decide to make a deal.[18]

With cattle ranching becoming a big business by 1882, the high prices commanded by beef in the Eastern markets brought a number of Eastern and European investors into the cattle business. They encouraged Western ranchers to put more and more stock on the ranges. The Cherokee Outlet was looking more inviting all the time to men with big investments in cattle. Changes were also taking place in the way cattle were handled. Cattle drifted on the open range until the 1870's, looked after by cowboys who attempted to keep the various herds separated and confined to a particular area. This was both inefficient and expensive in terms of manpower, but with the invention of barbed wire in the mid-1870's, inexpensive fencing became possible. The range could now be divided into separate pastures and cattle left relatively unattended. Fencing would also help keep out non-taxpaying cattlemen, making it easier for Cherokee tax collectors to find the herds and assess their owners. Barbed wire seemed to be the answer to several problems.[19]

The real impact for the cattle industry in the area came later with the leasing of land to individual ranchers. The difficulty lay in convincing the United States government that white cattlemen should be allowed to build permanent structures in the Cherokee Outlet. Complaints from Kansas cattlemen, who had been fenced out, brought the matter to the attention of the Department of the Interior. There were 959 miles of barbed wire fencing in the Outlet. The Cherokee Nation had given tacit permission for the fencing to be built but the federal government was alarmed by the fact that cattlemen were enclosing parts of Indian land. They demanded the fences be removed because of government policy. Cattlemen were faced with eviction from the prime grazing land of the Outlet, so they decided it was time to organize.[20]

And organize they did! The cattlemen's first meeting was an informal one in Topeka, Kansas, in January. 1883. They met again in March in Caldwell, Kansas, to formalize their organization. Nine men were chosen to write a constitution, bylaws and charter. Within two days they had produced the necessary paperwork to create the Cherokee Strip Live Stock Association. They organized under Kansas laws and the leadership of Benjamin S. Miller of Caldwell, Kansas. For a fee of $410, a rancher grazing cattle in the Outlet on undisputed land could join the organization. His brand would be registered and his range transactions recorded by the secretary of the organization. In case of a dispute with another member, the board of directors would appoint a committee of three ranchers to arbitrate the settlement. This decision could be appealed to the board of directors, but the board's decision was final. In short, the Cherokee Strip Live Stock Association meant to keep bureaucracy simple and let the cattlemen get on with the business of producing beef.[21]

To make certain this aim was accomplished, the association immediately began a campaign to end problems with both the federal government and the Cherokee Nation by leasing the entire Outlet. By July 5, 1883, an agreement was reached (though not without a great deal of controversy in the Cherokee capital) and the association was granted a lease that would run through 1888. For $100,000 per year, due in two semi-annual installments of $50,000, the association was allowed to restrict grazing in the Outlet to association members. Those who joined could build fences, corrals and construct housing for cowboys as necessary. At the end of the first five-year period, cattlemen had the option to renew the lease for two cents per acre.[22]

The lease did not satisfy everyone. The Cherokee felt they should also be allowed to graze cattle in the Outlet. If white ranchers could make money on beef production, they should be able to do the same. Cattlemen outside the association also objected, for they too were interested in leasing, if not buying the Outlet outright. Further, there was a growing agitation on the part of farmers in neighboring states to open the Indian Territory, in part if not in whole, for homesteading. The Cherokee Strip Live

Stock Association had control of the Outlet, but their tenancy was not by any means guaranteed.[23]

Ranchers in the Outlet got on with business. They surveyed, fenced and registered domains leaving little vacant space from the Arkansas River in the east to the 100th meridian in the West. A map of Kay County, in 1883, shows a patchwork of leased ranges. These ranges included the Stewart and Hodges range in the southeast, Roberts and Windsor in north central Kay County, Foss, Bridge and Wilson to the west of Roberts and Windsor, and W.B. Helm, southwest of the Foss, Bridge and Wilson's range. Around them were a dozen smaller holdings, as well as the Deer Creek pasture to the west of Helms, belonging to George Miller. The Cherokee were not the only Indian tribes to lease land to ranchers. The Ponca and Nez Perce leased surplus grazing land on their reservations to white cattlemen. George Miller leased a second range on the Ponca reservation known as the Salt Fork pasture.[24]

These were the years when much of the Cherokee Outlet legend was born, but life was probably not quite so romantic and glamorous as today's fiction presents it. In fact, it was hard work. In an 1950 interview, Burton G. Woodruff, Sr. recalled going to work in 1892, at the age of 17, on the Pryor Ranch about 10 miles southeast of Red Rock, Oklahoma. His experiences were probably typical of other cowboys. Woodruff was one of about 15 cowboys employed by the ranch to look after as many as 30,000 head of cattle on its four pastures. Each pasture consisted of more than 36 square miles. The cowboys were paid $20 per month, top hands were paid $25 and foremen were paid $125. The owner and foreman occupied log houses while the cowboys lived in large tents. The food was good---sourdough biscuits baked in dutch ovens, corn and tomatoes cooked together, dried beans, fruits and plenty of beef were consumed, since each week two 150-pound calves were butchered.[25]

The hours were long and hard. Woodruff, a line rider, was expected to get up, eat breakfast and be ready to leave camp by sunrise. He would spend the morning and early afternoon riding fence lines making necessary repairs. On his last trail drive before the opening of the Cherokee Strip, he was a wrangler caring for 65 horses. He had to get up at three in the morning, feed the horses and get them ready for the day's work. He helped herd cattle, worked night duty, carried water and peeled potatoes for the cook.[26]

On one particular drive, 2300 head of cattle were being taken to western Oklahoma, a 30-day trip. Care had to be taken, especially at night, not to allow the cattle to stampede. Drovers tried to choose a campsite with thick, high grass to help keep the cattle warm and content. Every night three cowboys would steadily circle the herd, singing "cattle calls" to help keep the animals quiet. Each cowboy kept a fresh horse saddled and staked nearby while he slept in case of an emergency during the night. The cowboy's bed was his "paddin", consisting of two five-pound red wool blankets, two Navajo blankets and a "sugan", or comforter. These were rolled up in a large tarpaulin during the day; at night the blankets were spread on the tarpaulin. It was then doubled back over the blankets and snapped up the sides to make a waterproof bed. Cowboys took care, according to Woodruff, to sleep with their feet toward the wind so the breeze would not creep down their necks.[27]

Life on the ranch itself was less harsh, yet offered few social amenities, especially to females. Very few women, except for the owner's wife, daughters and possibly a cook, lived in the Cherokee Outlet. Women who lived at the ranch headquarters were held in high regard and valued, due to their scarcity. With the harsh daily life and long distance between ranches. Outlet people looked forward to social gatherings, which were few and far between. These were usually dances attended by everyone within 20 or 30 miles.[28] However hard the life was in the 1870's and 1880's, old-time cowboys remembered it fondly. The Cherokee Strip Cow-punchers' Association was formed in 1920, meeting every year in Ponca City.[29]

Though ranchers in the Cherokee Outlet may have felt fairly well established in the 1880's, they endured chronic problems. One of these was the weather. In the mid-1880's, the weather over much of the Great Plains was more severe than usual. Hot, dry summers were followed by cold, stormy winters. Looking back, George Rainey remembers blizzard after blizzard sweeping across the Cherokee Outlet in the winter of 1884. He felt the fences that seemed such a benefit to ranchers were to blame for heavy cattle losses that year. Before fences were installed, cattle could drift ahead of a storm until they found shelter. Some would die, but losses usually amounted to less than two percent of the herd. Fences prevented cattle from finding shelter, many times huddling together in a fence corner only to freeze to death. Charles F. Colcord, an Outlet cowboy, told Rainey how he came upon several thousand head of cattle in the corner of a large pasture, standing knee-deep in snow, frozen upright.[30]

The following year the winter was just as bad. Snow lay on the ground from January to March, depriving cattle of pasturage. Ranchers suffered ninety percent losses that year causing many cowboys to be out of work. To help make ends meet they skinned the carcasses for hides. George Rainey recalled seeing fences in southern Kansas covered with so many drying hides that they looked like "...a huge washing on the line." For several years afterwards, people in southern Kansas and the Cherokee Outlet made extra money by picking up the bones of dead animals and shipping them East, where they were crushed for fertilizer.[31]

The situations faced by the Cherokee Outlet ranchers in the mid-1880's were common over most of the Great Plains. Ranges were overstocked in hopes to make a good profit due to the high price of beef in the east. But when the weather turned severe midway through the decade many suffered heavy losses. Late in the decade the cattle industry faced a new problem. Many homeless farmers looked upon the Cherokee Outlet and its good soil as a future home. Determined farmers became a major problem that bedeviled ranchers in the 1880's. Homesteaders were about as unmanageable as the weather. The territory appeared to ranchers as the last available cheap grazing land but to landless farmers it appeared as their last chance to own a farm. There was still land unclaimed in the far west but it was too expensive, too dry or too poor for crops. Indian Territory land, just over the border from Kansas, was fertile, well-watered and just waiting to be plowed. How frustrating it was that it belonged (or so the government insisted) to a bunch of Indians who refused to farm it! Instead, they were leasing it to an elite group of big-money ranchers for a few cents an acre. Ranchers could lease and fence large areas for their cattle, but homesteaders were denied even a quarter-section of land for a homestead. The unfairness of it was galling. To many it was a clear case of the "haves" and the "have-nots."

One has to remember the state of mind of many of the farmers on the Great Plains in the last half of the nineteenth century. They had been raised to expect that a man worked his land and by the sweat of his brow made a living for his family, not being dependent on anyone. Many farmers found reality to be a contradiction. The United States was becoming an industrialized nation and farming was becoming a big business and small farmers were being squeezed out. To compete in a market of steadily falling prices, many farmers went into debt to purchase expensive farm machinery and large tracts of land for cash crops. Human nature being what it is, farmers looked for someone to blame for their circumstances. Some railroads, banks, and other big businesses, concentrated back in the East, leased grazing lands through the Cherokee Strip Livestock Association. The farmers chose them as their targets. In the 1870's and 1880's, farmers saw a way out of their troubles, open Indian Territory for homesteading. Here there was good land and a chance to start over. The only obstacle standing in the way were the Indians and their tenants, the cattlemen.

Demands for Land Openings Occur

Demands for Indian lands to be opened for settlement began to be heard in the 1870's and gained strength all through the next decade. The focus of these demands were generally on the area known as the Unassigned Lands. This was a large tract in the heart of modern day Oklahoma adjacent to the southern boundary of the Cherokee Outlet. Following the civil War, the federal government forced the Creek and Seminole nations to sell their land to the United States for future settlement of other Indian tribes. Several reservations had been carved out of this tract but a large area remained "unassigned" to a tribe. People from neighboring states argued that this land, never having been assigned was public domain and available for homesteading. The government and the Five Civilized Tribes insisted that it was still Indian land ceded to the government for Indian use only. From time to time would-be homesteaders would move into the Unassigned Lands and lay out claims only to see the cavalry arrive shortly thereafter to evict them as intruders.[32] Homesteaders did not give up trying and about 1880 they consolidated around the leadership of David Lewis Payne. He was six-feet four inches, weighed more than two hundred pounds. Payne had a handsome face with piercing eyes and attracted hopeful home-seekers like a magnet. He had many shortcomings but his confident and friendly manner was enough to make his followers overlook them. Rarely doing a day's work, usually living on borrowed money that he seldom, if ever paid back continued his lifelong addiction to alcohol, usually conducting business in the local saloon. Payne even carried liquor into Indian Territory and selling it, a crime under federal law. He had a long-term relation-ship with Anna Haines by whom they had an illegitimate son. Payne staked several legitimate claims, none of which he ever proved up. His enemies, and there were many saw him as a scoundrel, but supporters saw the former soldier, scout, Indian fighter and legislator turned "boomer" as their best hope to force the opening of the Indian lands.[33]

Payne found his calling as a "boomer", one who encouraged or "boomed" for the opening of Oklahoma. In 1879, he helped found the Oklahoma Colony. Colony members paid Payne two dollars to file a homestead and $25 for a town lot in one of his prospective settlements. While waiting for an attempt to enter Oklahoma, his followers camped along the Kansas line south of Caldwell, Hunnewell, Arkansas City and other border towns. They held rallies, listened to Payne's exhortations and read the colony's newspaper, the *Oklahoma War Chief.* In general, merchants of the border towns supported the movement. After all, they were making money off the encamped immigrants. The movement was also supported by railroads that hoped to build lines through a populated Indian Territory. Ranchers of the Cherokee Outlet watched Payne's shenanigans with alarm and contempt.[34]

Fourteen times between April 1880 and July 1884, Payne led intrusions into the Cherokee Outlet or the Unassigned Lands. His target was usually the North Canadian River in the vicinity of today's Oklahoma City or the Cimarron River, north of modern day Guthrie. Before leaving boomer encampments in Kansas, he would assure followers. "This time we go to stay!" His routes across the Cherokee Outlet would not follow the main roads, for Payne knew the cavalry was aware of his plans and would be waiting. They would strike out across country, south from Hunnewell to the Bitter Creek crossing on the Arkansas City-Reno Road and across Nez Perce lands. The Nez Perce were not particularly friendly but permitted his parties to pass. Near the Salt Fork River they would go south across Red Rock and Black Bear Creeks into the Unassigned Lands. On every trip Payne promised his followers they would not be turned back, but on each occasion they were found and arrested. Payne never offered resistance, allowing himself and his party to be removed.[35]

Such actions were particularly frustrating to the soldiers charged with removing Payne's boomers, as well as the legal authorities responsible for punishing those who made such intrusions on Indian land. First offenders were ordered out or escorted from Indian Territory. Repeat offenders, such as Payne, might be held for a while at Fort Reno, then released, only to return to Indian Territory again at their first opportunity. Payne welcomed arrest and trial. He believed that by getting his case into court he could force a ruling as to whether or not the Unassigned Lands were public domain. But the only time he succeeded in being brought to court was in the aftermath of his attempt at a settlement at Rock Falls.[36]

Rock Falls, known to Cherokee Outlet cowboys as Rock Ford, was located on the Chikaskia River, just below the mouth of Bluff Creek, near today's Braman in northwest Kay County. In July of 1884, some of Payne's followers founded the Rock Falls Townsite Company and prepared to move into the Cherokee Outlet. They made no secret of their plans, claiming that 2,400 people would soon be building a town on this site. The town was actually composed of a small cluster of frame buildings, a small newspaper office, restaurant, hotel and drugstore, which also doubled as a saloon. Again, Payne hoped that by challenging the liquor-sale ban he would be arrested and brought to trial. During the next few weeks several dugouts and tents joined the four buildings in town. Payne and Anna Haines joined the Rock Falls group awaiting a reaction from the authorities.[37]

"Authority", in this case, was Colonel Edward Hatch. Hatch, who was well acquainted with the boomers and their intentions, visited the Rock Falls settlement on July 13. He found an average of 25 claims per day being sold to hopeful homesteaders with more settlers expected to arrive soon. Hatch was so impressed that he called for additional troops to repel the boomer invasion.[38]

With six companies of the Ninth Cavalry, Hatch encamped

at "Camp Hatch", 10 miles down the Chikaskia River just north of present day Blackwell. From there he kept a watch over boomer camps. Other interested parties, including Chief Dennis Wolfe Bushyhead of the Cherokee Nation, and Connell Rogers, clerk of the Union Agency at Muskogee, came as well. They worried that should the Cherokee Outlet be homesteaded the Cherokee Nation would lose its lease money. Payne refused to listen to their arguments or threats. Eventually word of what was happening at Rock Falls reached Washington. President Chester A. Arthur issued a proclamation ordering all intruders out of Indian Territory. Those who stayed would be forcibly removed by the army.[39]

Oklahoma Chief Newspaper printing office, Captain David L. Payne and his Boomers, at Rock Falls where the Taylor Trail crossed the Chikaskia River near Braman, Oklahoma. The first newspaper to be printed in the Cherokee Outlet was printed here on June 14, 1884. On August 7, 1884 the U.S. Army burned this Boomer Town and arrested Payne and his leaders.

On August 6 Colonel Hatch issued his last warning---boomers must leave Rock Falls and the Cherokee Outlet within 24 hours or face arrest. All of the "improvements", including the wells, fences and shacks, would be destroyed. Payne, who had been drinking heavily and steadily for the past several days, blustered, threatened and refused to budge, as did about 250 of his followers.[40]

The next day, August 7, 1884, Colonel Hatch's troops arrived at the Rock Falls settlement and surrounded the startled boomers. Some tried to hide in the brush but were flushed out by the soldiers of the Ninth Cavalry. They seized the newspapers office and arrested a bleary-eyed, "hungover" Payne. The entire spectacle was witnessed by several jeering cowboys from neighboring ranches and a crowd of people from nearby Hunnewell and Caldwell. By two o'clock in the afternoon the would be homesteaders started the weary march back to Kansas. Most of them went quietly but some women and children resisted. In fact, Anna Haines threatened Connell Rogers with a pistol, though there was very little violence. At six o'clock, four hours after the homesteaders started their trek northward, the Rock Falls settlement lay in ashes.[41]

At the same time Rock Falls was being destroyed, troops of the Ninth Calvary, under Captain Patrick Cusack, were making another raid. This one was on the settlement of Pearl City, also known as Staffordsville or Bodock, located "...twenty six miles east of Rock Falls and twenty below Arkansas City on the Bois de Arc Creek."[42] Pearl City was in the area just west of present day Ponca City.

Up to this time the law excluding intruders from Indian land had been rather ineffective. It merely provided for expulsion and fines for violators. This was of little consequence to Payne who was expelled but always returned. He had been fined but never seemed to have the money to pay them or the property to be confiscated. How could he be punished? This time the government did not intend to let Payne off lightly---he was to be brought before a federal court. It was decided that his time in custody would be highly uncomfortable. Payne could have been taken to the federal court at Wichita; instead, he was taken to Judge Isaac Parker's court at Fort Smith, Arkansas. The trip could have been made in a day or two by train from either Arkansas City or Caldwell, but the army packed Payne and five companions (including those arrested at Pearl City) into a closed wagon without springs and carted then three hundred miles through the late summer heat.[43]

Leaving in the pouring rain on August 11, with an escort of 60 troopers and several surly officers, Payne and his companions were soon soaked under the leaking canvas wagon cover and sick during most of the trip. Their route took them down the Chikaskia River to the Salt Fork River, southeastward across the Ponca reservation toward the Pawnee Agency, Sapulpa and Muskogee. It was early September when the circuitous trip was over and Payne was brought before Judge Parker. Parker fined him $1,000 (which Payne could not pay) and let him go.

By September 12, Payne was back in Kansas, a martyr to his cause.[44]

Payne's career as a boomer was nearly over. His health had never been good and the trip to Fort Smith had been grueling. He died suddenly on Thanksgiving Day, 1884, two months after re-turning to boomer camps on the Kansas border. Before the Fort Smith experience, many of his followers began to lose confidence in his ability to accomplish the goal of opening Indian Territory for homesteading. Many scorned him for his repeated capitulations to the army when arrested. The trial at Fort Smith and his triumphant return helped restore some of his image. Dead, he was a hero.[45]

Although Payne died without succeeding in his quest, his work was not a lost cause. One of his ablest lieutenants, William L. Couch, assumed leadership of the boomer movement. He led two more intrusions into the Unassigned Lands. Through the next five years, Couch and other boomers continued to demand that the territory be opened for homesteading. On April 22, 1889, their efforts paid off. The Unassigned Land were opened for homesteading in the first of the Oklahoma land runs. Other openings followed on land adjoining the Unassigned Lands. Ironically, a fatality of the Unassigned Land opening was William L. Couch, killed in a dispute over land title. He was buried the 22nd of April 1890, one year to the day of the opening.[46]

Little by little, time was running out for the ranchers in the Cherokee Outlet. In fact, it ran out abruptly for the Cherokee Strip Livestock Association in 1888. Association representatives negotiated a new five-year lease in the latter part of the year for a annual rental of $200,000 payable in advance. There was much discussion in Washington as to whether the association had bribed members of the Cherokee national government in order to obtain the original lease. Also, the voice of the boomers, amplified by railroad interests, was having its affect on the federal government. A short time after the renewal of the Cherokee Outlet lease by the Association, the United States Congress appointed a commission to deal with the Cherokee for the sale of the Outlet. Hopes for a continuation of the association's lease grew dim. At first, it did not appear to be possible for the government to deal with the Cherokee as they had already been offered $3.00 per acre in 1886 by a syndicate of cattlemen and were just entering into a new 5-year lease with the Cherokee Live Stock Association at twice the amount they had received for the previous lease.[47]

Secretary of the Interior, John W. Noble, ruled the Cherokee Outlet was an easement and therefore it was forfeited by the Cherokee failure to use it for its intended purpose. He further stated he would see the Cherokee release their Outlet lands to the government for $1.25 an acre or receive nothing at all. On February 17, 1890, President Harrison issued a proclamation ordering all livestock out of the Cherokee Outlet by October 1 of that year. Cattlemen grazing herds in the Outlet were not surprised at the decision; a similar incident had occurred years before on the Cheyenne-Arapaho reservation. This meant ranchers unable to find new pastures for their herds would be forced to sell their beef on a saturated market and take a considerable loss. Both the cattlemen and the Indians suffered from this action. The Cherokee, seeing they could no longer stand against the determination of the federal government, sold the Outlet on November 27, 1891, for $8,595,736. The era of the rancher was about to give way to the era of the homesteader.[48]

Time was also running out for Native American tribes of Indian Territory. There was talk of allotting lands of the tribes in severalty. It would break up the traditional communal tribal culture of Native Americans. Tribal members would be given 160 acres of land, the idea being to encourage them to become small, independent farmers. Since reservations included more than enough land to give each tribal member adequate acreage for a homestead, surplus land could then be opened for white settlers. This would have the additional benefit (in the view of the federal government) of placing white farmers near Indian farmers, providing the Indians with good examples. From the government's point of view, allotment seemed to be the right thing to do.

Most Indians were agriculturally oriented and did not agree with the federal government's proposed view. They were happy with Indian Territory and did not want whites crowding in. Further, they did not want allotments, a threat to their age-old customs. Indian lands were for the use of the entire tribe, not parcels to be owned by individuals. Thus, when the government began suggesting allotment of the lands in Indian Territory, they saw it as a threat and tried to resist.

The Dawes Act of 1887 became the official policy of the federal government and commissions were formed to visit each reservation in Indian Territory. The first step was to make up tribal rolls where each individual who could legitimately claim tribal membership would be listed. The person listed would be allotted an equal acreage of land, depending on available reservation land. Honest efforts were made by commission members to help individual tribal members select good land for homesteads. The whole process was disturbing to Native Americans and sometimes caused dissension within the tribes. Many problems arose and allotment selections dragged on for years.

Agents of the government visited the Tonkawa reservation in the summer of 1891 to make allotments to them and the Lipan tribe who shared the area. Seventy-three members of the tribe received about 160 acres each, leaving 79,276 acres in surplus lands for settlement. The government paid the Tonkawa $30,600 for these lands.[49]

The Ponca and Kansa were reluctant to take allotments and resisted efforts by government representatives. Some mixed-blood Kansa were prepared to take 160-acre homesteads but the full-blood faction was not willing, since no agreement had been reached in 1892. The Kansa, did however, divide up their surplus lands into 14 big pastures of 500 to 10,500 acres each and leased them to cattlemen for grazing land. It was not until 1902 that a committee of seven representatives including Chief Washunga

(Wah-shun-gah), Forrest Chouteau, Shot Arm (Wah-mah-o-e-ke), William Hardy, Mitchell Fronkier, Akan Pappan and W.E. Hardy, signed an agreement in Washington, D.C. and Kansa lands were allotted. Each tribal member received a total of 405 acres in 1904 by an act of Congress that said that the former Kansa lands were attached to Kay County.[50]

Equally reluctant to accept allotments were the Ponca. When the subject was presented to them in 1890, their agent reported objection was almost unanimous. President Benjamin Harrison issued an executive order in the fall that left them little choice. Agents of the government were ordered to visit the reservation, divide the land into 80 and 160-acre plots and all the acreage to the Indians whether they were willing or not. The special agent sent to carry out the allotments procedure was Helen P. Clark, a mixed-blood Blackfoot, and the only woman employed in this capacity. Her superiors hoped that her background would help persuade the Ponca to accept allotments; however, her Indian heritage had very little effect on their attitude. She received very little cooperation from her colleagues as they objected to the fact she was a woman. Miss Clark also worked with the Tonkawa, deciding to suspend work with the Ponca until they became more cooperative. Confusion reigned as officials in Washington assured two representatives of the tribe, Standing Buffalo and Frank LaFlesch, that no allotments would be forced on them unwillingly, yet the Department of the Interior allotment commissioners said just the opposite. Finally, in August of 1892, the Ponca, under the leadership of Chief White Eagle, began choosing acreage. By 1902, most had accepted allotments and on December 6, 1905, the Ponca reservation was abolished.

Another step had been taken to prepare the Cherokee Outlet for opening to white homesteaders. The land that had been Indian country, the cow country, was now about to pass through another transition. It would be the greatest spectacle the colorful West had ever seen, the Cherokee Outlet Run of 1893.

Rock Island Train at State Line September 16, 1893, opening of Cherokee Outlet, Caldwell, Kansas.

Photo courtesy of Walter B. Stover

CHAPTER FOUR:
The Run Of 1893

Getting the Outlet opened for homesteading was not easy. Many people, unfamiliar with the land, were convinced it was to poor and dry for farming. They contended that allowing unknowing farmers to homestead there was only setting them up for heartbreak and ruin. Cherokee Outlet ranchers, in an attempt to protect their leased lands, reinforced this view through the press and lobbyists in Washington. "Boomers", like David Payne and Gordon W. "Pawnee Bill" Lillie, combated this dreary image by continuously publishing information that made the Outlet appear to be a land flowing with milk and honey. Seconding these descriptions were railroad interests. T.C. Sears, an attorney for M.K.T. Said, "These lands are among the richest in the world."[1] In the mid-1880's the Southern Kansas Railway, a subsidiary of the Atchison, Topeka and Santa Fe, began building south across the Outlet from Arkansas City, Kansas. In 1887, they connected with the Gulf, Colorado and Santa Fe, another Santa Fe subsidiary. This line ran across mostly uninhabited lands of northern Indian Territory. Railroad owners supported the opening of the Unassigned Lands and the Outlet to settlement, because it created a demand for their services. Quickly, railroads joined the boomer lobby in calling for action on the part of the federal government.[2] People in Arkansas City, Kansas, supported the Outlet opening as a way to insure their survival. Located on the outer edges of the frontier, they needed the trade from Outlet towns to survive.[3]

Great masses of people, farmers, speculators, adventurers, businessmen, women, and numerous others from all walks of life began gathering along the borders of the Cherokee Outlet long before the opening. They waited through spring days as they dreamed about the land they hoped to claim and the crops they would plant in the virgin soil. They were sunburned, wind-dried men and women, who had dreamed about settling in the Outlet since the days of David Payne and his Oklahoma Colony. Some made the Run of 1889 that opened the Unassigned Lands. For many, this would be their first time to run, but all were hopeful they would get good land and the chance to start anew.

Would-be homesteaders, congregating along the Outlet borders, thought surely the opening would not be delayed once the cattlemen were driven out. The Cherokee agreed to sell the Outlet to the government in March, 1892, but the government delayed the opening through late spring and into summer. Anxious farmers, with an eye on the weather, began to hold mass meetings in the boomer camps. In late May they sent a petition to President Grover Cleveland and Secretary of the Interior, Hoke Smith, asking that the opening occur no later than July 1 to 15 to insure that they would still have time to plant wheat and harvest hay before winter.[4] Officials, far from the realities of western farm life, let the time slide through the summer months of 1893. By then, many who had flocked to the border towns in the spring began to drift away, their meager resources exhausted. They were replaced by others as the summer months dragged on, with no official word of the opening.

It was July before Washington bureaucracy began to take positive steps towards opening the Cherokee Outlet. Then the work of organizing the largest of the land runs began in earnest. Military units began moving the last of the reluctant Outlet cattlemen off their grazing lands, though many of them simply waited until the soldiers left and turned their herd back into the Outlet. Near the Salt Fork River, a detachment of soldiers came upon a herd of cattle and the cowboys in charge of them. The soldiers told the cowboys to take the herd north and out of the Cherokee Outlet, and they obeyed. A short time later, the cowboys turned back with the herd and a conflict ensued between the soldiers and cowboys. One of the cowboys shot and wounded a soldier. The detachment opened fire, killing one cowboy and about 50 head of cattle.[5] Homesteaders, waiting along the borders, snatched eagerly at every "waybill" (a map and information on springs and timber)[6] they could get, in an attempt to determine where bottom lands and good water might be found.

They continued to make plans for the big day. Local farmers profited from the delay, illegally cutting hay in the Outlet and selling it to the waiting crowds for their animals.[7]

The majority of the prospective homesteaders came from Kansas, Texas and Arkansas. Others came from as far north as Minnesota and Montana and from both the Atlantic and Pacific seaboards.[8] The method of reaching a suitable claim site was of prime concern. Some planned to ride the trains into the Outlet, while others planned to use horses or horse drawn conveyances. In anticipation of this need, enterprising ranchers shipped horses to border towns. They arrived by the train loads from Texas, Colorado, and as far away as Oregon, and were sold passage at prices ranging from $20 to $50 each.[9] Some people imported thoroughbred race horses but many knew these animals were only good for short distances, unable to withstand long distances. Seasoned cow ponies, accustomed to running cattle over the rough country, were acquired by some. All of the horses were cared for diligently, fed, groomed, and trained for the race of their lives. Owners knew that a claim would very likely depend on their horse.[10]

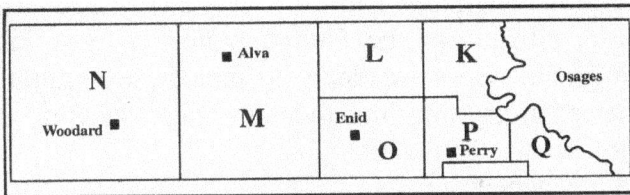

Surveyors moved methodically over the prairie, laying out sections, townships, range lines, locating county seats, and drawing county boundaries.[11] The Outlet, including the Tonkawa and Pawnee reservations, was to be divided into seven counties designated as K, L, M, N, O, P and Q. Surveyors set aside land for schools, roads, county seats, and other public uses. Within these planned towns, 80 acres were designated for courthouses, parks, and land for eight-foot sidewalks and 80 foot wide streets. Lots in county seat towns would be at a premium, so speculators began plotting as to how to get control of them. To prevent this, surveyors secretly relocated the county seats, keeping the information confidential. It was passed on only to the Secretary of the Interior, the Chief Land Commissioner and chief Platter of the land office in Washington.[12]

Bureaucrats, having experienced other land runs, tried to determine the best ways to prevent "sooners" from slipping into the Outlet. "Sooners" were people unwilling to take a chance in the race for homes. They would stealthily enter the area before the opening and hide. On the day of the race, they would dash out and stake claims on choice land. To prevent this, the Secretary of the Interior devised a novel plan. He decreed that every claimant would have to register before the opening and receive a certificate of eligibility. Registration would take place at one of nine booths opened once the official date of the land run was established by presidential proclamation. The booths would be located in towns already in existence in the area. In Oklahoma Territory, booth 1 would be at Stillwater; booth 2 at Orlando; booth 3 at Hennessey and booth 4 at Goodwin. In Kansas, booth 5 would be located at Kiowa; booth 6 at Cameron; booth 7 at Caldwell; booth 8 at Hunnewell and booth 9 at Arkansas City.[13] To be eligible, claimants had to be 21 years of age or head of the household, citizens of the United States, or with intentions of becoming one. Homesteader who met these requirements were issued a certificate entitling them to make the run. Those who owned more that 160 acres of land elsewhere or had perfected claims taken in earlier land runs, were not eligible.[14] Finally, on August 19, 1893, President Cleveland signed the proclamation opening the Outlet on September 16, 1893, at 12 noon, Central Standard Time.[15]

The registration booths, canvas tents, were furnished with

plain tables on which the   all important business of registering and establishing eligibility would take place.[16] It was impossible for the nine booths to accommodate the crowds that arrived when they opened for business at seven o'clock on Monday morning, September 11. The booths remained open until noon, closing for an hour while the clerks rested. During this time thousands of homesteaders waited in the dust and heat. They reopened at one o'clock and business was transacted until six o'clock.[17] At Caldwell, clerks processed 1000 registrations in 10 hours the first day, with another 5000 people still standing in line at closing time. At Arkansas city, some people stood in line two days and nights before the booths opened on Monday morning. They slept on the ground, wrapped in blankets. If, they were lucky enough to have one. The weather had been hot, but toward morning it became chilly. Hot coffee peddlers, who spent the night near the lines, were a welcome sight.[18]

During the day the weather turned hot again 100 degrees in the shade. The sun beat down, day after day, on the treeless, open plains that had not experienced a cooling summer rain for a long time. A pall of fine dust was hanging over everything. There was not water within two miles of the booth at Arkansas City. As thirst combined with heat, weariness and grime created real misery. Fifty people suffered from sunstroke in one day at the Arkansas City booth, resulting in six deaths. The story was the same at Caldwell, Orlando and Hennessey.[19] The grim homesteaders refused to give up. Many telegrams and letters were sent from the border towns to Secretary of the Interior Smith, telling of the miserable conditions being endured. Smith called for additional booths to be established to help the registration process go quicker. At Guthrie, Oklahoma Territory, the order to erect an additional booth was received at four o'clock in the afternoon on September 14. Ten minutes later, 500 people were in line at the new booth.[20]

It was supposedly the belief of the President and Secretary of the Interior that requiring applicants to make needed declarations, file affidavits, and secure a certificate would prevent "soonerism". Secretary Smith and his booth system was the brunt of many jokes, along with many a growl from dusty, thirsty men and women, patiently waiting for what they termed a "useless piece of paper".[21] They passed the time talking, joking, planning for the future, and making friends with the strangers next to them. It was the greatest gathering of people the Southwest had ever seen, twice as many as made the run in 1889. About 7,000 gathered at Stillwater; Hunnewell and Kiowa had approximately 10,000 each and Caldwell, Orlando and Hennessey each saw approximately 15,000 lined up. The greatest number, 30,000, gathered at Arkansas City. In all, over 100,000 people were prepared to make the Run of 1893.[22]

Homesteaders who staked a claim would have to present their certificates at the nearest land office to register their claim. They would then be able to purchase the land provided they gave proof of compliance with the homestead laws and the claim was not contested.[23] Payment (including filing fees and interest) could be spread over the next five years at four percent interest. Prices for the land ranged from $1.00 per acre in the western third of the Outlet; $1.50 per acre in the middle third; and $2.50 per acre for the better land in the eastern third, including Kay County. The final cost of a homestead for $2.50 would amount to about $500.[24]

As the time for the opening drew near, people picked their positions on the line. According to the procedures laid down by the Department of the Interior, homesteaders were to be allowed to line up 100 feet inside the Outlet.[25] This neutral strip was soon churned into dust by the trampling feet of men and horses. The wiser people in the crowd chose their positions, pulled their vehicles into place, then led their horses or mules away to a quieter, grassier spot to await the starting time.

In Kansas, people could hardly believe what was happening. Everyone, it seemed, was going to the Outlet. At Hunnewell, incoming trains brought more and more people into the town. Saloons and gambling houses flourished as they catered to the approximately 15,000 people that gathered there.

Most homesteaders brought food with them but a barrel of ice water cost between $25 to $30.[26] They were sure they would make their fortunes here. Many who lined up to make the race were ineligible to stake claims but planned to make the run for someone else. Others were there merely for entertainment; they simply wanted to see the show. It was the biggest spectacle anyone could imagine.

All manner of vehicles appeared for the run, sulkies, surreys, buggies, and lumbering farm wagons. While they waited, homesteaders greased axles, repaired harnesses, and trained their teams. There were many who planned to take advantage of the railroad lines that crossed the Outlet. The Secretary of the Interior issued a decree four days prior to the run, to the effect that trains would not run on these lines until 12 noon September 16, entering the Outlet with the other racers. The Santa Fe had 10 trains of 10 box cars each stationed at Arkansas City, with trains at Orlando, Kiowa and Cameron. Rock Island had trains at Caldwell and Hennessey, each pulling 42 cattle cars. Trains were to proceed at 15 miles per hour, stopping every five miles and at every station to let racers off. Federal marshals were to stand on the railroad lines opening day, not admitting passengers until 30 minutes before the noon signal. After conductors checked to see that no one without a certificate boarded, the ten to twelve thousand passengers expected to make the run by train would be permitted to board. The notion that 16 conductors could check and board that many passengers in 30 minutes made Santa Fe's officials snort in disbelief.[27]

Friday night, September 15th, finally came. Campfires flickered as far as the eye could see. Restless, hopeful homesteaders checked harnesses once more, fed and rubbed down their horses, studied maps, and memorized routes to the claim they intended to stake. Few slept that night as tension kept the crowd stirring. Then, slowly in the east, the sun began to rise. The crowd had grown larger during the night as latecomers arrived, going straight to the registration booths. Campfires were stirred, breakfast was cooked, then it was time to move to the line.[28]

All through the morning soldiers, stationed just inside the Outlet, kept an eye out for "sooners". They were standing at intervals of about one mile all along the line. Ponca Indians lined the boundaries of their reservations to see the show and make sure no one tried to claim part of their lands. Back from the line, spectators and journalists found a place to watch the show. On a specially built platform near the line, photographer William S. Prettyman and his assistants set up cameras, prepared to immortalize the moment in pictures.[29] Families and friends discussed where and when they would meet. A cloud of dust, churned by thousands of trampling feet, billowed into the hot wind.

When the trains arrived the crowd surged forward to board, only to find the cars already packed as people hung from every possible hand hold. Still more clambered aboard, pushing, shoving and elbowing. Courtesy evaporated in the urgency of the moment. A deputy marshal was stationed at the door of each car, unable to stop the rush. When the trains pulled out, so many people clung to the cars that brakes would not operate.[30]

Slowly, time crept towards 12 noon. At 11 minutes till noon, a shot rang out at Arkansas City. It was not the signal for the run to start, but no one stayed to find out. The horse belonging to James

Photo of the start of the Run taken at the west end of the Chilocco Reservation by Bill Graf's father.
–Photo courtesy of Cherokee Strip Living Museum.

Hill of Keansburg, New Jersey, bolted. Sergeant W.R. Willard yelled at him to stop. When Hill did not, Willard fired at him, striking Hill in the head, killing him.[31] This resulted in the first murder trial held in Newkirk, Oklahoma. Willard was exonerated.[32] The shot from the gun caused the earth to shake as the crowd spilled over the line. Troops were unable to stop the stampede. They could only watch helplessly as men spurred their horses into the Outlet. In the rush of so many close-packed moving bodies, some never made it over the line, as riders were thrown from their horses, wagons upended, and people on foot were trampled.[33]

Those able to clear the starting line raced headlong into the Outlet. Cowboys on tough cow ponies took the lead with light buggies and wagons following not far behind. Last of all came the lumbering prairie schooners, with their white canvas tops gleaming in the sun. Trains chugged with passengers hanging precariously on the sides and tops of the cars. Though the engines were supposed to stop every five miles and at each station along the line, some people did not wait, jumping off moving cars, risking broken legs or necks, many dying from injuries they sustained.[34]

From time to time, a racer would leap down from his horse or wagon, hammering a stake into the ground to mark his claim. Then they would plunk themselves down and defy anyone to move them. Within a few minutes flags were fluttering from stakes all over the prairie. Arguing, gesticulating men gathered around some flags as two or more people had staked the same quarter section. They would call up witnesses to defend their rights, wrangling over who should stay, and who should move on. While they argued, those who had yet to find an uncontested piece of ground rushed past.[35]

As if the confusion of the race and the extreme heat of the day were not enough, homesteaders had to contend with fires. There were varying theories as to how these fires started. Some say they were started by homesteaders to make it easier to find the surveyors' markers; others say the soldiers started the fires to flush out sooners; still another theory was that the first wave of racers stopped and set them in order to slow or stop those close behind. Whatever the cause, fires spread across the dry prairies, adding acrid grass smoke and soot to the day's miseries. Fires did not stop the homesteaders, many rode right through the flames.[36] Fires, heat, greed, accidents, and even murder took many lives that day. Man and beast alike suffered in the greatest horse race ever seen. Animals that carried their rider to a choice piece of land, and survived, were put to pasture, and were highly regarded as family members by their owners.

It seems odd that such determination should give way to charitable impulses, but in several instances that seemed to have been the case. A reporter from the *Chandler News* reported seeing two young men and a young woman jump off a train and race toward a barbed wire fence that separated the track from the prairie. The two men slipped through, but the woman got caught on the barbs in a very embarrassing position. The men ignored her at first, intent on hammering stakes into the same claim. Then, in mutual reaction, they stopped, looked at each other, and turned back to free her from the wire. Taking her stake, they hammered it into the claim and moved on to look for another unclaimed site for themselves.[37]

Another charitable act took place by a man named Charley Cooper, who came from Kansas to make the race. Once the line began to move, he kicked his mule into a gallop, tearing into the Outlet. Twice he dismounted to stake a claim and twice remounted to look for a better place. On his third attempt, he had just driven his stake into the ground when a weeping woman stumbled into view. Charley asked her why she was crying and she told him that she had been unable to stake a claim. "Well, take this one." Charley told her, and he rode on. His good deed was rewarded---he sold his fourth claim at a handsome profit to the railroad for a right of way.[38]

Most homesteaders held on to their claims with grim determination. They had come too far, waited too long, and endured too much to give up easily. When the sun went down on September 16, 1893, new towns dotted the Cherokee Outlet, with thousands of new Oklahomans prepared to put down their roots.

CHAPTER FIVE:
Pioneer Country Takes Root and Grows

On the afternoon of September 16, 1893, a small group of horsemen were riding across the Cherokee Outlet. They watched as a rider leaped down from his wagon and thrust a slim stick with a white cloth tied to it into the sod. The thin, elderly man, obviously an unsuccessful farmer, greeted them cheerfully. They visited about the Run taking place, his past and future. "All my life," he said, "I have been a poor man on rented land never able to own land of my own. And now, in the Providence of the Good God, at last I have a farm."[1] Such were the thoughts of many who made the Run of 1893. They had little or nothing before, but now they had a chance to make something of themselves. It was a gamble, one that some won and others lost.

A number of would-be settlers spent their first night camped near Yellow Bull Crossing on the Salt Fork River. Drought had reduced this usually fine spring to a trickle, taking three to five minutes to fill a cup.[2] Settlers came from every direction for the water, waiting up all night for their turn. The next morning the sun came up hot and angry, as a fierce south wind scoured the parched, fire-blackened prairie, kicking up clouds of grit and dust. Some who succeeded in staking a claim felt they had wasted their time and headed back to Kansas and civilization. One camper, an old farmer crossing the future site of Tonkawa, observed fresh mounds dug by gophers. "Look at that ground! I wouldn't give a dollar for a whole township of it. I will go back to Kansas and stay there five years and buy 160 acres, if I want it, for five or six hundred dollars."[3]

Homesteaders found that just staking a claim did not make it theirs. They might find several others claiming the same section of land. In some cases, organized groups conspired to support one another's claim of priority.[4] Either way, claimants were apt to find themselves tied up in litigation for years, spending their meager resources, and time, on lawyers and courts they could not afford. Many homesteaders gave up claims, feeling their case was hopeless. If they were lucky they might receive some payment for relinquishing their claim, but if they persisted with their case, they could still lose in the end.

Council Grove Crawford, who homesteaded in the northwest corner of the southeast quarter of Section 32, Township 27 North, Range 2 East, reached his claim at 1:10 p.m. on September 16. He immediately chose a hillside location for his home and began to dig a trench for a foundation. The dirt from the trench was thrown into a nearby pile. A short time later fire raced across the dry grass forcing him to abandon his work. Upon his return he found seven other claimants on his land. All but one dropped out of the contest. The remaining contestant began a stubborn fight for Crawford's land. The turning point in the case came when Crawford's rival described the land as burned when he arrived on the site. Crawford was able to prove he arrived first because the grass under the pile of dirt was not burned. The case took a considerable amount of time to settle, costing Crawford $500.00.[5]

Lucky homesteaders, not having to face contestants for their claims, still had difficulties those first years. Times were hard all over the United States. The Panic of 1893 began in May, leaving many people unemployed and without ready cash, like most of those who made the Run of 1893. One couple arrived with a family of three young children, a cow, a team of horses and one dollar and fifty cents.[6] Some had enough money to get them through the first year, but others got along the best way the could. As farmers had feared, the Run came so late in the year that they were not able to plant a crop. One man, with a family of six, spent the first winter cutting wood. One day he would cut the wood and the next day haul it to town in his wagon. For two days of work he earned 50 cents.[7]

Settlers used the barter system instead of cash, trading what they had for what they needed. Cottonwood and Cedar trees were cut and sold for humber and fence posts (five cents each). Chickens and eggs were traded to the grocer for flour, coffee, or a little sugar.[8]   Will Johnston, a Prairie Chapel farmer, grew sorghum cane the first years on his homestead. Sorghum was considered to be almost legal tender. Once he traded a barrel of sorghum for a young horse.[9]

Besides money, housing was a primary concern to homesteaders. A house was not only shelter, but also a way of proving up one's claim. Most houses were little more than one or two room shacks. In the Cherokee Outlet lumber was scarce and expensive since there were few stones and no bricks or cement.[10] Many homesteaders made do with "dugouts" or caves cut into a hillside.[11]   Sod houses were built using the thick turf of the prairie. Buffalo grass was the best sod for houses because of its fine, dense roots. Builders would use a span of horses or mules to pull a special sod plow through the turf. Its five long teeth ran four inches deep while turning the sod over, producing strips about a foot wide. The builder made sod "bricks" by cutting strips into pieces fourteen to eighteen inches long. These were laid grass side up to form interior or exterior walls, while doors and windows were framed with lumber. Saplings could be used across the walls in place of joists and covered with thick layers of sod.[12] Sometimes the roof was covered with wood shingles. Log or pole roofs were covered with straw or sod.   It was not uncommon to see cornflowers or weeds growing out of the roof of a sod home.[13] While not very elegant, sod houses were warm in the winter and cool in the summer, much better than the tents where people resided.

County Government Begins

Towns sprang up in Kay County the night of September 16, 1893. Settlers concerned themselves with getting their lives and surroundings organized. Claims were "proved up", crops planted, schools and churches were organized and built. Towns grew, with businesses being built as life took on a semblance of permanency. With its fertile soil and hard-working people. Kay County's future seemed promising. Settlers still had two important decisions to make, the election of a county government and a permanent county name.

A temporary government appointed by Territorial Governor William C. Renfrow, consisted of Commissioners G.W. Batchelder, Baxter Brown and E.R. Richey; Probate Judge, B.N. Woodson; Clerk of the District Court, F.M. Beale; County Attorney, A.A. Byers; Sheriff, G. S. Fenton; Register of Deeds, J.C. Jamison; County Clerk, C.S. Robb; Surveyor, W.R. Jouney; Coroner, J.D. Biggs and County Superintendent, R.A. Sullins. These men were to serve until November, 1894, when a general election would be held.[14]

Before the election, a vigorous campaign, by three political parties, took place. Besides Democrats and Republicans, the active Populists party joined in. Populism grew from farmers' discontent with the country's economic conditions in the late nineteenth century. By 1892, populism became political with the formation of the Populist Party. Populist candidates won offices in general elections that year, going strong and increasing in strength at the time of the Run into the Cherokee Outlet in 1893. Populist Hugh Owens, was elected from the second district to the Board of County Commissioners, along with Republicans J.B. Hart of the district and A.M. Thomas of the third district. They took their oath of office December 1, 1894, serving until January 1, 1897.[15]

The new commissioners were greeted with major problems, the first being an empty treasury. The General Fund, exhausted by the temporary commissioners, left the county more than $50,000 in debt. In the spring of 1894, the temporary commissioners made a basic organization of the townships, making assessments on asses-sable property. However, there was very little in the way of assess able property, since settlers had very little. Their property mostly consisted of a team of horses and a few household goods. These valuations were small and many levied taxes went uncollected. Now the new commissioners faced a quandary. The county owned these debts and was in need of operating expenses, but had very little income.

The small amount that trickled into the General Fund came from fines and licenses for saloons. They had to issue warrants in order to pay county officers, build and maintain the courthouse, build roads and bridges and care for the poor. They disbursed warrants at around fifty cents on the dollar. By spring, the new territorial legislature made some good laws and things began to look up. County officials were able to float a bond issue that allowed them to carry on county business.[16]

Another item on the 1894 election agenda was selecting a permanent name for the county of "K". The secretary of the Interior divided the Outlet into counties prior to the run, Designating county seats and temporary county names. The seven temporary county names were "K", "L","M", "N", "O", "P" and "Q". Each political party pondered the question of a name at their respective conventions. Republicans chose the name "Flynn" after Republican Territorial Congressional Delegate, Dennis T. Flynn, At the time, he was campaigning for the Free Homes Bill, a proposal that would permit homesteaders to receive free titles to their claims. This bill was quite popular in Oklahoma, but "K" county's Democrats and Populists did not agree to the name"Flynn" and joined forces, selecting the name "Kay". The election results were "Kay", 1,734 votes and "Flynn", 1,207.[17]

Flynn campaigned for his "Free Homes" bill the next two years. In 1896, the next presidential election year, he was confident of a third term re-election. He ran up against a stronger issue than his "free homes" proposal. The Populists, representing an economically hard-pressed agricultural minority, supported the inflationary measure of "free silver" (free, unlimited coinage of currency). When Democrats adopted the silver issue and nominated fiery Nebraska orator, William Jennings Bryan, as their candidate, Flynn found his issue overshadowed. He lost his bid for re-election and the chance to see his Free Homes Bill pass, but only temporarily. In 1898, Flynn returned to Congress and his Free Homes Bill passed on June 17, 1900. Word of this reprieve from debts for the settlers swept Oklahoma Territory like a prairie fire. They celebrated by ringing bells and tooting whistles.[18]

With the county's affairs in order, the debate was now on the location of the county seat. This decision, made by the Secretary of the Interior before the Run of 1893, or so he thought gave Newkirk the honor. However, Blackwell, Kildare and Ponca City pursued the honor of being the county seat. There was some discussion of dividing "K" county into two counties, with seats at Newkirk and Blackwell. The idea was dropped and county boundaries were left as originally set. The last serious attempt to shift the county seat came in 1908. Kildare fell out of the competition, leaving only Blackwell and Ponca City to pursue the issue. The question was placed on the ballot in the fall elections, with none of the towns winning a clear majority. As a result, a run-off election between Newkirk and Blackwell was held in December. Newkirk won by a bare 50 votes. With such a small majority Blackwell contested the count. The competition ended when the question was submitted to the Oklahoma Supreme Court, who ruled on January 30, 1912 that Newkirk, once and for all, was the county seat of Kay County.[19]

Crops Are Planted

By spring of 1894, people were ready to put in their first crop. Some crops were especially dependable in the virgin sod of the Outlet. The first two years after the opening saw drought take its toll. In the winter of 1895-96, crops of sweet potatoes and turnips pulled some families through. Kaffir corn grew readily and could be used for corn bread, pancakes and hominy.[20] Watermelons grew well in the bottom lands. When the weather cooperated wheat grew well, producing bumper crops. In 1894, Kay County produced 1,000,000 bushels. In 1897, the yield was 4,000,000 bushels and by 1900, the yield reached 5,000,000 bushels.[21] Other good grain crops were corn, oats, and alfalfa. Orchards and gardens began to bear within a few years, producing peaches, pears, plums, apricots, apples and grapes. Herds began to increase, making the county a production center for horses, mules, hogs and cattle. As productivity on the farms increased, farm-related businesses did well in nearby towns. Grain elevators dotted the horizon. Two-story gingerbread trimmed residences began replacing dugouts and sod houses. Those who had stuck it out on their quarter-sections were beginning to see some of their dreams come true.

Communities and Schools

Most people who staked claims in the Outlet arrived with some concrete ideas of what constituted a decent way of life. Almost always, this included a desire to be able to worship and provide an education for their children. Because travel was very difficult in the newly settled land most towns in Kay County were beyond easy reach of farm families. These families soon began forming communities and relying on their own resources to provide schools and places of worship. Communities like Bois D'Arc, along the creek west of Ponca City; Round Grove near Autwine, west of Ponca City; and Prairie Chapel, south of Blackwell, never developed into towns. These informally organized communities were important social, educational and religious contributors to people's lives. School and church often shared the same building, many times only a dugout, sod or frame structure. Little better than "prove-up houses", they served as a school during the week, the site of social gatherings on Saturday night and a place of worship on Sunday morning.

Bethel School, five miles northwest of Blackwell (two miles north of the present day Plainsman Motel in Blackwell), was such a school.[22] This school was a dugout, sixteen feet wide by thirty feet long. It had a dirt floor, a cedar shingled roof and a dirt wall at the north end, which was "sodded up" an additional three foot above the level of the ground. There was a window in this wall and a door on the south that was left open except on stormy days, allowing more light into the room. A large, round stove in the middle of the room furnished heat in cold weather. Long benches with backs were placed on the stage located at the front of the room. One class would recite lessons while the other students remained in their seats studying, listening or whispering.

Cracks in the dirt wall, large enough for a pencil to be inserted in, created entertainment for students.[23] Center School, west of Newkirk, opened in 1894. Classes in early rural schools were quite different from those of today. Students learned from simple books and chairs. They would memorize their work, recite it before the class, and work assignments on a slate with a slate pencil. To erase the slate, they would spit on it and rub the writing off with their sleeves. Anyone using a rag to clean his slates was considered a sissy. Every Friday afternoon visitors were welcome to attend programs put on by students, usually a ciphering or spelling contest. For the spelling contest two lines were formed on opposite sides of the room. The teacher would pronounce a word to be spelled. If a student misspelled it, he took his seat, and the word was given to the other side. The object of the contest was to be the last one standing. The ciphering contest was similar, except that math problems were used. It was a good drill in addition, subtraction, multiplication and division, allowing everyone to learn as they listened.[24]

Bethel and Center Schools were only two of many such rural schools in Kay County. Others included Fairview School, west of Ponca City, affectionately known as "Corn Bread College", because cornbread regularly appeared in the students lunch boxes.[25] Prairie Chapel School opened in 1894, one mile south and eight miles east of Blackwell; and Banner School opened near Newkirk in 1893. Round Grove provided education for grade school students until 1954 when it was absorbed into a larger district.[26] Rural schools were often subscription schools with parents contributing towards the construction of the building and the teacher's salary, usually twenty to twenty-five dollars per month. Ice cream socials and box suppers were popular ways to raise extra money when needed. In one such instance, Aldia Bissell baked a cake to be auctioned off. It sold for eight dollars, enough to buy the needed "potbellied" stove for the school.[27]

The people in the northern part of the county near Chilocco Indian School, established in 1884, were especially generous in building Dale and Grey Noret Schools, Chilocco

Creek split the established school district in half. Residents, not wanting their children crossing the creek during hazardous flood stages, established two new districts. Grey Noret was on the north side of the creek, on land donated by a man named Grey Noret. Dale School, on the south, was built of locally quarried limestone costing six hundred dollars. It was completed in 1894; perhaps the largest one-room school built in the county. Early schools might seem inadequate by modern standards but they provided adequate educations. Often their graduates went on to high school in a nearby town and some attended college in Tonkawa, Blackwell, Norman or Stillwater.[28]

Churches Play A Major Role

Equally important in rural community life were local churches. In the first days after the run, farm families often met in someone's home for informal services. These make-do arrangements lasted only until more permanent accommodations could be made. Often, the school building was used for church services until a separate building could be constructed. Within two or three years of the Run of 1893, permanent church buildings began appearing on the plains of Kay County. This was done through the spiritual and financial support of churches in nearby Kansas. Among the first was Riverview Church, eight miles southwest of Tonkawa in Owen Township. Services for what became the Riverview congregation began in the dugout of Timothy Chambers in the summer of 1894, moving into the new school building in 1895. During the winter of 1895-1896, H.A. Moulton solicited funds from people in the area, and Kansas, for a church building. It was the first frame rural church building in the county, named Riverview because it overlooked the Salt Fork river. Nearby was Riverview Cemetery, The first platted and recorded cemetery in the county.[29]

Like Riverview Church, Longwood Baptist Church was organized soon after the Run. Services began on August 30, 1894 in a sod house, under the leadership of H.J. Dykes, of Kansas. Nearby Coon Creek served as the baptistery. The eighteen-member congregation was ministered by W.J. Black, a circuit preacher, who preached three sermons a month. In August of 1896, a storm caused the north wall to collapse. A tarpaulin served as a temporary wall until other housing could be found. The congregation met at Oak View School for the next eight years. In 1905, a new $1,000 building was built, serving the congregation until 1966, at which time a new building was constructed.[30]

Round Grove Baptist Church organized in Round Grove School, April 26, 1896. Located five miles west of Ponca City, the congregation met from 1896 until 1963. Several years of informal services were held in Snyder Grove during the summer and the Robert Parmely home in the winter. Different denominations were represented each Sunday, but the majority were Baptists. Charter members included families by the name of Finley, Edwards, Dunn, Harris, Howell, Phelps, Smith, Keathley and Young. The Tyree family joined soon after.[31]

Most early church buildings were frame structures, but the Grey Noret Church, in the northern part of the county, was unique. The gothic building, constructed in 1907 of locally quarried limestone, stood until recently. Prairie Chapel Methodist Church, located eight miles east and one mile south of Blackwell, was typical of most prairie churches. A wood-frame building on a stone foundation, rectangular in shape with an imposing belfry, it was built in 1898 at a cost of $1,800 on ground donated by Jack Carter. Trustees Carter, John Ferguson, J.N. VanWinkle, S.J. Samuels and B.L. Long presided over its construction. After the building was completed, the question arose as to what denomination it would be. The families who helped organize and raise funds for the church were of several denominations. They settled the problem in the true democratic fashion of a vote. The Methodists won.[32] Middleton Church, near Newkirk, was organized in 1900. The church building was dedicated June 2, 1901. It continued to serve the congregation until January, 1966, when it was united with the First Presbyterian Church in Newkirk.[33]

There were many more rural churches founded soon after the Run, but better roads, bridges and the coming of the automobile caused attendance to decline. Members began attending larger churches in town. These were the same reasons for the demise of rural schools. It was more economical to have rural students attend larger schools in town than for the county to operate small one or two room schools in the country. One by one these rural schools and churches began to close. The buildings remained important to rural life. They continued to serve as community centers for organizations such as Grange, 4-H and home demonstration groups. Square dances, box dinners, picnics and ice cream socials held rural communities together in spite of the pull of nearer towns. Towards the turn of the century towns began to dominate Kay County life more and more.

New Towns Spring Up

Newkirk

Not everyone who made the Run, however, staked a claim on a quarter-section of farmland. Many headed for one of the new towns in the Outlet. In Kay County this might have been the proposed county seat, Lamoreaux (Newkirk), or any of the dozen government surveyed communities. Some towns were platted before the Run by private promoters who sold their town lots. This involved guesswork on the part of the promoters as to sites with the best potential for success. Homesteaders were advised not to put their money into these towns because some were fraudulent.[28] Towns planned by railroad companies chose sites along existing lines, some selected by Boomers, who worked for the railroads.[34]

The town with the best chance of success was Newkirk,

platted as the county seat, surveyed and laid out before the Run by government surveyors. It was named "Lamoreaux" in honor of S.W. Lamoreaux, Commissioner of the General Land Office of the United States.[35] Situated on the Atchison, Topeka and Santa Fe Railway line, twelve miles south of Arkansas City, was Kirk, a small Station two miles north of Lamoreaux. Confusion on the day of the Run caused some prospective citizens coming from Arkansas City to mistake the stop at Kirk for Lamoreaux and they got off the train too soon. By the evening of September 16, 1893, about 5,000 settlers had staked claims in or near Lamoreaux.[36] Anyone meeting the requirements as a claimant was allowed two town lots, one for a residence, and one for a business.[37] Settlers spent their first night in wagons, tents, or on blankets on the ground. It was a sleepless night for many, fearing they might lose their lots unless they kept watch.

It was just a tent city, but citizens of Lamoreaux did not forget that the next day, September 17, was Sunday. Church services were held at eight o'clock in the morning on the east side of the public square, with the minister, B.C. Swartz, using a bale of hay as his pulpit. In the afternoon, Congregational minister, the Reverend DeLong, of Arkansas City, delivered a sermon from an open buggy on the courthouse square.[38] During the day, settlers began putting down roots or trading off their lots to latecomers. One family, that of D.M. Hamlin, brought a "prefabricated house", a portable photography gallery, that they set up on their lot within a week.[39]

At ten o'clock Monday morning, citizens assembled to organize a city government under the direction of County Attorney A.A. Byers, Temporary officers selected were R.R. Talley, Chair-man; M.L. Harter, Secretary and L.M. Dolde, Assistant Secretary. One of the first orders of business was to change the name of the town to something other that "Lamoreaux". Since the Santa Fe Railway line ran through town, even though there was no depot, the name "Santa Fe" was chosen and forwarded to the Santa Fe officials. [40] Next, a committee of seven people was chosen to nominate permanent city officials.

Later that day, an election was held with N.L. Bowman elected Mayor; W.H. Line, City Clerk; P.W. Smith, Treasurer and W.B. Brown, City Marshal. W.L. Barnum, J.W. Dunn, A.C. Dolde, W.M. Ferguson, C.E. Wintrode and Robert Sutherland were elected Councilmen. These men governed until a general election could be held in January.[41]

It was late in the year before Santa Fe Railroad officials responded to the town's name change to Santa Fe. Officials announced other stations along the railway lines were named Santa Fe and therefore it would be too confusing and not acceptable. Once again the townspeople were called upon to choose another name. Since the station at Kirk had been abandoned, they voted to call their town "Newkirk".[42]

On January 4,1894, the first Board of Trustees for the new city under the name of Newkirk was elected. Officers were Jameson Vawter, President; A.C. Dolde, Vice President; Charles B. Apperson, City Clerk; H.C. McCant, Assessor; J.D. Biggs, Treasurer, W.B. Brown, Marshal and D.M. Hamlin, Justice of the Peace. Other members of the Board of Trustees were B.B. Burr, W.T. Whiteman and William M. Ferguson. Newkirk was permanently organized and incorporated as a City of the Second Class on January 8, 1894. At that time, the Board of Trustees chose W.S. Cline to be the City Attorney and the *Newkirk Times* as the city's legal newspaper. Newkirk's original 5,000 inhabitants had thinned to 2,108,[43] but those who remained took steps toward permanency. Tents disappeared, replaced by small wooden houses and business buildings. Construction of the first permanent stone building, the J.M. And C.E. Haynes Dry Goods Store, began in 1893 and was completed in the spring of 1894.[44]

Business was booming. By January, 1894, Newkirk had a post office, the first postmaster being William G. Jones. The Northern Oklahoma Telephone Company received permission from the city government to install and operate a telephone system September 3, 1894 and was in service by 1897. Dr. David D. Martin was one of the first doctors and Dr. A.J.M. Brazier one of the first dentists. Being the county seat, Newkirk attracted a number of lawyers including W. S. Cline, H.S. Braucht, C.L. Pinkham, Virgil Brown, William Rouse and a Mr. Smart. The city operated an opera house and dance hall. The Masonic Lodge organized in 1894 with several prominent civic leaders among its membership. The young town did not lack for excitement. There were 25 saloons and a rather rough and rowdy dance hall. Later, silent movies (ten cents for adults , five cents for children), traveling shows and stock companies provided a somewhat more sophisticated entertainment. Otherwise, the Newkirk people relied on their own talents for entertainment.[45]

Businessmen included George Alberti, who ran a furniture store; George Midgely operated a grocery store, and Hank Paris conveyed passengers around town in his hack service, delivered newspapers and boarded visitors in the "Paris Rooms". Joseph E. Hancock began to offer competition in 1908 with his Hancock Dray and Transfer Company. Visitors to Newkirk could stay in either the Endicott or Park Hotels. Kay and Kaw Mercantile, established in 1898, stocked just about everything the buyer could use, from farm implements and buggies to hardware items and glassware, as did Hoefer Hardware, Implement and Supply House. The J.C. Columbia Lumber Yard, later bought by Hufbauer and Son, provided building materials. Mrs. Ada Garside, a professional photographer, settled in Newkirk along with her husband in 1899. She had one of the finest studios in the Territory. Mr. and Mrs. Ed Chope set up an unusual business a cigar factory.[48]

The Bank of Santa Fe (which became Eastern National Bank in 1908) began operations on October 9, 1893, making it the first bank in the townsite of Santa Fe. It was founded by E.B. Eastman, who served as president, F.L. Flint, vice president and R.G. Bracken, cashier. Three days later, October 12, 1893, the Kay County State Bank was established by P.W. Smith of Udall, Kansas, who served as president. The Kay County State Bank became the First National Bank in 1900, later absorbed into the Eastman National Bank in 1933. The Kay County Mills, operated by James, George and Henry Ledbetter, sold feed to farmers and stored grain crops. Stone quarries, located five and one-half miles northeast of Newkirk, were operated by David L. Means and J.A. Feagins. They employed several men and furnished materials for the first permanent stone buildings in Kay County. The city's first bond election, October 9, 1899, voted 122 to 41 for a water works bond amounting to $2,500.[47] That same year P.H. Albright Investment Company of Winfield, Kansas opened a branch office in Newkirk, under the management of C. A. Johnson. On November 15, 1899, A.A. Slosson organized the Farmers State Bank. He served as president and J.H. Coleman served as cashier. The bank was purchased by Eastman National Bank in 1936. Another bank, the State Guaranty Bank, was established in 1909 with J.S. Eastman as president and P.S. Mason as cashier. This bank was taken over by the Eastman National Bank in 1911. On February 1, 1900, a population count was taken in Newkirk. It certified to the Governor of the Territory that Newkirk could be incorporated as a First Class City, reportedly exceeding 2,500 citizens. With growth came more modernization and electric lights were installed in 1903.[48]

Newkirk became a commercial center for this area of Kay County in spite of competition from several other towns. The Santa Fe Railroad shipped tons of farm produce out of Newkirk while the Kay County Mills, Cathcart and Cottrell Grain Company, and T.F. McGraw acted as middlemen. In addition, Newkirk profited by trade generated on the Kansa (Kaw) reservation east of the Arkansas River. The river was often difficult to ford and in May, 1894, city officials petitioned the Department of the Interior for permission to build a bridge across the Arkansas, east of Newkirk. The long wooden bridge was constructed, making trade much easier with both the Kaw and Osage further east.[49]

The *Lamoreaux Democrat* distributed only one issue before it became the *Santa Fe Democrat* September 20, 1893. Later it changed its name again to conform to the town's name, becoming the *Newkirk Democrat*.[50] Like most towns, Newkirk had several newspapers. In addition to the *Newkirk Democrat,* published by the Dolde Brothers, there was the *Kay County Populist,* published by Tom Smith; the *Newkirk Republican,* by Lincoln McKinlay; the *Kay County News,* E.F. Korns.;[51]and the *Kildare Journal,* by Jeremiah Johnson, which consolidated with the *Newkirk Republican,* becoming the *Newkirk Republican New Journal.*[52] As can be seen by the names, these often reflected the political affiliations of their publishers and subscribers.

The people of Newkirk were equally concerned with other aspects of community life besides commerce. The United Brethren built a meeting house soon after the town was founded. The Presbyterians began a church on November 21, 1893.[53] The Christian Church began holding services in 1893, building a permanent building in 1901. In early 1894, the Methodists bought a lot and moved the former Salvation Army Hall building onto it to serve as their church. Members of the congregation quarried stone east of town for the construction of a new building in 1901-1902. Father Isermann, a Benedictine from Sacred Heart Mission in Pottawatomie County, Indian Territory, offered Catholic mass in Newkirk just after the Run. In 1894 Catholic families acquired a building from Cross that served as a temporary church until 1898, serving as the home of the St. Francis of Assisi Congregation. In 1906 a two-story house was converted to a parochial school presided over by Father J.M. Kekeisen.[54]

Education for Newkirk's children began soon after the Run. There were no public schools only private subscription schools. Newkirk's first such school opened in a store building on Maple Avenue. Thomas J. Pate, assisted by two teachers, Mrs. Nellie Cook and Miss Ona Cochran, taught approximately 60 children from grades one through four. Both Mrs. Cook and Miss Cochran left their positions to teach in the first public school, opened in January of 1894. Mrs. Cook was in charge of intermediate classes; Miss Cochran, grammar classes; Professor D.J. Cowan was in charge of high school and Miss Mary Burke in charge of the primary. In 1897 classes were held for the first time in a new two-story, stone school building. Four years later another two- story stone building (replaced in 1915) became the first high school for Newkirk's older students.[55]

Fire dealt Newkirk a major setback in 1901, destroying the entire east side of the 100 block of Main Street between 6th and 7th streets. Flames raged when someone near the lamp-keeper lit a match. As a result, in 24 businesses were destroyed including two barbershops, two grocery stores, a dry goods store, four restaurants, a confectionery shop and four saloons. All were wooden buildings, one and two stories high, ready fuel for the flames that swept over them just before dusk on November 15. The owner of the confectionery shop ran back and forth across the street carrying buckets of merchandise he salvaged from the flames, but to no avail. He had not counted on the voracious appetites of the children who gathered to watch the excitement. Before the fire was out they had eaten his entire stock of candy. Citizens fighting the fire were helpless in the face of such a large conflagration. As a result of the disaster, the city com-missioners passed an ordinance requiring all future business buildings be made of brick or stone. They also bought new fire fighting equipment and organized a twenty-four man volunteer fire department. Several other Kay County towns faced similar fires and other disasters, but some were not able to overcome them. Newkirk's economy and vigorous character was such that the entire block was rebuilt by 1903. Most new buildings were constructed of non-flammable limestone from the Armstrong quarries four miles east of Newkirk.[56]

Life was similar in the other towns of Kay County during

115

these territorial days. Imposing stone buildings began to give dignity and permanence to the dusty streets while wood-frame homes gradually replaced the "proving-up" homes of the Run. Young Elms, Cottonwoods, shrubs and flowers began to change the once treeless prairie into shaded garden spots.

Kildare

Each town and community had its own character. South of Newkirk, down the Santa Fe tracks, lay Kildare. Promotional literature dated October 5, 1893, declared firmly "This will be the TOWN!".[57] Before the Run of 1893, Kildare existed as a stop on the Santa Fe line. Because of numerous ranches in the area, shipping pens and a small depot were already located there.[58] Approximately one mile to the northwest was Willow Springs, popular with ranchers and cowboys in the pre-Run days. Surrounding Willow Springs and Kildare was some of the richest soil in the Outlet. With its good soil, convenience to water and the railroad line, Kildare seemed likely to succeed as one of the prospective cities of the Outlet. There was considerable speculation that it would be the seat of County "K".[59]

Many men of strong will had a part in the development of Kildare. One of these was Dennis Wolfe Bushyhead, former Principal Chief of the Cherokee Nation. He had negotiated both the Cherokee Strip Live Stock Association leases and the sale of the Outlet to the government. A provision of the sale agreement (Article Two) allowed any Cherokee Indian who was a resident of the Outlet and who had made permanent improvements prior to November. 1891, to receive such lands as his allotment for a homestead. He could receive 80 acres each for himself, his spouse, and each of his children. However, an exception was made in the case of Bushyhead who was allowed 160 acres. Also, allotments had to be taken on land where improvements were made. On May 10, 1893, Assistant Attorney General John I. Hall, of the interior department, ruled that only the head of household had to take his allotments on property with improvements. Family members could choose their allotments where they wanted.

116

Bushyhead was again an exception. An article in the *New York Times* charged that these provisions were part of a scheme between Indians and land speculators to obtain the best land in the Outlet. Others, however, took the view that the homesteads selected by the Cherokee made it impossible for speculators to come into the Outlet on opening day and seize the best town sites.[60]

Bushyhead chose his allotment near Kildare. Tennessee Jane Jordan and Hattie Jordan chose their allotments adjoining Bushyhead's to the south. He had these allotments surveyed and divided into lots. The first one he reportedly sold for four hundred fifty dollars. Water for the Bushyhead town site was hauled from nearby Willow Springs. To end the necessity of hauling water, in early October, Bushyhead had three windmill driven wells drilled.[61]

Although it was well known the day of the Run that Kildare was not going to be the county seat of "K" County, numerous homesteaders headed for the area. Kildare, popularly called "Bushyhead's Town", was one-half mile west of the railroad. A lot could be purchased immediately with a clear title to it. Within a few days after the Run several businesses had set up shop. Most provided services or supplies needed for a town under construction. Architects, carpenters, contractors and lumber companies furnished a variety of building supplies.

The Kildare post office, established October 14, 1893, served as a distribution point for the surrounding area. The mail came by train and was picked up at the depot. The *Kildare Journal,* owned by Jeremiah Johnson, was the first newspaper. It later combined with a Newkirk paper, becoming the *Newkirk Republican News Journal.* By April, 1894, the town had street lights, and in August the Oklahoma Telephone Company began connecting Kildare with other Kay County towns.

Businesses prospered and the town began to take on a look of permanence. One of the first businesses to open was that of H.B. Owen, who operated a mercantile store. A frequent visitor to his store was Chief Washunga of the Kansa (Kaw) Indians.[62] Mr. and Mrs. Steve Paris moved to Kildare in 1894, where he worked for a lumber company. Their son, Madison Kildare Paris, born March 10, 1894, was the first white baby to be born in the new town. Chief Washunga and some of his braves came to see the baby boy, but Mrs. Paris, who was deathly afraid of Indians, would not let them in the house. When Mr. Paris came home from work, the Indians were still waiting to see the baby. He took the child outside and let Chief Washunga and the others hold him.[63] Around 1895 a three-room school provided facilities for 12 grades. Some of the earliest school buses or "kidwagons", orange and black wooden wagons drawn by a team of horses or mules, brought the children to school from surrounding areas. If one was in a hurry, the kidwagon was not the means of transportation to take. "Ross Hayes, a kidwagon driver, once offered Mrs. A.C. Beck a ride to which she replied, 'No thanks, I'm in a hurry.'".[64]

For the next several years Kildare was as prosperous as anyone could wish. A stagecoach line and a freight line that hauled supplies and grain, connected Kildare with Blackwell and Tonkawa. Kildare was the main railroad shipping point for Blackwell, thirteen miles to the west. Although Blackwell was the largest town in the county it was not on the railroad. At one time Kildare had three general stores, two meat markets, three doctors' offices, four lawyers' offices, a hotel, three lumber yards, two hardware stores, two livery barns, two blacksmith shops, two restaurants, three grain elevators, a bank, slaughter house, shoe cobbler, two bakeries, two drug stores, three saloons, a consolidated high school, Woodman Lodge and IOOF Lodge with their auxiliaries.[65] Kildare's Methodist Church was built in 1898 with money raised by the Ladies Aid Society. Some of Kildare's boosters still hoped they might yet snare the county seat, should it be removed from Newkirk, along with a state university.

On March 23, 1894, fire swept through the business area of Kildare, with an arrest being made for arson. Two more fires hit the town and each time many of the businesses did not rebuild. The same week of the 1894 fire, mother nature loaned her hand to the destruction of businesses when a severe storm hit.[66] In the early days Kildare had a high crime rate and horse-theft was not uncommon. Thieves would make raids on Kildare's livery stables and homes, then retreat across the Arkansas River east of Kildare. They took advantage of the rough country and dense timber with few caring to pursue them.[67] Kildare's population began to wane.

Willow Springs

Nearby Willow Springs got its name from a fine spring of clear, pure water, used for many years by Indians, cattlemen and travelers that crossed the Cherokee Outlet. A one and a half story house and large barn stood there prior to the run.[68] Though its population was never as large as Kildare's, it was the home of the Willow Springs Bottling Works, which existed as early as 1881. Water was peddled in tank wagons and sold at two prices: five cents a pint for drinking and fifty cents for a bushel-sized, galvanized tin-bucket full for livestock. Many families dipped from the fifty-cent water before offering it to the livestock.[69]

Willow Springs consisted of several stores, a bank and post office, but by 1895 most of the businesses and residents had packed up and moved east to Kildare. Another town site adjacent to Bushyhead's, on the east, was called Kildare City. This land had previously been claimed as a homestead by two different men. One man staked his claim east of the Santa Fe tracks which ran directly through the 160 acre tract while the other staked his on the west side. Although title to these lots was questionable, the location was apparently more desirable to many than Bushyhead's town.[70] On December 5, 1895, a decision was rendered on the Kildare City property issuing a patent allowing titles to be cleared on all the lots. Gradually over the next few months the population center shifted from Bushyhead's Town to Kildare City. The combined towns had a population of eight hundred by 1898, eventually it was named "Kildare".

Surrounding "Bushyhead's Town" of Kildare had been other hopeful towns such as Willow Springs, Kildare City, Cherokee and Pontiac. Cherokee was between Kildare and

119

Willow Springs. Pontiac was located south of Willow Springs. Kildare City later became part of Kildare. All of these tent cities had high hopes the night of September 16, 1893.[71]

Cross

Another townsite that appeared to have promise was Cross, located a few miles further south down the Santa Fe line. It had a railroad depot, express office and post office.[72] It was platted prior to the Run and promoted by the Santa Fe Railway Company, who planned it to be a dominant city.[73] When the dust cleared on the afternoon of September 16, 1893, Cross claimed 1,500 residents. A government-sanctioned distillery was located there, one of only two ever located in Oklahoma. Operated by a Civil War veteran, Captain W.B. Baker, he also ran a saloon and livery stable. The distillery and saloon were conveniently located across the street from the office of the justice of the peace. In some particular cases, the justice found for the defendant and then decreed "We will now go across the street to Captain Baker's saloon where the costs in the case will be liquidated."[74] Cross built a public school, had two newspapers, the *Cross Resident* and *Oklahoma State Guide,* hotels and a number of businesses.[75]

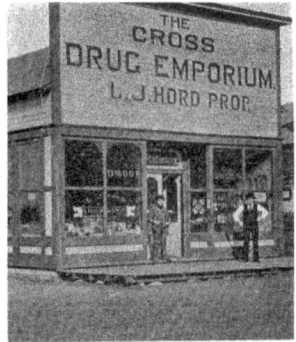

Ponca City

As a town, Cross was to be short-lived, for one mile further south lay another town, more aggressive than most, which became Ponca City. This second town was the product of a furniture manufacturer from Adrian, Michigan, Burton Seymour Barnes.[76] Like many businessmen of that time, he had been financially hurt by the Panic of 1893 and was looking for a way to start over. In June of 1893, he left his fine, ten room, two-story brick home in Michigan and set out for the Cherokee Outlet.[77]

Barnes toured the Outlet, not looking for a homestead but

120

a town site. He first stopped at the Enid and Perry town sites, but found little profitability in locating near government-owned land. Traveling east through the Otoe-Missouri and Ponca reservations, and then turning north, he came upon a spring just west of the B. and M. Ford on the Arkansas River. While watering his horses at this clear spring, he heard a train on the Santa Fe tracks about a mile away. Suddenly he realized that this was the place for which he had been looking. The railroad line, a good spring, and the nearby ford looked promising. Furthermore, he learned the water on the west side of the tracks at Cross was mostly "gyp" water. He was convinced that Cross would not grow into a large city, that this location, a mile to the south, was ideal for a town.[78] Barnes went to Arkansas City, where he organized the Ponca Townsite Company. For two dollars, Ponca Townsite Company members received a certificate entitling them to first call on town lots should the original claimants wish to sell out after the Run. The funds collected from the sale of certificates were to be used to survey the town and employ a city marshal. Barnes sold 2,300 certificates.[79]

Barnes joined the Run on September 16, 1893, staking his claim in the southeast quarter of the section he had chosen for his town site. He was convinced that he was first to stake a claim on the property; however, there were eight other people who also drove stakes into the land. All but three agreed to step aside for a small payment. There was a good deal of anger, arguing and a lot of bluffing, but Barnes won out. Later, when the plat was filed for the property, this quarter-section was named "Bluffdale".[80]

Five days after the Run, Ponca Townsite Company members got their chance for lots through a drawing, the surveying taking four days to complete.[80] Each certificate holder's name was written on a small card and placed in a box. Legal descriptions of the lots were also written on cards and placed in another box. On that Thursday morning, two little girls simultaneously began drawing a card with a name and one with a legal description for a business lot (or two residential lots). For the most part certificate holders abided by the luck of the draw. A

121

vigilance committee saw to it that "lot-jumping" was minimal. In one instance the committee, thirty strong simply appeared at the culprit's house. They placed poles under his house, trundled it down Grand Avenue, dumping it in a field on the far side of the Santa Fe tracks. Such impromptu moves were easy in those early days.[82]

Since final patents would not be issued for several months, or even years in most cases, people knew they might yet lose their lots. In spite of such insecurity, people of "New Ponca" as the town was called, got down to the business of establishing homes and businesses. Soon dusty Grand Avenue, the main east-west street, sported a ragged line of one-story, false-fronted, wood-frame stores. The town was incorporated on December 19, 1893 as "New Ponca". A post office was established January 12, 1894.[83] In February they elected the first city government consisting of B.S. Barnes, Mayor; J.W. Dalton, Treasurer, and J.M. McGuire, Clerk, Council members were F.P. Adams, W.M. Randall, J.L. McCarthy, P.I. Brown, and A.C. Foy.[84]

Ponca had almost everything it needed for success as a town except for a railroad depot. Cross had that. Trains stopped at Cross but steamed right through Ponca, much to the chagrin of Ponca's "aggressive" citizens. Before the Run, when Barnes was in Arkansas City campaigning to get members for his Ponca Townsite Company, someone asked him, "Will the trains stop in this new city?" Barnes replied, "The trains will stop just the same as at Chicago."[85] Yet, the trains did not stop and Ponca's Citizens were forced to go to Cross to collect freight and board the trains. This was a blow to their civic pride.

Barnes and his fellow civic leaders importuned the Santa Fe officials for months to locate a station at Ponca, but they refused steadfastly on the grounds there was not enough business to justify two stations located one mile apart. Quietly, Barnes made an agreement with the railroad agent at Cross that he would be given two town lots in Ponca if he would move there from Cross. Late one Saturday night, movers slipped into Cross, picked up the agent's house and rolled it towards Ponca. They were nearly out of Cross by dawn when the residents woke and realized what was happening. Angry men from Cross tried to stop the movers but were held off with a shotgun by the man in charge. That evening, the house was at the edge of Ponca City. It was guarded throughout the night and early Monday morning the house was placed on its new lot.[86] In September, 1894, one year after the town was founded, the Santa Fe gave in to pressure from some territorial legislators. The agreed to build a spur into Ponca and set up a station there. One week before the first train was to stop. Civic boosters were already planning for the big day and the town was humming with excitement. On September 22, 1894, at 9:27 a.m., the first train stopped at the new station in New Ponca.[87] Two young boys and two young girls met each train. Lady passengers received a bouquet of wild flowers and gentlemen were given a cigar. Everyone was given a small round-cornered card which quoted Barnes's promise. "The trains stop here just the same as at Chicago, Come and see us when you can.".[88] Ponca had won the railroad rivalry with Cross and now set about systematically dismantling and appropriating Cross.

Barnes bought the Midland Hotel, the largest in Cross, and moved it to Ponca. Later the Arcade Hotel was relocated from Cross. These were only the first of a migration that went on for months.[89] House after house and business after business crept on rollers across the mile that separated the two towns. Within six months little was left of Cross, it had all been incorporated into Ponca.[90]

With the railroad now recognizing the existence of Ponca, the future of the town seemed assured. Within a few weeks a post office was established and the name of the town was listed as "New Ponca". This did not please everyone, but on October 23, 1913, the name was changed to "Ponca City", which had a more impressive sound and the old depot known as "Ponca" near the Ponca Agency, was changed to "White Eagle".[91]

Good water was one of the concerns of the new town. There was a spring, but it was quite a distance from town, as much as three-quarters of a mile and always busy. William Evans, a Welsh immigrant, soon supplied a solution to this problem. Fastening barrels onto his wagon, "Water Billy" delivered water to

Grand Avenue, Looking East from First Street, 1897

homes in Ponca for fifteen cents per barrel.[92] This created a run on barrels, but the many saloons in the town quickly remedied the problem. The city government located a public well in the middle of Grand Avenue just east of First Street. A windmill and flat tank were added to the well, soon becoming an early day landmark.[93] Another public well was constructed at the rear of the J.S. Hutchins grocery store at 313 East Grand Avenue. In 1898, the city installed a city-wide water system. [94]

Education for the young people was one of the first concerns of the city government and within a few days after the Run, a large amount of both money and labor was pledged for the building of a school. Mayor Barnes suggested additional funding be obtained through voluntary contributions from non-resident lot holders and he received them. On November 16, 1893, the thirty-two foot by sixty-four foot school building was completed. It was a one-story building, partitioned into two rooms, by sliding doors that could be opened to make one large room. The cost of the building and equipment was $1,600. The Ponca Board of Trade claimed the school building as "the largest, handsomest and best public school building in the whole Territory of Oklahoma."[95]

The townspeople were understandably proud of their accomplishment and held a celebration on opening day. The program included a barbecue, banquet and ball along with games, horse races and Indian dancing. About 5,000 people, many of whom came in by special train from Kansas, watched the high point of the day as approximately 300 Indians took part in a race to capture 20 wild Texas steers.[96]

After a short three-month term that began in December 1893, classes in the public schools of Ponca resumed on September 24, 1894, with an impressive slate of teachers. Enrollment the first year was generally between 250 and 300 pupils. The first class graduated in May of 1896, consisting of two students.[97]

In the first two years the face of Ponca changed considerably. The scattered, ragged line of wood-frame buildings and "prove-up" houses gave way to more permanent structures. Grand Avenue was lined solidly with substantial two-story buildings. Early photographs depict traffic jams consisting of horses and buggies. At that time, South First Street was the main street of town. From the first, the people of Ponca liked to think of their town as progressive. It was the first town to have electric lights (within ten months after the Run) and the first flour mill (opened on April 9, 1894).[98] Around 1900, fire ravaged the north side of Grand Avenue between Second and Third streets. High winds helped fan the flames that destroyed the entire block. Firefighters were helpless. After the fire an ordinance was passed to build more fireproof buildings.[99]

Charles Welch built a brick yard, located on the south side of town (where Garfield Park is on South Avenue between Seventh and Ninth Streets). After installing a windmill to pump water, he took clay from the banks of the nearby creek, molded them, then dried them in the sun. These bricks went into many of the brick buildings in downtown Ponca City. He did masonry work on the Ponca City City Hall assisted by his son Nelson"Ted".[100] The City Hall, an elaborate two-story stone and brick building with a four-story bell tower, was built in 1900. It housed the police and fire departments as well as the city government. The bell in the tower warned bystanders when the fire engine was about to roll out of the double doors on the way to a fire. All of these changes were a part of Ponca City's transformation to the second largest town (population of 2,000) in Kay County.

Blackwell

Initially, Blackwell was the largest town in "K" county. Located in the western part of the county, northwest of Ponca and southwest of Newkirk, it was the brainchild of a group of businessmen from Winfield, Kansas. J.B. Lynn, William Whiting, F.T. Berkey, W.C. Robinson and E.L. Peckham formed a townsite company prior to the Run of 1893. They decided on a site for their town by selecting an area which had good agricultural land and was as centrally located in the proposed county as was practical. They felt a town built on their chosen site would have a good chance of becoming the county seat. Through the influence of A.J. Blackwell, a white man married to a mixed-blood Cherokee, they arranged for three Cherokee orphans, George Palmer, Mary Palmer and Mike Hendricks to be given allotments at the townsite they selected. Along with Blackwell's wife, each child received an eighty-acre allotment. The children's guardian secured a court order to sell the land to the townsite company. Once arrangements had been completed, Blackwell began touring southern Kansas advertising the town and recruiting potential townsite members. To aid in publicity, the townsite company started a newspaper called the *Blackwell Eagle*, making it the most publicized townsite in the Cherokee Outlet. On the day of the opening, many homesteaders ran straight for "Blackwell Rock".[101]

Like many townsites, an unexpected problem arose. Through some clerical error, or otherwise, only three of the four proposed eighty-acre plots making up the townsite went to the Cherokee heirs. One section remained public domain and open to homesteading. This allotment was approximately six miles north-

126

west of Blackwell and claimed by Frank Potts of Winfield, Kansas. For the right price, $1,050, this "townsite land" was purchased. The city government assessed those who settled on this "government eighty" to compensate for the additional expenses. This form of assessment was so satisfactory that the phrase "assess the government eighty" came to be a standing joke and standard operating procedure in Blackwell.[102]

Commercial transportation to Blackwell in 1893 was by Stagecoach. The public well is in the foreground.

Photo courtesy of Oklahoma Historical Society

As was the case with most new Kay County towns, citizens immediately organized temporary governments. The president of the town council was A.J. Blackwell; F.T. Berkey, clerk; Ed L. Peckham, attorney; M.B. Shields, treasurer and James Bethel, marshal. Blackwell, Berkey, Shields, John Sanger, E.M. Reynolds and William Whiting acted as trustees. On December 6, 1893, Blackwell became the first mayor and served through May 15, 1894. Like Ponca City, a Board of Trade was formed, a forerunner of the Chamber of Commerce, for the purpose of the town to recruit businesses. The Board met at Abe O'Harra's blacksmith shop and considered solutions to problems that affected the town.[103] One relatively minor problem was street names. Many were originally named by and for town boosters from Winfield, Kansas. In addition, A.J. Blackwell named the main east-west street for himself and others streets for his sons, King David (now Oklahoma) and Solomon (now Bridge), his wife, Rosa (now McKinley), and other family members. Shortly after the town was incorporated. Blackwell's citizens renamed the streets.[104, 105]

Another problem facing the new town was lawlessness. There were still plenty of cowboys around working on the ranches in the area. Some were vicious characters, but most were just hard working men who came into Blackwell's numerous saloons looking for a good time. Occasionally though, things would get out of hand. To help solve the problem, the town council hired a former Texas Ranger, but he soon found there was too much for him to handle. Marshal Josh Cox and his deputy, Alfred Lund, were able to get things under control. Lund, a former cowboy, captured the notorious Cherokee Outlet bandit, Ben Cravens, on December 4, 1896, while he was hiding out northeast of Blackwell on Lost Creek. During the conflict, Cravens was wounded and Buck McGregg, alias "Diamond Dick" was killed.[106]

Parker

Competition from the neighboring towns created another problem. Parker, a town organized by a Dr. Parker of Arkansas City, who, like the founders of Blackwell, expected his town to be the "premier" city of Kay County, was located about one mile south of Blackwell across the Chikaskia River. At least two two-story buildings were built and two newspapers established. Parker set about trying to convince a railroad to build a spur into his town then tried to convince the people of "Blackwell Rock" to give up their post office, even though they didn't have one yet and to merge with "Parker", giving up the name "Blackwell". A.J. Blackwell felt like this was Parker's lowest blow. Blackwell, an ambitious, energetic man, harangued fellow Blackwell citizens, accusing them of a lack of gumption by even considering the idea of letting a smaller town take over a promising place like Blackwell Rock. His persuasive arguments won out when the townspeople, who were already having second thoughts about the merger, came to realize that Parker meant to shift the central

128

business district away from Blackwell. Needless to say, the merger fell through, Blackwell kept its name and post office.[107]

Shortly after this turmoil, the Chikaskia River flooded the small town of Parker and practically washed it away. However, this was not the end of Parker. It went through two more incarnations, first as Chikaskia City and then as Kay Center. Kay Center at least had the distinction of having its own post office from October 9, 1897, to June 1, 1898, then, it too, ceased to exist as an organized town. Blackwell successfully met and defeated this challenge.[108]

Within 45 days of the Run, the town boasted twelve stores that stocked groceries and dry goods, a harness shop, boot and shoe store, three hardware stores, a drug store that also stocked paints and oils, a bank, seven restaurants, two bakeries, four feed stores, two meat markets, four saloons, three livery stables, four lumber yards, five blacksmiths, two well borers, two sign painters, two barbershops, two doctors, seven contractors, ten law and real estate offices, three stage line depots, many carpenters and a brick yard.[109] One of the more famous Blackwell residents was W.S. Prettyman, whose rare talents as a photographer captured the true west. He had a studio in Arkansas City but secured a claim south of Blackwell in 1893 when he made the Run into Oklahoma. He established his business in Blackwell, later building a two story brick building.[110]

In 1894-1895, Harvey J. Smith and his father built the first grain business, later purchased by John Royer of Nardin.[111] By 1896, some of the settlers' enthusiasm for the new land had declined and the population dropped slightly. In 1900, the population, about 3,000, made Blackwell the largest town in Kay County. A census showed 130 residences completed or under construction. The city fathers issued a building requirement limiting the construction materials for businesses to brick or stone in the business district. Fifteen brick or stone buildings were already built, including two banks, several stores, a warehouse, railroad depot, Odd Fellows Hall and the Hotel Maine. Several older frame buildings housed two hotels and several smaller businesses.[112] The boomer paper, the *Blackwell Eagle*, was joined by the *Blackwell Rock Record, Blackwell Times,* and *Blackwell Daily Spoon,* a paper that "dished up the news".[113]   Postal authorities established a post office, naming it Blackwell. Generally it was thought that Blackwell Rock had a post office, but this was not the case. The town had been so highly advertised from the start that letters written to persons there were sent to Kildare, brought over by Ferguson Brothers Stage and distributed from the Brown Brothers Grocery Store.[114] A short time later, telephone service came to town by way of Kildare. Ed Peckham, J.L. Waite, his son, Garrett Waite, and E.A. Hildebrand organized the Northern Oklahoma Telephone Company. This company installed and operated the first exchange system in Blackwell. By 1897, there were 180 telephone subscribers in town.   Garrett Waite installed the first electric system and brought in the first automobile, an 1894 or 1895 model with a surrey-like fringe around the top.[115] The largest problem facing Blackwell was no railroad line. In this area it was not the evangelical rhetoric of A.J. Blackwell that produced a solution, But the shrewd business sense of Ed Peckham.

Edward Lockwood Peckham, a lawyer from Kansas, homesteaded a claim adjoining Blackwell and quickly became one of the town's strongest boosters.[116] He soon realized Blackwell's distance from a railroad as one of the town's main disadvantages.   True, it was only 14 miles to the railroad at Kildare, where mail and passengers were transported over the connecting road by the Ferguson Brothers stage coaches, but a town with the agricultural potential of Blackwell needed its own railroad line.[117] The next problem was that the three main railroad companies in the area, the Missouri Pacific, the St. Louis and San Francisco (Frisco) and the Atchison, Topeka, & Santa Fe had a tacit agreement not to build any more lines into the Outlet for the time being. The Santa Fe had the nearest track to Blackwell; one that passed through Newkirk, Kildare and Ponca City. The other lines passed further away or terminated at the Kansas state line.

Peckham set out to persuade one of the companies to build a railroad line into Blackwell.[118]

Peckham spent five years negotiating with these railroad giants with only slight success. He was about to make headway with the Frisco line when another group of Blackwell businessmen completed an agreement with the independent company, Hutchison & Southern, to lay a track through Blackwell. To make the situation more interesting, Frisco, followed by Santa Fe, then offered to lay a track through Blackwell. Suddenly, Blackwell had the prospect of having not one, but three railroads. It appeared to be on the verge of becoming the railroad center of northern Oklahoma.[119]

Through the next several months, the three lines laid tracks furiously in an effort to be first into Blackwell. The Hutchison, & Southern, laying its line straight south along section lines, avoided litigation with the farmers who did not want their farms divided by a railroad line. They reached Blackwell first in March of 1898, with the Santa Fe and Frisco lines close behind.[120]

Upon reaching Blackwell, all three lines were ready to call a halt to more construction in the Outlet, but Ed Peckham did not agree. In his opinion, all of western Oklahoma was just waiting to be opened to rail transportation. He convinced some like-minded businessmen of the idea and began campaigning once again with railroad barons in New York City. Most laughed at Peckham's plans, but he found financing for an independent line, the Blackwell, Enid & Southwestern, otherwise know as the "BES Line". The BES line planned to build a track through western Oklahoma from Blackwell and on across the recently opened Kiowa country to Vernon, Texas. Work commenced, but before construction was completed, the BES line was purchased by the Frisco railroad in February 1902. The Rock Island Railroad eventually built a network of tracks across western Oklahoma, but it was Ed Peckham's independent Bes Line that forced larger railroad to take action and bring rail transportation to infant towns in western Oklahoma.[121] With a firm agricultural base provided by mother nature and accessibility to three railroads, Blackwell was sure to succeed as a town through the efforts of Ed Peckham and his colleagues.

Blackwell was no different than other Kay County towns when it came to its concern about education. At first there was no money for public education, so children were enrolled in subscription schools. Parents paid Miss Lottie Jerome, a brand new graduate of the teacher training school at Emporia, Kansas, from one dollar to two dollars per student to teach their children. In 1894, the county began levying taxes and dividing the area into school districts. Tax money was set aside for schools and Blackwell soon had a public school building and a high school was built in 1896.[122]

Religion was only slightly behind educational concerns in Blackwell. The first services were held within two or three Sundays of the Run. A union Sunday school began a short time later. A.J. Blackwell built the first church, the Church of God, on the corner of Third Street and Blackwell Avenue, often delivering sermons himself. Other denominations such as the Methodists, Baptist and Christian Churches used A.J. Blackwell's church building until they could construct their own. In 1896, the Presbyterians established a church in Blackwell, followed by numerous others, including the United Brethren, Episcopal, Lutherans, Spiritualists and Christian Scientists.[123] The Salvation Army usually took their position in front of the busiest saloon in town.[124]

Blackwell became the home of Oklahoma Baptist College. Founded in 1899 by the Oklahoma Baptist Convention, the first school term began on September 4, 1901. Blackwell was selected because "All leading denominations of Christians are represented and have good houses of worship. It is in the center of one of the richest agricultural regions in the world and is reached by rail from six directions.".[125] The college's first president was J.A. Beauchamp, who occupied the post through 1903, followed by A.P. Stone, 1904-1908; J.R. Jester, 1908-1909; J.H. Moore, 1909-1911 and A.E. Baten, 1911-1913. In 1911, enrollment was 208, but financial problems caused it to close its doors August 12, 1913. It was located on West College, where Washington School now stands.[126]

Social life in Blackwell was active. People entertained themselves in a variety of ways including dance clubs, church sponsored socials or pound parties. Everyone brought a pound of something to pound parties; flour, sugar, coffee or other staples, not only providing a good time but often paying the minister of poor congregations. Music was popular and the first town band was organized at J.C. Phelps drug store in November, 1893. For men there was a Masonic lodge, for men and women, lectures were popular as were Chautauqua's which first came to Blackwell in 1901. Being midway between Wichita and Oklahoma City on the railroad, touring companies frequently stopped there. One show, the "American Hobo", originated in Blackwell, written and directed by lawyer, Bob Neff. His daughter, Aline, played the leading role and for many years the company began and ended each season in Blackwell. Baseball was a popular spectator sport at the turn of the century, as were political rallies.[127]

Less respectable, but no less a part of life in Blackwell, was gambling, with poker the favorite of those who frequented saloons. Cockfighting brought in crowds though it was not openly practiced. As the community began to mature, citizen groups pressured elected officials to make such activities illegal.

Nevertheless, they continued in someone's back room or at a cockpit in remote areas of the country. Dog-racing was also a part of Blackwell's history. The real father of dog-racing in Blackwell was J.W. Pickett, who served as president of the National Coursing Association one year. He brought the national meet to Blackwell. R. S. "Dog" Howard kept a kennel of fine animals near the Chikaskia River, boasting he did not have to work his dogs did it for him. Ed Peckham was a horse-breeder with a national reputation. His horse, Dan Patch, was known all over the United States.[128]

Before statehood, men in Blackwell could find entertainment in one of the town's nine saloons. The swankiest place was Wiley Monroe's Manhattan Bar, with its eye-catching display of birds, monkeys and animals in the front window, yet maintaining a reputation for spotlessness. Card tables, pool tables and games of chance could be found in a back room for the discrete clientele. A city ordinance stated saloons had to close by midnight on Saturday for a day of rest, but determined drinkers could usually find a place open for a price. Anheiser-Busch built an ice plant and brewery in Blackwell, selling both ice and beer from a decorated brewery wagon drawn by a team of Clydesdale horses. When statehood came in 1907, saloons were forced to close, but Blackwell still had its share of early-day speakeasies.[129]

By 1907, Blackwell was a well-to-do community with railroads, telephones and electric utilities. It had the amenities of any other well established town of the day. Though noisy, smelly automobiles began to compete with horses on its city streets, there were still more livery stables than gas stations. Even then, Blackwell was destined to become a long enduring town.

CHAPTER SIX
The Growth of North Central Oklahoma Continues

Tonkawa

Slower to start than Blackwell, or any other town in the area was Tonkawa. Located in the southwestern part of the county and unlike Newkirk, Ponca City or Blackwell, it was not platted before the Run of 1893. Instead, it was laid out on the homestead claims of Eli V. Blake and William W. Gregory, two Kansas farmers, who claimed adjacent quarter sections during the Run. After looking over their homesteads, they believed their locations were ideal for a town. The Yellow Bull Ford and Yellow Bull Spring, located one-half mile west, were near the Salt Fork and Chikaskia Rivers, surrounded by rich land capable of supporting a town. Their nearest competition for the agricultural market was eight miles to the north in Blackwell.[1]

A surveyor, J. Elmer Chapson, was hired in March of 1894 to lay out their town, named "Tonkawa" after the nearby Tonkawa Indians. An Irishman, Thomas H. Martin, joined their venture as a partner. The three men, with several other investors, made up the board of directors for the Oklahoma Townsite Company.[2]

During the spring of 1894, the town company engaged in a vigorous campaign to entice potential settlers to come to Tonkawa. Adverse publicity about land fraud by some Cherokee Outlet townsite companies deterred many who might have been interested. Thus, only a few determined settlers made their way to Tonkawa. By the end of 1894, forty people had taken up residence there. This was fewer inhabitants than the prairie dog village first claiming the site. Still, a cluster of frame buildings made up the business district, consisting of Charles H. Martindale's store; the post office operated by town founder, Eli V. Blake; C.S. Reed's dry goods store; Moses Truesdale's grocery and bakery; Charles W. Robison's blacksmith's shop; John A. Hell's feed store; Robison and Abe C. Plummer's Tonkawa Restaurant; and Frank Rohr's meat market. The weekly newspaper, the *Tonkawa Chief*, kept the town in touch with the rest of the world, followed by the *Tonkawa Register, Salt Fork Valley News,* and *Tonkawa Chieftain,* as did stage coach service to and from Ponca City. A major deterrent to the growth of Tonkawa was a problem Blackwell struggled with--- the lack of railroad service.[3]

Tonkawa's growth continued at a slow pace for the next two years. Drought resulted in poor harvests in 1894 and 1895, keeping farmers reliant on the only successful crop, broom corn. Tonkawa enjoyed a different source of income in 1895, when the Tonkawa Indians received part of their annuities, spending the money in the town bearing their name. This "prosperity", slight as it was, allowed Shorty Brookhoven and Joseph Hamil, Sr. to open the first two saloons in Tonkawa, while Thomas Martin and Edward J. Richard opened a lumber yard and real estate office. Telephones came to Tonkawa in 1896.[4]

Things began looking up in 1897 as harvests improved. Farmers were able to get as much as fifty bushels of wheat per acre, a trend which continued and saw businesses prosper as the farmers' lot improved. Sylvester James' Tonkawa Hotel (probably a boarding house) opened its doors; Joe Hedrick's barbershop provided haircuts and baths and Cornelius Richards added a harness shop to his hardware store.[5] The town's first bank was established in 1898, but not after some difficulty. W.H. Poffenberger, an Iowa banker, surveyed the town with the intention of opening a bank and was impressed. Returning to Iowa, he consulted his partner, Dr. Samuel T. Goodman. Dr. Goodman preferred to locate a bank where corn was produced rather then wheat, which was a predominate crop around Tonkawa. Forewarned, the town fathers made sure that Goodman visited farms specializing in corn

136

production during his inspection visit that summer. Reassured, Goodman agreed to support a bank, approving the organization of the Bank of Tonkawa, but the town still lacked accessibility to the outside world. In 1895, travelers continued to ford the Chikaskia and Salt Fork Rivers in order to reach Tonkawa. Amos Thomas, an area farmer, was also a county commissioner. He sponsored a drive to improve Kay County roads and bridges. By the end of 1895, a bridge was constructed and in use across the Salt Fort River. The following year one spanned the Chikaskia, allowing greater access to Ponca City and the Santa Fe Railroad.

Tonkawa procured a railroad link in 1899 when Thomas Martin, Edward Richard and William Gregory formed the Santa Fe Construction Company to bring in the Atchison, Topeka & Santa Fe. Farmers were now able to bring their crops to Tonkawa for shipment.[7]

Education was not neglected. A subscription school with about twenty students convened in April 1895, under the instruction of J. Calvin Richard. In the fall, the first school building was built. It was so poorly constructed that when cold weather set in, it was useless. A solid two-story school was erected in 1896. It was built on Seventh Street, a block north of Grand Avenue.[8]

Churches took priority as the Presbyterians began holding services in June of 1894 for people of all denominations. The following year Baptists organized a denominational congregation, hiring a full-time minister and building a church dedicated in April of 1898. The Methodist Episcopal Church organized in 1896, held services in the school.[9]

A major change came to Tonkawa in 1902, with the opening of the University Preparatory School, established to provide secondary education for Cherokee Outlet and Oklahoma Territory students at a time when high school facilities were almost non-existent. Many local primary schools were founded soon after the Run of 1893, but young people in the Outlet who wished to attend high school or preparatory school before going

137

on the college could find them only in Guthrie, Newkirk, and across the state line at Wellington, Kansas. Tonkawa owed its candidacy for the site of a preparatory school to the enthusiasm of James Wilkin, a member of the Territorial Legislature and farmer from the Tonkawa area. He campaigned diligently for the establishment of the school. The board met on May 2, 1901. The members were Territorial Governor, Cassius M. Barnes; Newkirk editor, Jeremiah Johnson; and Thomas H. Martin, of Tonkawa, who presided as president.[11]

Classes convened on Sept 1, 1902, with seven faculty members under the leadership of President James Herbert Kelley. There were 217 students. They met in Central Hall, a newly finished, four-story, brick and limestone building constructed by O.F. Keck, a Ponca City contractor.[12] The school's curriculum, as a feeder school for the University of Oklahoma at Norman, closely resembled that of the university. The student body yell was "Hi rickey whoop di doo! Preparatory for O-Kla-U!". Though the curriculum was classical, courses in sciences and commercial practice were offered. By 1903, enrollment had reached 315 students, 146 preparatory students, 83 commercial students and 86 special students studying art and music. The first class commencement took place in 1904. After 1904, a Department of Military Science and Tactics was added. This was the beginning of a long association between the Tonkawa school and the military.[13]

The University Preparatory School had a great deal of influence on the town. First was the physical addition of the campus, beginning with Central Hall on East Grand, followed by a number of buildings over the years. Wilkin Hall was dedicated in

138

1905. It was designed with classical lines, white columns and a dome, which added elegance to the prairie town. Ivy transplanted from England, as well as rows of Elms, Poplars, Maples and Black Locusts, set off the buildings. At first there was a housing shortage as the small town tried to accommodate the sudden influx of newcomers, but within a short time, houses, designed for student rental, began to appear. The people of Tonkawa supported the school, taking pride in its presence. They supported the school's usually superior athletic teams, the military science department and shared the many cultural activities. Among the music programs and lecture series were such well known attractions as The Royal Hungarian Orchestra; The Wesleyan Quartette; the Cleveland Ladies Orchestra; The Dunbar Company; The Kellogg Haines Singing Party; impersonator, Leland Powers; lecturer, Lincoln McConnell and Shakespearean reader, Frederick Warde.[14]

As the school continued to grow, campus acreage grew, more buildings were built, and the school's operating budget increased through 1911. Lynn Glover, third president of the school, came to the Tonkawa campus in 1911. When the campus was further beautified with fountains, paved drives and decorated classrooms.[15] Meanwhile, in the Legislature, the Aikin Bill was introduced. This bill was designed to abolish three normal schools, both university preparatory schools, and five district agricultural schools. Aikin and his supporters claimed "...self-interested individuals have elected an entrance into the pockets of the taxpayers of this state." Their claim was rebutted by Glover, who stated, "...school costs to the taxpayers amounted to less than three cents for each $1,000 of property valuation."[16]

In November, 1912, President Glover stated in the *Tonkawa News*, "The function of this school is to teach the practical things of life without depreciating the cultural subject." Glover encouraged an expansion of courses to be offered by the school. At this time, there were still few high schools in the state; therefore, few students completed a high school education. U.P.S. offered free tuition to ambitious students and a chance to prepare themselves for college. Since only about 15 per cent of students graduating from secondary schools attended college, U.P.S. aimed to help prepare them for society and the working world. In 1913, President Glover attempted to better serve the state when he changed the direction of the school by expanding the curriculum to include technical courses, as well as those of the "old normal school". He also changed the name of U.P.S. To the Oklahoma Institute of Technology, though this name was never officially recorded. Under the auspice of President Lynn Glover, who encouraged the scope of courses the school had to offer, the legislature did not pass the Aikin Bill. The Oklahoma Institute of Technology had survived.[17]

On April 7, 1914, Wilkin Hall, the pride of the campus, burned. Firemen from Tonkawa, using Horse-drawn equipment, tried to put out the blaze but were hampered when they could not locate a wrench to open the fire hydrant. Students managed to save some furniture, records and museum specimens, but the building was a total loss. Only part of the facade was left standing, with losses estimated at $80,000, including the building and contents. Insurance covered only a portion of the loss. State law required the $52,000 insurance payment to be deposited in the state treasury, but Governor Robert L. Williams refused approval to rebuild Wilkin Hall, even though the state legislature had appropriated the money.[18]

Glover's vision for the school did not suit everyone. There were some in Tonkawa who felt the school had departed from its original purpose of providing high school level work for potential college students. On May 20, 1915, the state superintendent recommended that the school return to the status of an ordinary high school. This meant many classes would be discontinued, the staff would be reduced by one-third, and there would be less money for expansion. "Must We Lose Our School?" the *Tonkawa Chieftain* asked on May 25. The *Ponca City Democrat* advised, "Wake up Tonkawa, you have shown in the past that you were fighters and since this means life or death in your hustling city, now is the time to show your mettle." In June, 1915, the

State Board of Education ruled the school must operate under its University Preparatory School name and curriculum.[19]

U.P.S. Survived many crises, but the worst of times were yet to come, as World War I was to have its effect on Tonkawa and the campus. In 1917, young men began to leave the town and campus as they entered the armed services. U.P.S. shut its doors too many students had gone to war. North Hall was turned over to Tonkawa for one dollar and was used as the first high school. Faculty member, Walter G. Hopkins, became the superintendent. Central Hall was dismantled and the library, printing machines, and much of the school's equipment was distributed to other institutions around the state. Of the more than 60 former students of U.P.S. who served in the military, four died. They included Fred L. Allen of Tonkawa, Cecil R. Bottenfield of Blackwell, Francis H. Bush of Tonkawa and Ralph Brown of Tonkawa. Brown was the first casualty from Tonkawa and later the American Legion Post was named in his honor.[20]

It appeared that after 30 years of growth, Tonkawa had lost one of its main sources of prosperity. This same pattern of growth was found in several Kay County towns. For a few years they flourished, then dwindled away. In some cases, there was simply not a large enough population to support the towns. In other instances, smaller towns were overshadowed by larger more aggressive ones as in the case of Cross and Ponca City. More often though, around the turn of the century towns lived and died by the railroad. Those with access to railroads survived, while those who had none died. Still, some towns did not last as long as Newkirk, Ponca City, Blackwell and Tonkawa. However, their days were just as important to their residents and to Kay County history as the more successful ones.

Rock Falls

A case in point was Rock Falls, located north of Blackwell. David Payne and his boomers established it as an illegal boomer town in 1884. It was located at the site of the well-known Rock Ford, 75 feet from a three and one-half foot waterfall known as Rock Falls, on the Chikaskia River. Payne's Rock Falls settlement was destroyed by Colonel Hatch's troopers, but in December of 1893, A.J. Blackwell, one of the boosters of nearby Blackwell, laid out a new town of Rock Falls. He acquired the 80 acres for the town from a Cherokee allottee on December 21, 1893. Within a few months a blacksmith shop (where church services were held), several stores and a hotel were opened. A post office opened February 12, 1894. Ironically, David Payne's cousin served as the postmaster. A school opened the same year. A.J. Blackwell sold the Rock Falls township to A.B. Crawford on May 29, 1894 and it prospered until 1898, when the Santa Fe railroad arrived in Blackwell.[21]

Braman

The downfall of Rock Falls started when J.W. Whistler and B.J. Templeton bought 160 acres from homesteader, Sam Garrison, and platted 80 acres for a town site. Dwight Braman, a railroad surveyor, surveyed and platted the townsite, beside the railroad line, free of charge.

Citizens in the area donated three thousand dollars for the construction of a railroad depot. Farmers discovered it easier to transact business in Blackwell or Braman, rather than Rock Falls, causing it to decline and lose its post office in 1898. As Rock Falls declined, Braman grew vigorously and was incorporated January 9, 1899. Many new stores opened, including a general store, meat market, lumber yard, implement and hardware store, three elevators, two saloons, a hotel, livery stable, two doctors and three barbers. Citizens State Bank was organized in 1899 by W.J. Whistler, B.J. Templeton, W.A. Searles, L.W. Hamilton and D.L. Westmore. The First National Bank of Braman was opened November 14, 1899, by W.H. Franks, J.N. Wommack, A.O. Via and R.E. Burkes. The post office opened on April 11, 1898 and the first newspaper, *The Braman Star*, was published on

December 30, 1899 by W.J. Krebs. Raul Gordon Krebs was born in Conway Springs, Kansas, on July 18, 1899, to William Joshua Krebs and Katherine Bosch Krebs. He was six months old when his parents moved to Braman, Oklahoma, where his father published that paper. The *Braman Leader* followed in 1902. Two years later, his father became agent for the new town which was being promoted by the Kaw City Townsite Company. The first Mayor of Braman was Bert Payne, formerly of Rock Falls.[22]

Braman's first school, which employed three teachers and had 121 students enrolled, was a three-story frame building. By 1900, three churches, Baptist, Methodist and Christian, were established. The first Church of Christ in Kay County, with 44 members, was built in 1907. Active organizations included the Royal Neighbor, Modern Woodmen, Masonic Lodge and Rebekahs. The town formed a band and a Baseball team.[23]

Nardin

The town of Nardin began to grow only after the railroad by-passed the existing community and trading center of Vilott. Vilott was one and one-half miles north of Nardin, near the Grant County line in western Kay County. Ed Vilott opened a post office and general store on his claim soon after the Run of 1893. He later published a newspaper called the *Vilott News,* However, when word was received in the spring of 1898 that the Hutchinson and Southern Railway, a division of the Santa Fe, was to build a railroad between Medford and Blackwell, many area farmers felt it would be better to establish a town site near the railroad. They wanted a trade center where their wheat could be sold, eliminating long hauls to Hunnewell, Kansas. Local farmers created a town company, bought 60 acres for $1,200 from a farmer named George Nardin, and paid the railroad company $1,500 to build a switch and depot there. George Roberts later said in his memoirs, "It doesn't sound like much today, but in those days that was a lot of money.".[24] The town site was divided into lots and sold for $10 per lot, in order to help defray costs. These efforts indicated the importance people placed on railroads.[25]

Nardin, established in 1898, soon had an energetic population. Within two weeks of the drawing for lots, a dozen or so buildings were under construction. Ed Vilott moved his *Vilott News* to Nardin, where it became the *Nardin Star*. The Vilott post office was relocated to Nardin and Daniel E. Mahaffey became the first postmaster. In 1898, the first school was built. When the town was platted, the north side of the main street remained a wheat field. At harvest time, the wheat in this field was cut and threshed by the citizens, with the proceeds going to support the school. This school was rebuilt on the same location in 1904.[26]

The first business was Charley Vilott's grocery store and the town quickly prospered, as more and more families moved into the area. By 1899, the town had a hotel, two restaurants, short order house, two saloons, billiard hall, drug store, coal dealer, general store, meat market, poultry market, livery stable, harness shop, four grain buyers, a flour and feed store, grain elevator, jewelry store, lumber yard, two real estate agents, one hardware and implement dealer, one hardware and furniture store, barbershop, two blacksmith shops, two livestock dealers and a cigar factory. John Eilers, a hardware store owner became the first mayor and G.W. Coffey and William Beacham became council members.[27]

A flood the first year saw six inches of water cover the main street of Nardin. Fire ravaged the business district in the spring of 1899, winter of 1901, and in 1903. The fire of 1901 was the worst, resulting in the loss of 10 stores. Transformation from wood-frame to brick buildings resulted, earning the block the reputation of the "handsome brick block". The "Roberts Block", named for the owners of a mercantile store, George Roberts and his brother Harry, was an example of the new face of the downtown. In 1904, the Bank of Nardin occupied a two-story brick building. The upper floor served as a town meeting hall, able to accommodate 500 people. Unlike some towns, Nardin had the reputation of being a tranquil place. Congregations of

Baptists, Methodists, Christian Church, and later, Lutherans, dominated its character. These temperance people and the town council "kept the lid on the saloons", seeing that the town's peace was rarely disturbed. In the early part of the nineteenth century, the town had several flourishing businesses and a good location, making it seem that Nardin would endure.[28]

Ghost Towns

Some early towns were never much more than a post office, grain elevator or general store. **Batchelder**, six miles east of Ponca City, was such a town, It consisted of a general store, housing a post office from February 4, 1895 to October 31, 1903. A dance hall, on the second floor, accommodated the Odd Fellows and Rebekahs. Batchelder was located on the Arch Kenyon homestead, with Kenyon serving as postmaster. Carson S. Williams carried mail on a small burro to Batchelder from Cross for the nine years the post office was in existence. **Ed Kelly** was a trade center between Ponca City and Tonkawa. It consisted of the Kelly Elevator, with its 100 foot corn crib and large coal storage. Ed Kelly worked for the Santa Fe Railroad, though no one ever knew in what capacity. The elevator was used until 1950, when Tonkawa built the Tonkawa Co-op elevator. **Tyner,** consisted of a grain elevator three miles south and one-half mile west of Blackwell. **Grainville** consisted of an elevator operated by Blackwell Co-op Elevator Association on the Frisco line. It is unknown as to when it was built or how it came by its name. **Erie** was located on the Kansas-Oklahoma State Line road. In the early 1890's, as the Frisco Railroad worked in the area, construction workers lived in shacks and tents in Erie until their work was completed; then they moved south. **Alcorn** was southwest of Tonkawa and consisted of an elevator beside the Rock Island tracks. The town was named after John Scott Alcorn, a Vice-President of Marland Oil Company. **Wilber**, eight miles west of Chilocco, was a grocery store run by Deci L. Wilber, who served as postmaster from May 9, 1894 to November 30, 1908. The post office was located in the store until free mail delivery from Braman started. **Vernon**, one and one-half miles north of

Peckham, was a post office on the Tom Trenary homestead. **Lillivale** consisted of a store and post office on the James E. Lilly homestead from May 3, 1894 to April 30, 1903.[29]

Bain was a store and post office located four miles south and one mile east of **Uncas** on the corner of a farm owned by Dan Bain. Around 1900, one of the two brothers operating the store and post office started another store across from the **Longwood** post office, which was about one and a half miles southwest of Kaw City. The brothers took the post office charter from Bain, made a few changes, and took it to the new store. Gus Pellman, operator and owner of the Longwood Store and post office, did not know it was a forgery and turned his mail center over to the brothers. They operated for about six months before the federal government caught up with them. This is the only post office in Kay County that was stolen.[30]

Sometimes these towns included a cluster of houses or perhaps a store. Such was the case with **Alert**, near the Grant County line in southwest Kay County. Alert was the home of a large general store operated by brothers Swan and Will Olson and their wives. They bought lots for the store from a homesteader and opened for business on March 5, 1894. A post office opened three months later. They stocked merchandise most needed by the farmers; windmills, hardware, farm machinery, dry goods and groceries. The store prospered, but the brothers sold out to a Mr. Shirley. A new postmaster named Mr. Geller was appointed. The two men changed the towns's name to **Geily** (a combination of their two names). When the Frisco Railroad passed three miles to the north, the store began to lose its customers to **Eddy**, a newer town on the railroad line.[31]

Owen, five miles south of Tonkawa, lived a very short life. It had a blacksmith shop, grocery store and a post office. The post office began operations December 8. 1898, with Charles O. Howe as its first postmaster. It operated until August 31, 1901, reopening September 6, 1901 for several more years. Owen never developed as a town, even though the railroad line ran diagonally through the twonship.[32]

In the southwest corner of the county, the counties of P.O.L. And K met. It was here that a town called **Polk** was started shortly after the Run. Leo Miller gave land for a sod school house with a wood shingle roof. Don Lawhead and Mr. Neikirk ran a general store and post office near there. The store was blown away by a tornado in the fall of 1894, but the following spring, George Meece built a new store one mile east, on the Maston Riley farm, and it was named Polk. Meece also served as postmaster during the two years his store was in operation. Meece raised his six children alone after his wife's death. His daughter, Flora, recalled how the store kept them from having to pull up stakes and move again. John Prather had a general store and blacksmith shop on his claim about two miles north of Meece's store. It was located on his homestead on the Northeast Quarter of Section 30, Township 25 North, Range 2 West. When the Meece store closed, Prather moved the post office to his store and became the postmaster of Polk. Due to Mr. Prather's ill health, the post office was discontinued and the store closed in 1904.[33]

Middleton, located three miles south of the Kansas border on the southwest corner of the Chilocco Indian School reserve, like Nardin, started late. It became a town site when the railroad established a stop there. With the farming industry having a prosperous year, the town obtained a post office in 1900 (originally established at **Gray**, two miles north of Middleton). It became a cattle-shipping point the next year when the Middleton Stock Yards were built. The town was platted and a small business district developed. A number of people lived in the vicinity, establishing several rural schools and churches, but these were communities, rather than full-fledged towns. Several families moved into town and a Presbyterian church was soon erected. The first school was held in the vacated 12x12 foot homestead shack of Sarah Lewison. Businesses included Bill Stevenson's store, David McHugh's store and post office, Burney Allen's lumber yard, John Spohn's restaurant, Elmer Cummings's blacksmith shop, James Lockwood's hotel and John Landon's telephone switchboard. These gave the town substance. Even so, Middleton never grew to be large, holding on for two decades.[34]

Railroads were directly responsible for some of the towns which popped up beside the tracks. At the turn of the century, major railroads threw a network of branch lines across Kay County. From 1900 until Oklahoma's constitution was adopted in 1907, there was a period of railroad booms in Oklahoma and Indian Territories. Many companies financed construction of lines by selling lots in towns they promoted along their railroads. When Oklahoma Territory and Indian Territory became the state of Oklahoma, a provision in the constitution restricted railroad activities, hindering further development in the state. By the time this provision was revoked, the Panic of 1907 had depressed railroad construction across the nation. The previous decade saw a dozen new Kay County towns born. These new towns included: **Eddy**, 1901, on the Frisco line where it crosses into Grant County; **Sumpter**, 1900, north of Blackwell on the Santa Fe line; **Peckham**, 1899, on the Frisco line in the north-central part of he county; **Autwine**, 1899, on the Santa Fe line between Blackwell and Ponca City; **Uncas**, 1902, on the Santa Fe line in east central Kay County; Kaw City, 1902, on the Santa Fe line in the Ox Bow Bend of the Arkansas River in the eastern part of the county; and **Owen**, founded about 1898. Peckham and Eddy had the distinction of being named for railroad builder Ed Peckham and his son, Ed E. Peckham, respectively. Unlike many of the other towns mentioned, Kaw City is still a thriving community.

The town of **Peckham** is located seven miles west of Newkirk. It was named for Ed L. Peckham, who encouraged the Frisco Railroad to build a line from Arkansas City, Kansas to Enid, Oklahoma in 1899. The town was built by farmers on a quarter section of land and once had a population of around 400.[35]

Peckham built a school in 1894 with 47 students in attendance. Business establishments included a furniture store, four lumber yards, a bank, livery stable, realty company, restaurant, grocery store, drug store, an implement store, general store, meat market, candy and confectionery store, barber shop, hotel and a post office. Business thrived during the teens and twenties. At one time, the town had Catholic, Methodist and Christian Churches. Churches were the scene of many fellowship gatherings.[36]

Eddy, another community that failed to become an incorporated town, should have changed its name to "Disaster", being hampered by one disaster after another. Charles A. Spencer started the community when he moved his post office from Osborne, in Grant County, to Kay County, primarily because of the new railroad line. The post office opened January 3, 1901, named "Eddy" after the son of DES Line builder, Ed Peckham. At one time or another, Eddy claimed two grain elevators, a livery stable, four or more grocery stores, a restaurant, two lumber yards, a general store, the Hayes Hotel, Baptist Church, Methodist Church and a fine big depot. Then came disasters. Fires burned out whole sections of Eddy in 1907, 1920 and 1939. Tornadoes demolished much of the town in 1904 and 1914. Eddy's post office, established January 3, 1901, remained open until February 22, 1957, but the town never was able to overcome the many disasters it endured.[37]

Most railroad towns never became prosperous or sizable. **Autwine**, originally platted June 17, 1899 by W.A. Bradford, west of Ponca City, was given the name "**Virginia City**". A man by the name of Pierce was successful in locating a post office on his homestead just a mile and a quarter south of Autwine. The post office was called "Pierceton" causing a bit

Antoine Roy

of confusion. When the Santa Fe Railway Company called it Virginia City depot "Arta", the townspeople decided "enough". A town meeting was called to settle on a name and they decided none of the names were acceptable. They chose the name "Antoine", in honor of Antoine Roy, a Ponca Indian, who was very popular and respected by both white and Indian neighbors. The name was sent to Washington, D.C. To be recorded, but an error occurred. Either the town clerk wrote Antoine carelessly, or the official who recorded it spelled it incorrectly. At any rate, the "n" became "u" and the "o" became a "w", recording the town as "Autwine".[38]

Both the Big V and 101 Ranch used Autwine's shipping facilities, as did cattleman Ola Goodson and hog-grower, Jesse Bainum, making it one of the leading hog and cattle shipping point in the area. Bill Vanselous, owner of the Big V Ranch, shipped his White Wonder seed corn from **Autwine** to many parts of the country. His corn storage building was said to be a quarter of a mile long. Besides the railroad facilities and the three grain elevators, the town had about 20 homes and a nine-block business district, consisting of three grocery stores, a blacksmith shop, an implement yard, general store, dry good store, hardware store, bank, restaurant, drug store, Woodman Hall, Royal Neighbors Lodge and an Anti-Horse Thief Association office. There was also a post office, telegraph office and railroad depot. Elementary school children in Autwine attended nearby Round Grove School, while high school students took the train to Blackwell. Autwine appeared destined for prosperity until about 1904, when it could not keep up with the competition of Blackwell and Ponca City. Large-scale livestock shippers began taking their business elsewhere and Autwine's railroad traffic decreased. In 1904, the bank and restaurant closed; then, in 1905, a fire swept over nearly the whole business district, taking the life out of Autwine. For a time the last remaining business, a general store, stayed open, but closed in 1930. In 1966, when the railroad removed its whistle sign, Autwine went back to where it had come from—the prairie.[39]

Sumpter was merely a community, rather than an incorporated town, located five miles north of Blackwell on

Highway 177. The site that became Sumpter was homesteaded by John R. Sumpter in 1893. When the railroad came through, around 1900, several others came to the area. The Cope, Clark, Watson, Hine, Kinnear, Easterday, Nichols, Courtney, Wood, Carr, Alexander, McAdams, Geiger, Wymer, Sharp, McIntire families and two families named Jones made up the community. A post office was established in 1901 in the Sumpter home but closed February 29, 1908. There was a grocery store and elevator, as well as a school, established near Bitter Creek, that had to close when flood waters rose. Later, they moved outside of the flood plain. The real hub of the community was the stone Grange hall, built in 1919, which helped maintain social ties in the wide-spread farming community.[40]

Retta, located six miles from Blackwell, was named after a 16 year old town resident, Retta Richmond. Retta's post office was established April 3, 1902 with Joshua Bean, postmaster. The town included a pool hall, dance hall, boarding house, grocery store, blacksmith and grain elevator. The Retta Methodist Church was the last building to close in 1959. The building was moved to Nardin in 1960, where it became the Asbury Methodist Church. As for Retta, she married Harry B. Patten on November 15, 1905, and died February 20, 1973 at the age of 91.[41]

The Ox Bow Region and Kaw City

Another late-starting town was Uncas, located near the Black Dog Crossing in the Ox Bow Bend of the Arkansas River, in eastern Kay County. The town of Uncas, named for a Mohegan Indian chief, was platted in 1902. At the time, the Santa Fe was building a branch line through the site. Several families homesteaded this area after the Run of 1893. Lafe Devore farmed there while James Kenton and Gano Dawson operated trading posts, drawing trade from the Kaw Agency and lands east of the river. A post office was established on June 21, 1895, named Uncas. The mail was brought from Kildare and anything going to the Kaw Agency was taken across the Arkansas River at Dawson's Crossing, located about a mile east of the trading post

151

and a mile south of Black Dog Crossing.[42]

The first school was built of native stone, located a mile west of the Uncas town site. It had an enrollment of 94 students until other district school houses were built. Pupils walked, rode horses or traveled to school in wagons.[43]

Railroad construction created jobs for local men and brought new businesses. L.E. Bacher and Sons General Merchandise, Sam and Andy Booster's hardware store, Margaret Chapin and Mrs. George Jacques's candy kitchen, Bertha Baker's hat shop, John Springer's barber shop, C.O. Spurlock's contracting business and George Beardsmore, blacksmith at the trading post, were early day businesses. A quarry, grain elevators and stockyards profited from the railroad and remained for several years. John and Fred Pearce, Earnest and Forrest Armstrong, George Danhour, Arthur Pasley and Mr. Kohler were stone masons who built structures in Uncas, Newkirk and several other towns, using limestone quarried at nearby Lewis Rock Quarry. In addition, Lafe Devore pioneered a brick making factory on his farm, using soft red clay material to produce bricks and for cistern purification. The first medical doctor was Dr. LaMiller; later, Dr. Sewell settled in the town. Dan Bain, an early day sheriff, feared by horse thieves, lived in the Uncas area.[44]

An early day bridge with wooden piling was built across the Arkansas River, near Uncas a few years after the Run. It washed out in the flood of 1904 and was replaced with a hand ferry one and one-half miles north of Uncas, operated by Doc McCaskey. The rich farm land produced fine grain crops and an abundance of fresh fruits and vegetables. The land north of Coon Creek, across the river, was called "McClung's Bottom". During the winter the farmers would bring wagons full of corn, going to the elevator at Uncas, across the river's thick ice.[45] A great deal of livestock passed through the stock yards as Uncas flourished during the teens and twenties.[46]

Kaw City, located in the Ox Bow Bend of the Arkansas River, was one of the few new railroad towns that prospered. The Kansa (Kaw) Indians lived on their reservation just north of the Arkansas, with several families homesteading the lands in the area before Kaw City was developed. Among this small community were the Fleharty, Kneedler, Randall, McSmith, Taylor, Acker, Brown, George and Ramsey families. Pioneers who settled in the timbered lands along the Arkansas built log homes for shelter while turning their claims into farms.[47]

Kaw City was established in 1902 by the Kaw City Townsite Company, consisting of William M. Jenkins, the fifth territorial governor of Oklahoma Territory, N.F. Frazier, C.W. Carey and W.E. Brown. They purchased a 480 acre site owned by George M. Murff.[48] The town was ideally located on the threshold of the Kaw Indian reservation to the north and Osage Indian reservation to the east. In the midst of the most fertile and productive farm land, it is said to be the finest corn, wheat and cattle country in Oklahoma. The Kaw City Townsite Company had the site surveyed in May 1902 and offered lots for sale shortly thereafter. It was advertised as "the finest townsite in Oklahoma, having as a place for businesses land as level as a floor with gently sloping upland for residences.".[49]

Kaw City was located twenty miles southeast of Newkirk, twenty miles northeast of Ponca City, forty miles north of Pawnee and thirty-five miles west of Pawhuska.[30] Among the many things favorable to its growth was the fine building stone found within a mile of the town, an inexhaustible supply of water, and a natural gas well, located around nine miles away.[51] In addition, the Atchison, Topeka and Santa Fe Railway Company was building a line at that time, stretching south and east from Newkirk, through Kaw City and the Osage reservation and then south to Pauls Valley in Indian Territory.

From the town's inception, building progressed at a rapid rate and within three months the first lot was sold. Kaw City had a bank, newspaper, two lumber yards, a mill and a dozen or more substantial business filled with stocks and goods. Some of the earlier businessmen were; C.B. Bendure and Jack Frost, dealers in dry goods, groceries, feeds, etc.; G.D. Rohr and C.L. Shidler, lumber dealers; Frank Randall, livery barn; C.F. Kneedler, restaurant owner; W.J. Krebs, newspaper publisher; A.H. Eudaily and John W. Piece, barbers; H.G. Diamond, harness shop; Dill Reed, operator of a peanut stand; Ed Lewis, druggist; B.F. Smith, hardware store; W.T. and M.C. Conklin, hardware merchants; Hutchison Brothers, owners of a meat Market; A. Gumbiner, clothing store; T.E. Smith, dry goods store; I.F. Lowder and John Taylor, saloon operators and H.E. Guy, owner of the mill. E.B. Eastman of Newkirk established the Bank of Commerce with J.S. Eastman, cashier and general manager and John E. Hoefer assistant cashier. Later, bank officers were J.E. Hoefer, W.S. Cline, H.E. Guy and A.J. Sanderson. The bank suffered a financial loss in the spring of 1915 when robbers stole $2,000.[52] W.S. Cline of Newkirk built several business buildings on main street during this period.[53]

With the population increasing rapidly, nearing three hundred by September, 1902, it was necessary to provide facilities for children to secure an education. The only school was the red school west of town, but it was in an inconvenient location. The Kaw City Townsite Company agreed to build a schoolhouse on the northeast corner of Main Street and Fourth Avenue. It opened in November with Professor Warner employed as the instructor of 56 students. This school soon proved inadequate and was succeeded by a four room frame building three blocks west of Main Street on Walnut, between West Sixth and West Seventh Avenues. In 1910, a two-story brick building with a vestment replaced the frame schoolhouse. A high school was built in 1922, adjoining the grade school on the south.

With the opening of the Kaw City town site, the village of **Longwood**, earlier opened during the Cherokee Outlet run and located a half mile south and a mile west of Kaw City, was abandoned.[54] Its three merchants, G.H. Pellam (Longwood's postmaster), C.D. Bendure and Jack Frost, who had a combined hardware and grocery store, moved their buildings and goods to Kaw City in 1902. The Woodman Hall's two story building followed in short order. Dr. J.B. Irvin opened an office and became Kaw City's first physician, later joined by C.S. Barker.[55] The deputy postmaster in Longwood operated the post office out of this home after the buildings of Longwood were moved to Kaw City.

W.J. Krebs received notification in the early part of October, 1902 that he was to open the Kaw City post office on October 15, with him being the commissioned postmaster.[56] Although the notification he received issued the name "Kaw", Mr. Krebs stated that business would be conducted under the name of **Kaw City**. Until now, all the mail had come through the Longwood post office. G.H. Pellman received notice that the Longwood post office would be abolished the day Kaw City opened. As the year 1902 came to a close, Kaw City looked forward to continued progress. With the railroad passing through town, a railroad bridge, across the Arkansas River, was being constructed. A contract was let for a wagon bridge to be constructed to the north that would bring in more trade from Kaw Country.

In the years following, Kaw City's growth continued with the completion of the north bridge. Another bridge was being built across the Arkansas, but this one was to the south. A large two story hotel was built, telephone lines were brought into the city, as well as two grain elevators, the mill and the Curtis (Santa Fe) Hotel. The Bank of Kaw City was established, having as its officers H. Barnum, president, and E.S. Shidler, cashier.[57] A new grade school was built on the hill to the west; telephone service was expanded; an opera house, the center of social activity for many years, was built by W.T. Conklin and cement sidewalks replaced the wooden planks. New merchants opened their doors for business; several churches were built and Dr. C.J. Barker and Dr. J.T.B. Widney became an important part of Kaw City, establishing practices at an early date.

Kaw City became an important shipping point for both cattle and farm products. Texas cattle, by the thousands, were shipped to the vast pastures of the Osage, stopping briefly at the Soldani Stockyards east of town. There they were dipped in order to eliminate the Texas tick, carrier of dreaded Texas fever in cattle. The same cattle, along with locally raised stock, subsequently made their way to eastern cattle markets. Thousands of bushels of corn, wheat and other farm products were also shipped to the market place from Kaw City.

By the end of 1903, Kaw City had a population of over 1,000 people. It was supplying more business for the Santa Fe than any of the stations on the line from Newkirk to Pauls Valley. Local shippers included ranchers like Ralph Graham, I.M. Clubb, E.S. Shidler and Hugo Milde, as well as stock brokers who shipped trainloads of livestock out of Kaw City.[58] Other companies leased land along the tracks and sidings. These included Tulsa Sand and Gravel Company, Oilwell Supply Company, the White Swan Oil distributors, Conklin Grain Company and Kaw City Canning Company.[59] Although it remained a relatively small town, Kaw City was a happy and prosperous place enjoying a good business with farmers, Kaw Indians and cattlemen. Kaw Indians, living near the agency at Washunga, were an ever present part of Kaw City's life. They would drive to town in light wagons, the men on the seat and women and children in the wagon bed. Shopping in the stores, many of the Kaw Indians wore beautifully colored blankets and

156

the traditional beaded moccasins.[60] However, the real days of prosperity were yet to come.

Washunga was established in 1903 and named for the third chief of the Kaw tribe.[61] The Kaw Indian lands had taken allotments in 1902 and town lots went on sale June 25, 1903. "Washunga is now a full fledged city." reported the *Kaw City Star*, on November 13, 1903. City officers were J.C. Columbia, mayor; H.D. Early, clerk and William Hardy, treasurer. The city was composed of six wards. Aldermen were Dr. Compton, D. Early, C.J. Hill, General Hardy, M.L. Leopard and D.W. Bush.

A post office had existed at the Kaw Agency since June 28, 1880. The original Kaw Agency office was named "Washungo", then "Washunga" in 1906. Mr. Davenport was the first postmaster of Washunga and Forrest Choteau was appointed to the position on September 4, 1904 when he resigned the position after serving for only eight months. The post office closed November 15, 1918.[62]

An Indian boarding school was built and in operation in 1893 near the Kaw Agency. The school included a one-story building for classes and a huge four-story dormitory, both built of native stone. In later years the school building was used as the Kaw Council House and was moved to a location above Washunga Bay, being the only Kaw Agency building to survive the construction of Kaw Dam. The large dormitory was destroyed by fire in 1910. A small white school was constructed for use as a public school and later the dormitory was rebuilt for use as a public school. One of the more popular teachers who taught was Miss Louise Burgert. Alice Clubb Romine, one of her first grade students, remembers an Easter when Miss Burgert brought Easter candy for her students and carrots for the ponies the children had ridden to school that day.

Children attended school in the old Kaw Agency school building (the Rock School) until the winter of 1927. Late that first semester, their new, more modern frame school, built on the west side of Main Street, was completed. The children helped carry books and supplies across the street to the new Washunga School. There were many fine teachers who taught throughout the years. Among them were Roy Grantham (later an Oklahoma Senator); Homer Main; John Hohmann and his wife, Juanita; Emma and Nellie Barlow; Katherine Pierce Bowker; Effie Chamberlin; Patricia Cline; Geneva Fink; Lela Shaw and Mrs. Jerry Brown.

Thomas Early, a white settler, built the first store in town. He owned an entire block, known as Early Park, which served the town as a community meeting place. Lou Hedges had a store one block north and three west of the Early Store. There was a jail and livery stable on the east side of Hedge's store and a bakery on the north. Washunga had a pool hall and grist mill. Other businessmen were Jack Frost, Ira Yager, Elzie Randolph, Coleman Peters, Joh Allen, Jake and John Streets, Jim Auld Jr., Joe Karball, Red Eslewell, Jim Barker, John Eads, Ike Doney, Johnny Cooper, Jim Sierman, Harry Crouse and Lee Key. Washunga had grocery stores, a butcher, blacksmith, service stations, garage, trading post and several other stores.[63]

One of the memorable characters in Washunga was Silas Conn, a Kaw Indian, blind from childhood. Silas, along with four others, Claude McCauley, Rufus Test, Barkley Delano and Bill Jones would greet the early morning sun from the east-facing porch of the Early grocery store. Silas, who would walk from Washunga, across the Arkansas River bridge to Kaw City, said "We get up early and face the east, to face the rising sun, and thank God we have lived another day. But things are changing and our younger generation will be facing the west and not thinking about the day." He would walk the streets of Washunga calling everyone he met by name.[64]

Another memorable character of the Kaw tribe was Julie Pappan's grandson, Charles Curtis. Julie convinced the orphaned Charles to stay in Topeka, Kansas with the Curtis family and receive a good education, instead of returning to live with her at the Council Grove reservation. He remained in Topeka and went on to serve Kansas in Congress for 34 years. He also became Vice-President of the United States under Herbert Hoover, from 1929-1933. Charles visited Washunga often, never forgetting his Indian heritage.[65]

Hardy was established in the northeast part of the county early in the twentieth century, on the Midland Valley Railroad. Hardy and the land surrounding it were not a part of the Cherokee Outlet, but played a major role in the development of Kay County. Named for General W.E. Hardy, the elderly secretary to the Kaw Tribe, it was organized by a group of Arkansas City businessmen to serve the reservation. Hardy was located on 240 acres surrounded by a cattleman's paradise with bluestem grass as high as a horse's back.[66]

On February 1, 1906, at 4:30 p.m., the first train ran into Hardy on the Midland Valley Railroad, an occasion to celebrate. The track force stayed several days before moving on to a camp at Silverdale, Kansas. An impressive feature of the railroad was the long trestle over Myers' Creek, made of wood, requiring 566,000 feet of lumber and 20 tons of bolts and nails.[67]

In the early days, ranchers known as "the big four", Fulton, Jacques, Olsen and Hammon controlled most of the pasture land. Thousands of head of cattle were shipped by the trainloads from Texas, to be fattened on the bluestem grass before being shipped on to Kansas City. Elevators operated by Dean and Towner held bumper crops of corn, so much that sometimes it had to be piled on the ground. Businesses in Hardy included the Hardy Bank, three general stores, two hotels, two pool halls, a barbershop, livery stable, lumber yard, hardware store, blacksmith shop, confectionery store and a saloon.[68]

When Midvalley Railroad moved its depot in 1930, a section foreman named Fowler was left behind. Mr. Fowler had two sons and four daughters. The youngest daughter's name was Patti. She was too young to attend school but her older brothers and sisters would take her to school to visit. Later she became known as Patti Page, singer and television entertainer.[69]

Hardy's first schoolhouse was a wooden frame building. Soon outgrown, a brick building was built beside it, but both were destroyed by fire. A new school building was constructed that had two classrooms and an auditorium which was used as a basketball court. The school building, the hub of community events, hosted church, Sunday school, box suppers, plays and benefits. Hardy, like several other early towns, declined with the withdrawal of railroad service.[70]

The life of these towns and their hardy pioneers cannot be taken lightly. Pioneers watched as towns and homesteads came and went. Those lucky enough to survive the droughts and cold winters saw their dreams become reality. "It was a time of excitement, calamities, quick changes, floods or drought for the pioneers. Yet through all those years ran the golden thread of the "American Spirit, high hopes, faith, courage, character, honesty and integrity (when a man's word was as good as his bond). It was work or starve, so the early Oklahomans were a rugged breed.".[71]

By the time Oklahoma became a state in 1907, many towns founded as a result of the Run of 1893 were already memories. Others, born in the railroad boom, were feeling death throes, realizing that just having a railroad did not insure success. Kildare learned this when Blackwell obtained its own railroad line in the 1890's and too many farmers no longer needed the railway in Kildare. Two other factors affected towns with the coming of the twentieth century. Automobiles and highways drew customers away from these small town markets and into larger ones. Hardy found itself by-passed by prosperity when freight trains gave way to trucks. At the turn of the century, towns such as Nardin, Autwine and Eddy were finding it difficult to compete with larger towns. Each setback, a tornado, flood or fire was harder to overcome. What had been thriving town sites, with homes and businesses mushrooming after the Run, were becoming little more than abandoned depots surrounded by a few straggling houses on dirt roads. A new era, though, was approaching Kay County.

CHAPTER SEVEN:
Oil Country

By 1907, many small towns had passed into memory, but Blackwell, Ponca City, Newkirk, Tonkawa and Kaw City led the ranks of those surviving the first struggling years. Once the transition from trains to automobile began in earnest, the wheels of change set their course upon Kay County. This new era was destined to create new towns and rejuvenate others. The cry heard in Kay County and throughout the world still reverberates today.

OIL !!!

Newkirk maintained its dignity as the county seat despite the controversy. The first courthouse was built in 1894, but the frame building burned to the ground around 4:00 a.m. on March 4, 1897. It was replaced by another frame building, two stories tall, with a cupola centered on the roof, surrounded by rows of trees planted on the town square, where it remained for 30 years. A new courthouse was dedicated on October 28, 1926. Costing $280,000 to build, the Kay County courthouse is an imposing building with a classical style. The old courthouse building was sold at auction for $750.00 on November 18, 1926, a month after the new one was dedicated.[1]

Other changes continued to take place in Newkirk. The Presbyterians established a preparatory college, the Presbyterian Academy, in 1901, but it closed by 1906.[2] The Newkirk Study Club began a library in 1908 and the State Guaranty Bank was established in 1909, with J.S. Eastman, president, and P.S. Mason, cashier. It was taken over by E.B. Eastman and the Eastman National Bank in 1911. Newkirk's extensive business district was built of brick and stone by 1910. That same year a steel bridge was built across the Arkansas River, east of Newkirk, replacing the earlier wooden bridge. Much of Newkirk's continued prosperity was due to its rich agricultural land. In 1910, wheat farmers harvested 20 to 40 bushels per acre, while corn production was from 20 to 75 bushels per acre. The First Presbyterian Church dedicated it's new building in 1911. It was constructed of limestone taken from local rock quarries. By 1915, a three-story red brick high school was completed and Catholic children were attending a constantly growing parochial grade school and high school. In 1916, Santa Fe built a handsome red brick depot. Another bank, the Security State Bank of Newkirk, was established in 1918, with P.S. Mason serving as president; F.S. Midgley was cashier and W.S. Cline was one of the directors. This bank became the Security National Bank in 1919, later consolidating with the Eastman Bank in 1927. In 1918, a board of Freeholders for the City of Newkirk was elected to prepare a town charter. These men, J.M. Hoefer, Wilmont Jones, J.S. Thomas, Charles Peel, T.J. Sargent, J.J. Cronan, D.S. Ford and Claude Duval submitted a charter, approved May 28, 1918, making the City of Newkirk a city of the first class.[3]

At the turn of the century, Blackwell and Tonkawa possessed institutions of higher education. The closing of the University Preparatory School in 1917, as a result of World War I, was a factor in Tonkawa's slow growth. Blackwell continued to prosper, even after closing the Oklahoma Baptist College in 1913. A brick plant in Blackwell closed early in 1910, when the clay deposits were worked out. It was replaced by an industry which was even more valuable, natural gas. In 1902, half a dozen gas wells were drilling northeast of town, with the first coming in at 750 feet. Soon, the Blackwell Gas and Mineral Company was formed, with a capital of $10,000. Natural gas provided light and heat for Blackwell homes and businesses. In 1913, the Blackwell Oil Field came in when Marland Oil drilled 28 wells without one dry hole. This abundance of natural gas, in conjunction with three railroad lines, was enough to draw more industry to Blackwell. In 1916, Blackwell Zinc Company began operations. They were the owner of the largest multicondenser, horizontal retort smelter in the world, and employed 700-800 employees. Later, Acme Foundry and Machine Shop, Turvey Packing Company, International Milling Company (an oil field tool factory), and other industries increased the number of people, adding to Blackwell's prosperity as farmers continued to make it their market. Farmers found buyers for their products in the town's five elevators, two poultry houses, creamery and flour mill, one of the largest in Oklahoma. Four banks, a building and loan, six lumber yards, six oil well supply houses and three refineries gave Blackwell a population of 18,000 by 1923, with a $10,000,000 annual payroll.[4]

In the teens, Kay County towns took on a more modern look as automobiles began to compete with horses for space on city streets. Garages began to replace livery stables; Ponca City paved its streets with brick in 1921, but still remained in many aspects a Western Frontier town. Cowboys came to town on business or pleasure, adding color to the local scene. Ponca, Kaw, Tonkawa and Otoe-Missouri from surrounding areas were frequently seen on the streets of Kay County towns in traditional dress. Merchants appreciated the trade Native Americans brought to their businesses. Dry goods merchant, Charles F. Calkins, of Ponca City, recalled, "We had a good trade with the Indians. There never was any trouble with the Indians. They were always friendly fellows."[5]

Most Kay County towns suffered disasters at one time or another. Fires were the most common type of disaster. In November, 1901, an entire block on the east side of Newkirk's Main Street burned down. Subsequently, an enlarged volunteer fire department of twenty-four men was organized and fire equipment ordered, with the hopes such a large conflagration could be prevented in the future. Ponca City already had a volunteer fire department which was organized in 1899. In 1914, it became one of the earliest towns to use a motorized fire truck. Blackwell had a progressive fire department. Fire Chief J.E. Taplin, a former school teacher and Blackwell's first fire chief, directed one of the first state training schools for fire fighters. He wrote what may have been the first instruction manual for fighting fires in the United States. His book, "The Essentials of Firemanship" written in the 1920's, was widely used in Oklahoma and was the forerunner of the "Redbooks", still published by Oklahoma State University and used in many countries.".[6]

Less could be done about natural disasters Kay County towns experienced. The Flood of 1923, the largest ever to occur in north central Oklahoma, could not be forgotten by those who lived through it. Rains in June sent the Salt Fork, Arkansas, and Chikaskia Rivers out of their banks. Flood waters inundated many square miles of low lands, drowned crops, swept away herds of cattle, poultry, horses and hogs. It swept away railroad and highway bridges, and washed away buildings. Towns such as Tonkawa, Kaw City, and Ponca City were isolated by the high waters. The 101 Ranch was also flooded. The water reached the second floor of the ranch store and came within inches of the porch of the White House. People from miles around were transported there by boat for refuge until the waters went down. The situation was aggravated by the fact that many visitors had arrived for one of the ranch's spectacular shows and an exhibition fight featuring Jess Willard. Many of these visitors were stranded for days, becoming members of the "Order of Noah".[7] When the waters receded, they left behind untold devastation, having demolished entire towns. In the aftermath, there were heaps of debris, rat plagues and typhoid epidemics.[8] Floods were not the only natural disasters to plague Kay County. Blizzards, hail storms, tornadoes, droughts, extreme heat (116 degrees on July 19, 1936) have all taken their toll on residents of the area formerly known as the Cherokee Outlet.[9]

Even more memorable to the people of Ponca City was the tornado of 1912. Late in the afternoon of Thursday, April 25, dark clouds from a spring thunderstorm began to move into Kay County. Just west of the Big V Ranch, located to the west of Ponca

April 25 - 1912   Ponca City Okla

City, a huge funnel formed about 4:45 p.m., moving erratically

164

north and east. Traveling about 50 miles per hour, towering perhaps a mile high, it churned across the prairie, damaging farm buildings and oil derricks in its path. At 5:25 in the afternoon it arrived near Ponca City, scouring the Wylde Addition west of the Santa Fe tracks. One woman was killed instantly by a falling house and several other people were injured. The tornado crossed the tracks, destroying houses in Cross, on the north edge of Ponca City. Again, there was considerable damage but few injuries. After leaving town it roared on eastward, overturning several box cars at Uncas and demolishing its depot. Although the sun came out briefly just after the tornado passed through, another storm arrived only a few minutes later with wind, followed by hail and a deluge of rain. This left streets of Ponca City, already torn up for paving, a mass of mud. The tornado was remembered for the damage it did on its path across the county. Because of the photograph made by photographer Jerry Drake, the tornado is still remembered. The funnel took fifteen minutes to arrive in Ponca City after it was sighted. This gave Drake time enough to set up his equipment and capture the awesome dark cloud on a photographic plate. His picture, one of the best tornado pictures made until recent times. It was widely circulated as a postcard.[10]

101 Ranch

Towns like Ponca City were able to recover from such blows and take them in stride, while smaller, struggling towns, like Kildare and Autwine, could not. In fact, Ponca City was gifted with not one but two, resources that made it a thriving town. The first of these was the 101 Ranch. The 101 Ranch had been in business since before the Run of 1893. It had grown continuously over the last three decades until it dominated the southern part of Kay County and Ponca City. By 1903, when its founder, Colonel George Miller, died, it sprawled over 50,000 acres of land leased from the Ponca Indians. Miller's wife, beneficiary of a $30,000 life insurance policy, used the money to purchase 3,720 acres (nearly six sections of Ponca land already within the confines of the 101). Over the next several years, the Miller family continued to buy small parcels of land, most of

165

which contained Indian allotment lands in Kay, Osage, Noble and Pawnee counties. Eventually, their holdings consisted of owned and leased land reaching 110,000 acres.[11]

To manage a ranch of such size, the three Miller sons formed a partnership. Each had his specialty: Joe, the eldest, was interested in stock raising, crop production and breeding new hybrids; Zack, the youngest, was the stockman, while George, the middle brother, was the financial manager. George and Zack loved to buy and sell, traveling frequently on ranch business. Together they engaged in a great number of different enterprises that literally turned the 101 Ranch into a showplace.[12]

Enterprises stemmed from a philosophy of diversification

Zack   George   Joe C.

started by Colonel George Miller when he put 5,000 acres of grazing land into wheat following the Panic of 1893. That economic depression forced Miller to sell much of his livestock to pay his debts. To help recoup his losses, he turned to wheat production and harvested 70,000 bushels the first year. The quick profits enabled him not only to pay off his debts, but buy more livestock including horses, mules, hogs, ducks, geese and buffalo. Miller's lesson in diversification was one his sons took to heart.[13]

They continued to grow wheat, plant cotton, corn, oats, sorghum, barley and rye. Under Joe Miller's direction, they experimented with crops that were difficult to grow until an acceptable

101 Bull

166

hybrid was found. Many acres were put into garden vegetables, onions, cabbages, sweet potatoes, peas, beans and tomatoes. Plots of cantaloupes, melons and acres of berries, fruit trees, walnut and pecan trees were planted.[14]

Similar experiments were carried out with livestock. The brothers began to bring new breeds of cattle to the 101 Ranch. Brahmas, Jerseys, Durhams, Holsteins, and Herefords were added to their Texas Longhorn cattle. When Joe Miller decided to raise hogs as well as cattle, he purchased $75,000 worth of purebred Durocs. He bought and experimented with the breeding of buffalo, zebras, ostriches and other exotic animals.[15]

The 101 Ranch diversification programs did not stop with crops and animals. The Miller brothers were determined to make the 101 Ranch self-sufficient. The result was a series of ranch industries organized to process and sell ranch products on the ranch itself. They opened a meatpacking plant capable of handling thousands of animals, 12,000 hogs and 5,000 cattle in 1926 alone. The processed meat and hams were shipped out in the 101's refrigerated trucks for local delivery. Hides from the slaughtered animals were made into leather goods and harnesses at the ranch tannery and leather shops. Milk from dairy herds was processed into cheese, ice cream, and butter at the ranch creamery. A cannery turned vegetable garden and orchard produce into canned goods, cider, and apple butter. These products were sold at the ranch store.[16]   In addition to the aforementioned industries, the ranch had its own electrical plant, water system,

telephone system and internal mail delivery. Machine shops, woodworking and blacksmith shops kept modern farming equipment in repair, and a ranch refinery produced gasoline from ranch wells. So impressive was the 101 Ranch operation that Oklahoma Agricultural and Mechanical College (now Oklahoma State University) required agriculture students to visit the ranch two weeks each summer to see how the diversified ranch operated.[17]

For the most part, it was not ranching and farming operations that brought thousands of visitors each day, but the 101 Ranch Wild West Show. What began as a ploy by the Millers to bring the National Editorial Association to Guthrie, Oklahoma Territory in 1905, turned into another business for the 101. They promised cowboys, Indians, a powwow, buffalo hunt and promised to have the Apache leader, Geronimo, brought from imprisonment at Fort Sill to take part in the buffalo hunt. Some 30,000 people came to see the dress rehearsal held in the fall of 1904.[18]

The 101 Ranch Train

When the actual event took place in June, 1905, 30 trains brought spectators to Ponca City. From the railway they walked to the Ponca City area then watched a mile-long procession of performers enter the arena. The show was everything the Millers promised---buffalo herds, pioneer wagon trains, bronc-busting, Indian dancing, Geronimo, and Lucille Mulhall, along with her trained horse. A crowd of 65,000 attended this first official performance.[19]

The Millers found it profitable to make the show a regular feature. Subsequently, they began to take it on the road in Oklahoma and neighboring states. Three years later, the show was combined with Edward Arlington's Ringling Brothers Circus and began to tour the county. Each year new attractions were added with gratifying results. Between 1908 and 1916, the show grossed the Millers' around $800,000 annually.[20]

The 101 Ranch Wild West Show was just as much at home in Madison Square Garden as in Ponca City. They toured Mexico, Canada, and were just embarking on a tour of Europe, with a performance scheduled in London. After displaying their version of the Wild West for queens of England, Greece, Romania, and the czarina of Russia, they were suddenly brought up short. In August of 1914, England entered World War I, immediately confiscating the Miller show horses and equipment for the war effort. Joe Miller, who usually accompanied the show, managed to get the troupe home to help keep some American commitments, but with only his most highly trained show horses. In 1915 and 1916, Joe again took the show on tour, but with the United States on the verge of joining in the war effort, he sensed the public had little time for such spectacles. Joe disbanded the show in 1916.[21]

The show remained disbanded until 1924 when, once again, the Millers helped bring the National Editorial Association to Oklahoma. Joe persuaded his brothers to put up $100,000 each to reassemble it. They put together the same type of Western entertainment presented in earlier days. This time they purchased the Walter L. Main Circus, with its elephants, tigers, lions, monkeys and other exotic animals. An Arabian troupe, Scottish and Russian bands, and several other circus acts were added to create the new 101 Real Wild West and Great Far East Combined Show. It left on its first tour in the spring of 1925.[22]

An impressive show, it attracted larger audiences than before the war, but it was also more expensive to operate. Sometimes the show made money, but some times it ran in the red. In general, the public was more sophisticated in the 1920's, having lost its appreciation for wild west shows. In addition, the 101 show was in competition with other circuses. The stock market crash of 1929 saw problems for the Millers begin to accumulate. Even though they carried on the show, it began to lose as much as $100,000 annually. In 1932, the show ran out of money while performing in Washington,D.C.[23]

The 101 Ranch Wild West Show had a profound effect on Ponca City and Kay County. Many performers lived in the Ponca City vicinity and many Indian performers were Ponca. When the show wintered on the ranch, Kay County's population included a variety of nationalities from Mexican to Russian and a constant stream of visitors visited the ranch complex and Ponca City. The guest book of the Millers' White House home was a register of famous names. Novelists, Mary Roberts Rinehart and Edna Ferber, used the ranch for background material; John Philip Sousa, "The March King:, came to discuss joining the tours and Admiral Richard Byrd rode elephants. Presidents Theodore Roosevelt and Warren G. Harding, along with Vice-President Charles Curtis, Senator Arthur Capper and General John J. Pershing were guests at the Miller ranch. William Jennings Bryan, Will Rogers, William Allen White, "Pawnee Bill" Lillie, "Buffalo Bill" Cody, Nancy Astor, John D. Rockefeller Jr., Jack Dempsey, William Randolph Hearst and Chief Bacon Rind found

themselves equally welcome, enjoying the famous White House hospitality. Less famous, but just as welcome, were thousands who flocked daily to the ranch complex to watch shows, look at animals, buy ranch produce or eat at the ranch restaurant.[24]

It did not matter how famous the White House guests were, the Millers never forgot their cowboy heritage, helping found the Cherokee Strip Cow Punchers' Association. Eligible members, including the Millers themselves, were required to have worked cattle in the Cherokee Outlet before the Run of 1893. When the group was organized in September of 1920, it had about 400 members. Ave Banta, of Billings, Oklahoma, was the first president. The following year, Joe Miller was elected president for life. Oscar Brewster, of Crescent, Oklahoma, continued as

170

secretary-treasurer. The group was so large that President Joe Miller appointed Ike Clubb and Hugo Milde of Kaw City, Link Barr of Dover, George Laing of Kingfisher, and Monte Tate of Oklahoma City to an executive committee to help with the work. The Cow Punchers also enlisted the help of the wives who were eligible for membership in the "ladies auxiliary". Zack Miller gave the organization a lifetime lease on 101 Ranch land for annual meetings. The hill on the south side of the Salt Fork River, across from the original 101 Rodeo grounds and southeast of the White House, was chosen as the site for these annual meetings. The site was named "Cowboy Hill" and a large frame building was built for the CSCPA reunions held every year at the time of the annual round-up and terrapin derby.[25]

The 101 Ranch also brought the movie industry to Kay County. Movies were still in their infancy and the ranch provided both the background and performers for some of the first western films. The serial "Wild West" combined western adventure with circus life; "Trail Dust" featured a buffalo stampede starring the ranch's own herd. Several early movie stars got their start at the 101: Ken Maynard, Tom Mix, Hoot Gibson and Jack and Lucille Mulhall, who rode and roped their way into the movie industry.[26]

A series of misfortunes struck the 101 Ranch, seriously affecting it. In 1927, Joe Miller, the agriculturalist and showman of the family, was accidentally killed by carbon monoxide poisoning, George mortgaged the 101 holdings to pay off the show's indebtedness, concentrating on the oil business in hopes of recovering their losses. In 1929, George Miller, the financial manager, was killed on an icy road near the ranch. Zack Miller, the remaining brother, was left to handle the monumental task of managing the entire operation. The stock market crash of 1929 ushered the nation into the Great Depression, sending farm prices to rock bottom. This era watched oil prices decline and the wild west show lose money each year. Zack found himself and the ranch in a financial bind. He tried to recoup as his father had in 1893, but was unable to salvage the show and began to sell it, bit by bit, to other circuses. In March, 1932, Zack was forced to sell all the ranch animals and farm equipment at auction. The White House was heavily mortgaged, and due to be liquidated. Disheartened, he barricaded himself in the mansion in an attempt to resist the court-order to liquidate the 101 Ranch properties, threatening intruders with his six-shooter. Friends talked him out and Miller was arrested and jailed in Newkirk. Governor William H. "Alfalfa Bill" Murray used his executive powers on Miller's behalf. He sent a squad of state militia to release Miller, with the militia instructed to use force if necessary. Everyone cheered when they learned that the colorful old westerner had been freed. Loan companies granted him a moratorium of two years in hopes he could redeem the Ranch. Zack turned to his friends but they too had their backs against the wall. The depression had hit everyone.[27]

Over the next few years the lands from the ranch were sold off in small parcels; ranch buildings were torn down for their materials; and the White House deteriorated. Zack Miller made several valiant attempts but failed to save the 101 Ranch. Zack moved to Texas, where he died in 1952. He was buried atop Cowboy Hill, across the Salt Fork from the 101 Ranch White House.[28]

Oil Boom Days

The 101 Ranch helped shape the image of Kay County well into the twentieth century with the discovery of oil. In those days there was little use for oil, other than for lubrication and medicinal purposes. Oil was discovered in Indian Territory in 1859 when a settler, drilling for water, struck oil, regarded as more of a nuisance. The same year the first well was drilled at Titusville, Pennsylvania. Around 1900, the invention and development of gasoline-fueled internal combustion engines created new high-speed machinery coming into industrial use. This development, along with automobiles, helped create a market for petroleum products. The search for oil had been under way for some time in Oklahoma and suddenly men were traveling over the country looking for it. They found it in eastern

Oklahoma at Red Fork and Glenpool. This transformed Tulsa from a sleepy crossroads cow town into a boom town within a few years. Other fields were discovered, each a little further west than the one before. Most oil prospectors believed there was no oil west of the 96th meridian and the Osage Hills where Red beds, a layer of deposits from the Permian Era, lay. Their reddish color gave much of central Oklahoma's soil its reddish tint, but inspired little interested in Kay County.[29]

The indications of oil in Kay County were there. In 1894 Marcus McCaskey was having a water well drilled on his farm southeast of Newkirk when it struck gas at 90 feet. One of the drillers, experienced in eastern oil fields, showed McCaskey how to pipe the gas into his house for heating and lighting. McCaskey kept his gas well a secret for two years while he finished "proving up" on his claim. Only when he was sure of his ownership did he let the news of his strike get out. By 1898 there was enough interest in oil prospecting that the Newkirk Oil and Gas Company was organized. Local businessmen, Jim T. Brown, John Hoefer, John Miller, Joe S. Hayes, all of Newkirk; Lincoln McKinley, of Wichita; and Peter Hollenbeck, of Arkansas City were disappointed when their first well made only a barrel or two a day, but it was enough to keep their interest alive.[30]

Between 1902-1903 the Santa Fe built a line from Newkirk southeastward to Kaw City. Drilling in this area continued for several years. The first successful shallow well was on the property of Jens and Marie Christensen, about a mile northeast of Mervine. Jim Young, Dennis Mooney, Clifford Leatherman, Henry Bucker and Jim M. VanWinkle, all of Ponca City, drilled this well. They used the first names of the Christensen couple and named their organization the Jens-Marie Oil Company. A hotel built in Ponca City was also named the Jens-Marie. Shallow drilling continued, but several years passed before drilling in the Mervine (or Newkirk) sand became extensive.[31]

In 1903, Charles H. Ruby formed the Ponca City Oil, Gas

and Mineral Company, in order to prospect near Ponca City. Several local businessmen, C. DeRoberts, W.E. Scott, A.G. Soldani, George Brett, and C.F. Calkins were on the Board of Directors. They persuaded investors to buy shares in the venture and drilling began. The first well struck a small flow of gas, but the second proved much more productive. By 1905 a number of gas wells were drilled near town. This made it practical to install gas mains throughout Ponca City. Though the company never struck oil, Ruby never lost confidence that there was oil in Kay County. Ruby's company was the only one in the county exploring for both oil and gas.[32]

The real boom for Kay County came in the spring of 1910. Like Ruby, Ernest Whitworth Marland believed there was oil west of the 96th meridian. Unlike many early wildcatters, he applied the new science of petroleum geology in his quest for oil. A native of Pittsburgh, he came west in 1908. The 34 year-old Marland made his first million dollars as a promoter in the West Virginia oil fields, but like many others, lost it in the Panic of 1907. Marland stopped in Chicago, where he met Colonel F.R. Kenney, an army officer formerly stationed in Oklahoma. They discussed the possibility of oil in the western area of the new state. Kenney arranged for Marland to visit his friend, George L. Miller, at the 101 Ranch. The two men arrived at the ranch in December, 1908 and began surveying the prairie for rock formations indicating the presence of anticlines, where oil might be trapped in porous sands. They found such a formation at the site of the Ponca Indian Cemetery.[33]

The Millers agreed to lease Marland about 10,000 acres of the 101 Ranch. The Ponca, however, were not willing to allow drilling in their cemetery, deemed hallowed ground. Landowners, Running-After-Arrow, Willie Cries-for-War, Little-Man-Stands-Up, Peter-Knows-the-Country, and Thomas-On-Two-Lean-Bears'-Ear agreed to let drilling take place on their land as long as the cemetery was not disturbed. They leased 4,800 acres to George Miller, who in turn leased one-half interest to Marland.[34]

Drilling got underway in February, 1909, but not without complications for Marland and his drillers. The nearest oil equipment supply houses were 125 miles away at Tulsa, making it necessary to ship everything by railroad. The nearest railroad siding was at Bliss (now Marland), several miles south of the 101 Ranch White House. All of the equipment shipped to Bliss (most old-fashioned even at the time) had to be hauled overland to the drill site near the ranch headquarters. To make matters worse, the 101 Ranch could not supply the heavy draft animals needed to haul these loads of cable, timber, tools, boilers and casings to the well. It was necessary to use teams of oxen for the freighting. Marland finally abandoned his first well without ever reaching oil producing sands. Moving to another site, a second well was sunk and completed in the spring of 1910. The drillers were excited about their success, but the Poncan, Running-After-Arrow, was dubious. He forecast sadly, "No good,no good. Beautiful country all die now. Cattle die. Ponies die. No good, no good, Beautiful country soon all gone.".[35]

Willie Cries-For-War

Marland, with only this one success, made plans to develop what he was sure would be a large oil field. With W.H. McFadden; J.C. McCaskey, Pittsburgh businessman and sauerkraut king; Colonel F.R. Kenny; George L. Miller; James J. McGraw, and others, Marland organized the 101 Ranch Oil Company. He continued sinking wells in the vicinity of the first, with seven gas producers out of eight attempts. Marland marketed his gas in Tonkawa, fifteen miles to the west, after building a pipe line and obtaining a franchise to distribute it there. The profits did not return the investment of $500,000 Marland and his associates invested, but provided his company with the needed money to keep drilling. Their ninth well struck oil in June, 1911, on the allotment of Willie-Cries-For-War, the proof Marland needed that there was great oil deposit in the area named the Mid-Continent Field.[36]

This was the beginning of the oil boom in Kay County, lasting for several years and reshaping the face of the land. Soon, other wildcatters arrived in Kay County to scout for likely geologic formations. Fortuna Oil, Watchorn Oil and Magnolia Petroleum followed Marland into the new territory. Marland continued to get production from the Ponca Field, but moved his exploratory to the Newkirk Field in 1912 and the Blackwell Field in 1913. Soon pipelines fanned out from discovery areas to towns in north central Oklahoma and southern Kansas. By 1912, Marland formed the Marland Refining Company and absorbed the original 101 Ranch Oil Company. He built a refinery on the south edge of Ponca City, expanding his operation into refining and marketing petroleum products. The Kay County Gas Company, which he controlled, took over natural gas distribution. In 1920 Marland incorporated the refinery into the Marland Oil Company, creating an integrated company engaged in oil exploration, production, natural gas distribution, refining and marketing.[37]

Soon Marland Oil's "red triangle" insignia was a familiar sight in Oklahoma. In 1921 he opened his first filling station at Pawhuska. On opening day visitors were given free oil with the purchase of gasoline, women were given flowers and the children toys. In addition, they enjoyed the sight of sweeping approaches and drives landscaped by Marland's gardener, Henry Hatashita. This was the first of many stations to be opened in the following years, as money flowed into Marland's pockets as easily as oil flowed out of his wells.[38]

Marland was not the only one to make his fortune in Kay County oil. Another new oil millionaire who came to call Ponca City his home was Louis Haines Wentz. Also a Pennsylvanian, he came to Oklahoma at the request of J.G. McCaskey, one of E.W. Marland's partners. Wentz, a baseball coach and semi-

176

professional player, knew little about oil, but McCaskey, liking Wentz's work in sports and Republican politics in the Pittsburgh area, brought Wentz into his business. McCaskey sent him west to oversee investments in the new Ponca City Field.[39]

Wentz arrived when several new fields were coming into production. Using slender resources and good judgment, he began acquiring leases, first in the Peckham-Braman and Blackwell areas, and later in the Tonkawa area. In 1921 the Tonkawa Field came in. By this time Wentz had bought out McCaskey's interests including the McKee lease just south of the Tonkawa Field. This one well brought in a $3.000.000 profit, putting Wentz in the millionaire category.[40]

Wentz was farsighted while others were not. By 1927, the independent Wentz Oil Company was making $1,000,000 a month and its founder was one of the richest men in the United States. Two years later, the stock market crash of 1929 sent oil prices plunging, ruining many oil entrepreneurs. The inherently cautious Wentz saw the crash coming, sold his oil interests and invested in government bonds. Later, while other businessmen were watching their investments collapse, Wentz reinvested his wealth in a variety of ventures and profits continued to flow into his pockets.[41]

Indeed, oil money washed over much of Kay County throughout the decades of the teens and the 1920's. A changing agricultural market turned towns into oil boom towns in a matter of weeks. Heavy machinery churned country roads into muddy bogs as derricks sprouted up like weeds on the prairie. Population figures ballooned as oil workers and those providing services to them flocked into the newly opened oil fields. Tonkawa's population of 1,500 in 1910 expanded to 10,000 plus following the discovery of oil in 1921. Ponca City blossomed from 2,500 to 15,000 within a few years.[42]

Towns like Three Sands were created overnight, just as towns had following the Run of 1893. Others that grew slowly before, such as Mervine and Dilworth, experienced a flood of newcomers and sudden prosperity. Mervine, named after D.T. Mervine of the Wells Fargo Company and Santa Fe railroad, sprang up in the vicinity of the McCaskey well. Drilling in the area started around 1898 by the Newkirk Oil and Gas Company and flourished between 1915-1916, following the discovery of oil. By 1918 **Mervine** had four grocery stores, three lumber yards, a blacksmith shop, tire shop, Methodist church, feed store, two rooming houses and Roy Gill's two story furniture store. Mervine children attended Stony Point School, with 70 students attending between 1915-1916. One-half mile west of the railroad depot was a nitroglycerin depot. Heavy equipment rumbling through Mervine's main intersection always had the right of way.[43]

Dilworth sprouted in the mid-teens, enjoying its own Oil Field Short Line Railway. It was platted by W. Matthews and John A. Frates, president of the Dilworth Townsite Company and an employee of the Santa Fe Railroad. The town sprawled over 60 acres of the Charles Dilworth farm, ten miles northwest of Newkirk. The Lew Wentz Oil Company, Empire (later Cities Services), 101, Sinclair, and Marland Oil Companies converged on Dilworth. The population of Dilworth, according to Homer S. Chambers, "...Rose as by magic to 3,500 to 4,000 within a few months." Chambers became postmaster when the post office opened March 17, 1917. Two thousand people (some estimates were 4.000) lived in Dilworth's new homes and rooming houses; sent their children to Dilworth's new Pleasant View grammar school and high school; and shopped in Dilworth's business district. On October 23, 1917, the town voted to become incorporated.[44]

Several false-front buildings lined the broad, unpaved main street. Among these businesses were the Fred Davenport Bakery, the Empire Pipe Yard, a clothing store, telephone office, W.R. Pickering Lumber Company, Hillsdale Rooming House,

O.F. Graff Rooming House, Star Rooming House, a hotel, Maltby Grocery and Garage, Maw and Dad Holmes Grocery, John Lewis Garage, Mike Trapp Barber Shop, Keith and DeRossett Pool Hall, Bob and Babe Morrell Pool Hall, Allen's Drug Store, O.C. Munn Hardware Store, physicians Pryor and Bishop, Tom McQuirt General Store, Dilworth Bank , Roy Hill Furniture Store, a theater, refinery and the Charlie Rollins Elevator.[45]

A new $60.000 sewer system had just been completed when disaster first struck Dilworth. The first indication of problems was a rapid decline in oil production. The final blow came in 1922 when Dilworth's tinderbox business buildings went up in flames. Fire fighters struggled to save what they could from what was felt to be arson. The town never recovered, since too much of Dilworth's business district was lost. Dropping productivity in the oil fields saw the oil boom move on. On February 7, 1924, Dilworth's population was 72, as the town faded away with its post office closing March 29, 1929.[46]

While Dilworth was a thriving town, **West Dock**, also known as Dock, one-half mile west of Dilworth, also thrived. Located on the Frank Dilworth homestead, it consisted of three stores and a bunk and boarding house. When it was obvious that Dilworth was going to be the town to survive, West Dock yielded to its competition. Another place that prospered during Dilworth's prosperity was **Clifford**. Clifford was not a town, with neither a post office nor many residents. The one thing it did have was plenty of travelers and shipping from its depot. Clifford was at the end of the "Oil Field Short Line Railway" and had a turnabout, boxcar depot and large auger to load grain. It was originally named "Berenice", but this caused confusion with a town in eastern Oklahoma named "Bernice". Clifford, established in 1916, closed in 1929.[47]

As might be expected, many of these towns attracted rough characters: some of the oil field workers themselves, gamblers, bootleggers and prostitutes. One of the roughest boom towns was **Three Sands**, located on the Kay-Noble County line, five miles south of Tonkawa and thirteen miles east of **Marland (Bliss)**. Drilling for oil in Three Sands began around 1920 when E.W. Marland's geologist drilled test wells in the Tonkawa vicinity. Results were very discouraging at first, as eight dry holes were drilled. Well number nine showed traces of oil and on Friday, June 30, 1921, more than 1,000 barrels of oil a day began flowing from this well eight miles due south of Tonkawa in Noble County. It produced high grade crude and this excited the oil industry so much that several companies, Royal Dutch-Shell, Roxana, Carter, Comar and Gypsy were soon moving into what become known as the Tonkawa Field. Farmers struggling to get by on some of the less productive land in Kay and Noble Counties found themselves courted by oil "lease hounds". Many farmers leasing their land to oil companies, quit farming and moved into Tonkawa.[48]

Most of the drilling was centered around the Sam McKee farm, but activity shifted northward along the highway that lead to Tonkawa. At each successive crossroad a cluster of stores and houses would spring up. Businessmen sought to profit by providing goods and services to the oil field workers; groceries, dry goods, equipment, repair shops, entertainment, food and places to sleep. As the drilling activity would move, another town would spring up at the next crossroad. **Hatchville**, a grocery store east of the discovery well, was operated by Charlie Hatch. Mayor of his establishment. **Murray**, two miles into Noble County, consisted of a barber shop, grocery store, filling station and dry goods store on the F.H. Murray farm, **Four Ways**, **Kanolka** and **Three Sands** made their appearance known at three corners east of Marland's discovery well. Other business centers in the area were **East Side**, one mile east of Three Sands' original intersection; **Foster**, one mile west; **Riverview**, seven miles west (Three Sands' greatest rival); and **Blue Ridge**. These business districts never disappeared completely as oil activity moved and the business district for the oil field eventually stretched three miles.[49]

The main business center for the Tonkawa field was **Three**

Sands. Like earlier business districts, Three Sands started out as a grocery store and cafe in a shack on the C.C. Endicott farm. At first it was called "Comar", after one of the seven major oil companies engaged in exploiting the field, ("Comar" meant "companies of Marland"). The *Tonkawa News* complained about the confusion of names in the oil field business district. Merchants and officials from the Comar company met and agreed on the name "Three Sands" because, at the time, oil was being produced from three separate oil sands, Endicott, Carmichael and Tonkawa. (If they had waited six months, they could have named the town "Seven Sands" for the same reason.)[50]

Three Sands was like other oil boom towns of the day. By December, 1922, 11 boarding houses and several cafes served meals to hungry oil field workers. These types of businesses usually came first, followed by oil tool supply houses, machine shops, boiler shops, markets and stores. Within a month, the Cozy Theater was under construction and the town's first two-story building, a dance hall, was planning to offer entertainment. By March, 1923, citizens were petitioning for a post office, claiming there were 2,000 people living in town with around 3,000 more in the vicinity. On June 15 of that year, the post office located at **Four Corners** (also known as **Murray Corner**) was moved to Three Sands. Carpenters worked day night to put up frame buildings for businesses and housing. Neat company houses were built and painted green for Comar, gray for Gypsy, gray with red roofs for Amerada and gold for Carter. Lumber was so much in demand that carpenters did not dare leave it unattended at night. Until houses were built, many people lived in tents, shacks or dugouts. Accommodations were less important than making a quick profit from the oil being produced at 200,000 barrels a day. "Two-Ton Tilly" and "Three Sands Blanche", boarding house operators, and the "hunchback" who made deliveries for a local bootlegger, rubbed elbows with geologists, oil field workers and housewives. A writer for the *Daily Oklahoma* in April, 1923, described Three Sands as "... a crowd and not a city. A struggling, shoving, pushing, determined, reckless, maddened, coldly calculating mixture of human beings who have forgotten for the time being that they are alive. Who don't seem to care how long they live, who, in fact, are bent on one thing, the getting of all the money they can as fast as they can. The person visiting Three Sands today finds himself in a traffic jam surpassing that of any city of 300,000 inhabitants. There isn't such a thing as the 'right-of-way'. The man who tries to make his way through the street is 'in the way' of everyone, including himself. All he can do is keep going. He can't turn around, he can't stop, he can't become impatient. He can only keep going and at the same speed decided upon by a mile of automobiles, motor trucks, and pedestrians. If he took a notion to get away from the throng and speed through the fields to his destination, he would find himself trying to dodge oil well rigs that are so thick it's pretty hard, sometimes, to walk between them without getting oil on your clothing.".[51]

Most people who appeared at the opening of the Tonkawa field were law-abiding citizens, intent on their own business, but some were not. The arrival of rowdy oil field workers in Three Sand gained it the reputation of being a disorderly and violent place. The 1920's were prohibition days, but a drink could be had in Three Sands at any time of the day or night. Moonshining, brewing "Choc beer" and bootlegging were a fact of life, as was prostitution, gambling and fights. Free-for-alls were so common on the main street that passers-by paid no attention to them. Robberies were epidemic. One night thieves went from one oil rig to another, taking the crew's valuables, then committing another robbery at the next rig. Since most payrolls were paid with cash, hijackings and kidnappings were frequent. Wealthy local families were objects of this type of lawlessness. There were two reasons for such lawlessness. Three Sands never established a town government to help control what was happening and the other was partially due to the fact that Three Sands and the Tonkawa field sprawled across the Kay-Noble County line. Each county appointed a deputy to oversee its jurisdiction, but neither man really did the job. The deputies could blame their problems on the basis it was the other's jurisdiction. In addition, their salaries were so low that oil companies, businessmen and civic organizations increased them with contributions. This practice encouraged payoffs and the selling of "protection". There were no facilities for jailing lawbreakers, with one deputy chaining his prisoners to a telephone pole until delivery could be made to the county seat. Eventually, Kay County authorities built a special wire stockade at the Newkirk jail to hold the prisoner overflow from Three Sands until the next court session or the next train left for the state prison.[52]

Three Sands' two deputies, John "Two Gun" Middleton and George 'Three Finger" Miller, each came to a violent end. In July, 1923, Miller, a former member of the Red Buck gang and ex-convict, tried to extort protection money from Jackson "Chief" Burns, a full-blood Choctaw oil field worker. He chained Burns to a bed post in a Three Sands boarding house room and beat him until he agreed to pay. Then Miller let him go. At 12:20 p.m. on Saturday, July 21, Burns shot and killed both Miller and Middleton on the street in front of the Blue Front Cafe. Witnesses testified Burns shot in self-defense while others swore that he ambushed the deputies. Either way, the jury quickly acquitted Burns, saying his killing the two notorious deputes was a clear case of "kill or be killed".[53]

Even more outrageous was the killing of a man named Askren, a disabled World War I veteran, who was murdered on a Three Sands' street by a recently paroled convict from federal prison. The death of the victim, a member of the American Legion and Masonic Lodge, infuriated law-abiding citizens of Three Sands. The following Saturday night a crowd of public-spirited men gathered on the Comar baseball field and demanded Three Sands be cleaned up. A mob atmosphere threatened, but some of the wiser men cooled the temper of the crowd. The meeting ended by resolving that if the town were not cleaned up within 24 hours by authorities, they would do it themselves. Editorials from across the state called for an end to the lawlessness in Three Sands. A series of raids shut down most houses of ill repute, with many undesirable elements escorted out of town. Three Sands citizens cleaned their own house.[54]

Only two years old, Three Sands had already reached its peak. By the fall of 1924, the town had an active Methodist mission, several new elementary schools, a high school and was the state's largest common school district. Organizations such as the American Legion; Free Masons; a 300 member Klu Klux Klan and auxiliary; and several semi-professional baseball teams, sponsored by Wentz and Comar, existed. A $60,000, 2,500-seat basketball gymnasium was built, but oil production, the reason for Three Sands existence, was on the decline. Production continued in the Osage fields to the east and new fields were opened in California. For a few years, oil field workers alternated between Three Sands and the Osage as productivity fluctuated. By 1930 only a few hundred of the original 2.000 inhabitants still resided in Three Sands. The high school closed in 1946 and a grocery store, the first, as well as the last business in Three Sands closed in 1951. The post office shut its doors in 1957 and like many a boom town before it, Three Sands became little more than a memory.[55]

That was not true of **Tonkawa**, for which the oil field in southwestern Kay County was named. Unlike Three Sands, Tonkawa had existed as a town since the Run of 1893. The founding of the University Preparatory School in 1901 ensured the town's survival, but after 1910, when the population had reached 1,776, Tonkawa ceased growing. A railroad spur and U.S. Route 60, one of the nation's earliest transcontinental highways, passed through town, keeping it active as a farm center. A writer for *Harlow's Weekly* wrote that Tonkawa always knew it was meant for something bigger.[56]

That something was oil. Anticipating the day when Tonkawa might become part of the oil industry, city fathers saw to the paving of the city streets and to providing utilities for the whole town. The Tonkawa Chamber of Commerce, founded in 1919, was very progressive and farsighted. They actively promoted oil business in town as they watched over the installation of telephones lines and the grading of roads. In addition, Tonkawa already had an oil well supply house before the first well was completed in the Tonkawa field. When the day came, Tonkawa was ready for business.[57]

Tonkawa's businessmen welcomed the oil boom which began in the spring of 1923. Old businesses expanded to meet new demands. The American State Bank, the Bank of Commerce and the Farmers National Bank met the boom with a total of about $1,000,000 in deposits, increasing to approximately $13,000,000 by 1927. Receipts at the Santa Fe depot ballooned to 10 times what they were before 1923, amounting to $250,000 per month as 800 carloads of oil field supplies were shipped in and 120 tank cars of high-grade crude were shipped out. By April, 1923, there were 150 new businesses in town, including 15 oil field supply houses.[58]

All of these new businesses served the 10.000 or more people who moved into Tonkawa during the peak of the boom. South Main Street was the center of the business district and resembled the congested streets of Three Sands. Stricklen's Cafeteria (once the Main Garage), Coppage's news stand, Bertwell's shoe store, a theater, lumber yard, feed stores and restaurants lined the east side, while boarding houses, cleaners and royalty offices were on the west. Lots that once sold for $50 to $75 brought $1,500 each and building space was at a premium, with a six by twelve foot office renting for $100 per month. Builders constructed a trestle over a wide drainage ditch and constructed buildings on the trestle. South of the Salt Fork, a farmer, leasing 1,000 feet of land on each side of the road, began building a town called "**Smackover'**. It was named after an earlier oil boom town, Smackover, Arkansas. Shacks and tents quickly filled the area along the road. Smackover quickly became notorious for its crime. One area resident best described Smackover as"...the sin-filled, oil boom addition of Tonkawa...".[59] The town was short lived, when in June, 1923, flood waters inundated Smackover, leaving its main street under 10 feet of water. It never recovered as most of its residents moved away. South Main Street, north of the bridge, then gained a reputation almost as evil as Smackover's. Robberies, fights, prostitution, and gambling were commonplace, but they never reached the epidemic proportions occurring in Three Sands.[60]

One reason may have been the presence of the Ku Klux Klan in Tonkawa. The 1920's were an active period for the Klan across the nation. Unlike the Klan of the 1870's and 1880's, directed against "un-Americanism", the Tonkawa Klan was against crime. Not only was it a vigilante force but it was also a social organization; membership was not necessarily a stigma. The Klan first appeared in Tonkawa on a Saturday night in April, 1922. A double file of hooded, white-robed marchers paraded down Grand Avenue, leading the way with a fiery cross held between two American flags. A bugle blast announced their presence as banners proclaimed, "We Are 100 Per Cent American" and "We Are Here Today and Tomorrow and All the Time". One woman was said to have shouted, "Oh, why were you not here yesterday?" Over the next several months, the Klan grew stronger in the Tonkawa field area. Cars lined the roads for one of the larger rallies, with more than 2,000 people in a pasture north of Tonkawa. One hundred new members were initiated. Members of the Klan were usually local businessmen, prominent citizens, oil men and local farmers. Many who did not join were sympathetic to the Klan's cause. It maintained that its purpose was the suppression of crime and in support of the public's welfare. The organization made contributions to oil field accident victims or threatened a perpetrator of injustice when the law did not offer a proper recourse. Surprisingly there was little Klan-related violence in the Tonkawa area.[61]

Crime was only one problem the oil boom brought to Tonkawa. There was an acute housing shortage in the fall of 1922, as the vanguard of the boom arrived. Many had no choice except to camp out in the city park since the town's three hotels were packed, with sleeping space in the lobby going for 50 cents a night. By January, 1923, about 3,000 more people arrived, the population reaching 8,000 by that summer. Many Tonkawa householders rented out spare rooms, attics, garages, stables, any place that a person might sleep. Some families in small houses would move into one room and rent out the rest of their house. Students who arrived in Tonkawa for the 1922-1923 term at the University Preparatory School, reopened in 1919, simply went back home because they could not afford the rent. To answer part of the problem, investors spent $100,000 to build the Hotel Tonkawa. This hotel became the headquarters for oil men in town. House building flourished with 500 new houses, ranging from $500 to $10,000, being built by April, 1923. Sam McKee, who had the first oil well in the area, built a home costing $35,000, the first house in Tonkawa to exceed $10,000. Many other homes in Tonkawa were built with oil royalty money.[62]

Tonkawa enjoyed many benefits from the 1923-1924 oil boom. Besides town growth and business expansion, Tonkawa built several new facilities it could not afford before, including a new city hall, high school and hospital, while many churches built on new additions. The oil boom could not last forever. As the boom moved elsewhere, Tonkawa's population declined to 4,635 by 1927.[63]

Kaw City **benefited** from the oil boom period. Excitement swept the town in 1919 with the discovery of oil! Strangers walked the streets, oil company officials, trucking contractors, oil well supply contractors and all that go with an oil field appeared. People crowded into town seeking quarters and unheard of rental prices were asked for rooms and houses.

A building boom started; roads were widened; new culverts built; gas was piped into town; main Street was paved; and old buildings were torn down, replaced by new ones. Bonds were voted on for a city water and sewer system. The oil field spread in all directions, with many individuals profiting through investments. The town's population more than doubled and Kaw City became a first class city. The showing of oil disappeared in the direction of Kaw City, but left behind new businesses, new

187

wealth and a vastly improved city.[64]

On June 11, 1923, disaster struck Kaw City in the form of a spring flood of the mighty Arkansas River. Many businesses and homes were inundated, with both the north and south bridges washed out. The economic loss was devastating as Kaw City, surrounded on all three sides by the river, was for all practical purposes isolated except from the west. The north bridge to the Kaw Country was soon reconstructed, but the south bridge was lost forever. The town settled back to the life of a quiet farming community, its farm trade now coming from the north and west. The vast trade from the Osage lands would never again cross to Kaw City from the south.[65]

On December 16, 1923, a post office was established two miles north and three miles east of Washunga. Hickman was located on the Lemon Hickman property south of Ike Clubb. Though the town consisted for a grocery store, it lost out to Cooper, two miles east in Osage County, surviving only a year.[66]

Many other towns enjoyed this period of oil prosperity but decreased in size and population as oil production declined. Some towns like Tonkawa, Ponca City, Blackwell, and Newkirk were able to survive the economic downturn, while others with a less solid base like Mervine, Three Sands and Dilworth vanished almost as quickly as they appeared. The decline that began in 1927 continued into 1929 when the collapse of Wall Street sent prices spiraling downward. As prices on all kinds of commodities dropped, manufacturers shut down factories and laid off workers. The price of oil and gas dropped also, contributing to hard times in Kay County.

Although the oil boom was short lived it made a lasting impression on Kay County towns. First of all, the county had experienced a population explosion as oil-industry workers flocked in to work in the oil fields during the teens and 1920's. They brought their families, meaning new houses and schools and the establishment of oil-related businesses and many service oriented businesses. With all this came new money, as people, who 20 years earlier pioneered the opening of farms on virgin prairie, now leased mineral interests of oil prospectors. Those who were fortunate became well-to-do when oil was found on their property. Perhaps more subtle than the oil boom, was the new cosmopolitan air emerging in Kay County towns, especially Ponca City. With so many newcomers to the county drawn by oil fields, it was inevitable that new ideas would come with them. Probably more influential than anyone else was E.W. Marland.

Although Marland's oil company rapidly expanded into new localities, he made Ponca City his company headquarters, putting down permanent roots in town. After living at the Arcade Hotel, he built his first home on East Grand Avenue in 1916. This Spanish-style home was surrounded by 80 acres landscaped into formal gardens and a golf course.[67] Marland and his wife, Mary Virginia; Marland's sister, Lottie; as well as his wife's niece and nephew, Lyde and George Roberts, lived with them. Marland adopted George and Lyde in 1916, wanting them to grow up in the great southwest where he felt they would have a better chance to develop.[68]

Marland's interests in the Blackwell, Mervine and Tonkawa fields made him a multimillionaire. He had greater visions and to expand, he sold a considerable amount of Marland Oil Company stock in 1924 to J.P. Morgan and Company, who then became the Marland Oil Company bankers. An executive committee was elected consisting of six members whose actions had the authority of the board of directors. Three of these members were Morgan representatives; therefore, Morgan's interests dominated the company.[69]

Marland, no longer being able to direct the policies of his oil company, channeled his energy in other areas. In 1925, he began construction of a new home such as Ponca City had never seen. The Marland Mansion, modeled after the Davanzati Palace in Florence, Italy, stood in the midst of a 2.500 acre estate on the eastern edge of Ponca City. It was constructed of locally-quarried limestone. Imported master artists were hired to paint, sculpt, carve and completely decorate the villa. Surrounding the mansion were gate houses, an artist's studio, guest house, riding stables, dog kennels, swimming pool, lake and a boat house. It took approximately three years to build. Japanese horticulturist, Henry Hatashita, landscaped the extensive grounds with rare trees, shrubs and bulbs which he also propagated for Marland's neighbors. Formal gardens and young trees soon appeared on the once treeless prairie. Collectors in Europe purchased art objects and after furnishing the mansion, the total cost amounted to approximately $5,500,000.[70]

Mary Virginia Marland died in 1926. Two years later, after having the adoption of Lyde set aside, Marland married her. They moved into the mansion shortly thereafter and kept open house as they lavishly entertained hundreds of guests from around the nation, as well as Ponca City. Marland, a horse enthusiast, maintained a large stable, employed a riding instructor and made the facilities available to any guest who cared to take advantage of them. Kay Countians who knew how to ride cow ponies now learned to sit on English saddles, fox hunt and play polo.[71]

Another family that benefited by the discovery of oil was Ike and Laura Clubb of Kaw City. Ike Clubb, a former Cherokee Outlet cowboy, made his first homestead in 1891 on a claim he purchased on Skeleton Creek in Logan County, Oklahoma. In 1898 he established a ranch on Little Beaver Creek in northeastern Kay County. By 1919 the search for oil moved east of the Arkansas River into the Kaw and Osage country. A strike made on the Clubb's ranch near Kaw City in 1922 enabled Ike Clubb to build the Clubb House, a modern four-story hotel in Kaw City. It was started in 1923, completed in 1924, and was unrivaled in its day. The strike also allowed Laura Clubb to indulge in her life-long interest, art. A former teacher, she started her teaching career in a one-room sod school, later teaching at the

Oklahoma Baptist University in Blackwell. Laura visited Europe with her graduation class from Northwestern University and admired the art she saw there.   Now able to purchase the paintings, books, linens, china and antiques she loved, the collection soon outgrew her home. She began to hang paintings in the lobby, dining room and halls of the Clubb Hotel, "I will be pleased, " she said, "if even a small majority of the guests find some inspiration or emotional lift from the paintings."[72]

Included in the collection were works by George Innes, John Singer Sargent, Gainsborough, Sir Peter Lely, Paperitz, Chase, Rosa Bonheur, Benjamin West, Gilbert Stuart, Felice Schiavoni, Sir Thomas Lawrence, John Constable, Thomas Moran, George Romney, Sir William Beechey, Elliott Dangerfield, Sir Henry Raeburn, Murillo, Kirchback and many others. Kaw City became one of the great art centers of the United States. *Harlow's Weekly* called it "The Finest Private Collection of Paintings in the World".[73]   Tourists came in droves, filling the lobby and halls, viewing art by the old masters brought to the little town in Oklahoma. On Sundays an average of 500 to 1,000 visitors viewed the masterpieces owned by Laura Clubb. The register in the front lobby listed visitors from every state in the union, as well as from England, China, Egypt, British South Africa, Australia, India, Yucatan, Germany and numerous other countries. Guests could eat a wonderful meal in the dining room for$.75 or spend the night for $2.00.[74]

Ike and Laura enjoyed sharing their time and money with others. They helped many schools, churches, hospitals, libraries and worthy organizations through the years. In 1947, with the intent that her art collection would always be kept together, available for the people of Oklahoma, Laura presented it to the Philbrook Art Center in Tulsa, Oklahoma. She presented the majority of her library of rare books to Oklahoma City University and 319 volumes of rare, distinctive books on art, artists, and art history to the Philbrook.[75]

Six men and one woman were added to Oklahoma's "Hall of Fame" on the twenty-fourth anniversary of Oklahoma's statehood. The woman was Laura Clubb, honored because she brought to the southwest one of the finest art collections in the United States. She was also honored for her service to youth as a pioneer school teacher.[76]

Ponca Citians, Mr. and Mrs. Charles F. Calkins, also collected a variety of art works including European, American. Oriental and Native American. The Calkins first settled in Cross in 1884, where they opened a store. However, the next year they joined the exodus from Cross to Ponca City. In 1901 Mr. Calkins built a three-story brick dry goods store that he operated until his retirement in 1926. C.F. Calkins was one of the men who organized the Ponca City Oil and Gas Company in 1900. Mr. and Mrs. Calkins used their wealth to collect paintings by prominent artists of the National Academy; Thomas Moran, A.P. Lucas, Ralph Blakelock, William Ritchell, Richard Miller, E. Irving Couse and Albert Bierstadt. They also collected along with modern paintings, paintings from the Taos school; cloisonne and brass work from Nepal, India; and art from throughout Asia. Mrs. Calkins collected early American glassware while Mr. Calkins treasured hand-made Navajo pieces from the Southwest, such as moccasins, beaded vests, silver belts and ceremonial objects. These art works were displayed at their home at 505 West Grand for many years.[77] They shared their home with Richard Gordon Matzene for several years. He was a leading professional photographer in his day. Matzene was born in Devonshire, England in 1880 and educated in England, Denmark and Italy. His interest in art and photography led him to set up studios in New York, Chicago, Los Angeles and Simia, India. Matzene, a veteran traveler, was in China at the time of the Boxer Rebellion in 1900 and was hidden from the hostile "Boxers" by a Chinese friend who later helped him acquire treasures from the Imperial Palace. He visited Nepal and photographed the royal family when Nepal was still closed to foreigners. He made eight trips around the world and accumulated many rare art works. In 1937, he gave a $300,000 collection of Oriental Art to the University of Oklahoma. Upon his death in 1950, he left a fine collection to the Ponca City Library.[78]

Culture was not the only thing the newly wealthy dispensed. Several were remarkably open-handed, giving money away as easily as it seemed to come to them. Marland was one of the leading philanthropists of Kay County. He took part in numerous charities and benevolent causes, contributing to several religious denominations, the Boy Scouts and Girl Scouts, donating money to the University of Oklahoma and financing a dictionary of the Osage language for the Smithsonian Institute. Marland, along with W.H. McFadden built the American Legion Home for destitute children. He was generous with his employees, paying them adequate wages and bonuses for excellent work. For the bachelors in his company he built the Qush-to-see-dah Club, a large Spanish-style dormitory and classroom facility, later becoming the Ponca Military Academy. He provided land for an athletic field near his office building. One of his most notable gifts was the Bryant Baker statue. "The Pioneer Woman". Erected at the foot of the Marland Mansion drive. It was unveiled on April 22, 1930 to pay tribute to the pioneer mothers of America and remains a lasting memorial to Marland's philanthropy.[79]

Less ostentatious in his generosity, but no less open-handed, was Lew Wentz. He began his philanthropy in Ponca City long before he became wealthy. He would borrow money to buy Christmas toys for the town's poor children, a custom he carried on for years anonymously. He was well known in Oklahoma for establishing the Oklahoma Society for Crippled Children. During the Great Depression, Wentz ran a free movie theater, entertaining thousands who could not afford the price of a ticket. A former semi-professional baseball player and coach, he believed in athletics. One of his contributions to Ponca City was Wentz Camp, a recreation area with one of the most beautifully landscaped swimming pools in the country, and the Lakeside Golf

Course, completed after his death.[80]

Another Pennsylvanian who made an oil fortune in Kay County and gave some of his fortune back was William H. McFadden. He was sent west due to poor health in 1911. He camped out on the 101 Ranch while involved in the Miller-Marland drilling operations. When Marland ran short of working capital, it was McFadden, who helped financially. McFadden's health improved and he remained in the oil business, serving as a vice-president of Marland Oil Company. McFadden involved himself in Ponca City affairs and served as mayor from 1914 to 1920. Like Marland and Wentz, he was generous with his wealth, especially where children were concerned. He helped found the American Legion Home and built Camp McFadden, donated by him to the Camp Fire Girls.[81]

Not all of the life in Kay County during the teens and 1920's revolved around the oil industry and its endeavors. Kay Countians enjoyed various activities; among them were spectator sports and horse racing. Baseball was an early popular sport played by all ages in many communities. The first Ponca City ball team, formed in 1894, played teams from Cross, Perry, Newkirk and Blackwell. Most teams played all corners, using whatever pasture was available. An early Ponca City team was managed by J.S. Hutchins, a grain dealer. Members included M.B. Shire, mayor of Ponca City; S. Van Vorhees; Henry Gott; Ralph Morrison; B.C. Wieck; Albert Bemis; Claude Bake; John Given and Hans Broadboil. One of their opponents was a team sponsored by the 101 Ranch. This team called Bliss it's home and included Colonel George Miller, along with the future circus performer and movie star, Tom Mix. In 1920 one of the prominent local teams was the Marland Oilers, a semi-professional team sponsored by the Marland Oil Company.[82] Through the Years, baseball remained a popular sport, with Ponca City and Blackwell having semi-professional teams. In 1935 the Ponca City Angels came to town, affiliated with the Los Angeles Angels, then a Chicago Class A farm club. In 1938 the Ponca City club won their third straight Western Association championship. Shortly thereafter, their league was dissolved. Football was a popular spectator sport on the high school and college level, as was amateur boxing. Professional boxing interested some sports fans early in the century.[83]

Blackwell and Ponca City had race tracks where racing fans could watch trotters compete. Ponca City's track, complete with a grandstand and barns, stood on the north side of Grand Avenue between Osage and Ash streets. With the development of the gasoline engine, car and motorcycle racing became popular between 1915 and 1925.

Though parts of the county were caught up in the oil boom, most were still concerned with agriculture. Each September many paused to enjoy the end of the harvest season by attending the Kay County Free Fair, first started about 1900 in Newkirk. The first year was a financial failure; the next year, F.B. Hutchison and Sylvester Spore, of Newkirk, took over the operation. It was a complete disaster due to rain that started on the second day and continued for four days. Attendance was low due to poor roads and flooding streams. Newkirk nursed the fair through several more bad years and their persistence paid off. Many fine fairs were held at the fairgrounds concentrated one-half mile east of Newkirk. Each September Kay Countians flocked in to look at exhibits, compete for ribbons, watch races on the oval track and enjoy entertainment provided by such performers as Will Rogers. In 1909 many Kay Countians saw their first airplane at the fair. By 1910 the fair began to have financial difficulties again and in 1917 Blackwell and Newkirk jointly established the Kay County Free Fair with Blackwell providing the facilities. It continued very successfully over the years and is still in operation.[84]

In 1917 the good times in Kay County were interrupted by World War I. Although it was relatively brief, young men of the county had to temporarily set aside education and business to enter the armed services. Americans were involved in the war for about 18 months and then the soldiers returned home to try to pick up their lives. The sacrifices of these soldiers were not forgotten by the citizens of Ponca City. Under the leadership of the Ponca City Chapter of the Daughters of the American Revolution, a lighted fountain was built in 1925 in front of the Ponca City Civic Center. It was a tribute to those Ponca Citians who served in World War I. Ponca City closed its schools and gathered around the fountain for dedication with its bronze plaque inscribed with the names of the 293 veterans who gallantly served.

As the country tried to return to normal after the war years, new oil fields were being found and opened in Kay County, refineries were in full swing, automobiles were replacing the horse. All of this meant prosperity for Kay County. Still, trouble was looming on the horizon. During the twenties, farm prices had risen while the United States attempted to feed Europe and the United States' populations. Now these prices were beginning to slide. Wheat dropped from $1.05 per bushel to $.33 per bushel while stock prices, on the other hand, rose and factories turned out more goods than people could use. Toward the end of the decade, the national economy began to falter, collapsing with the Wall Street Stock Market Crash in 1929.

For Kay Countians this meant the end of many things which seemed like institutions. In 1928, Marland, no longer in control of Marland Oil Company, resigned as president and chairman of the board. Not long afterward, Marland Oil Company merged with Continental Oil Company, the surviving corporation. Marland was hurt and bitter, unable to maintain the mansion where he lived a little more than three years. Deeply in debt, Marland was down but still optimistic. He and his wife, Lyde, were forced to move into the artists' studio on the grounds.[85]

The oil boom was over. The Roaring Twenties were about to give way to the Great Depression. Though most Kay Countians did not have as far to fall as the Millers and Marlands, the next few years were going to be difficult ones.

CHAPTER EIGHT:
The Beautiful Country

In many ways, the years of the Great Depression were not as difficult for Kay County as they were for other parts of the nation. Even so, general economic conditions caused widespread hardships throughout the country. These lean years ended a decade later, with the coming of World War II.

Unlike western Oklahoma, Kay County did not suffer as extensively from the Dust Bowl. The Dust Bowl extended from southeastern Colorado, through the Oklahoma Panhandle, and into the Texas Panhandle. Kay County was affected by droughts of the 1930's, though, as was all of Oklahoma. Clouds of dust darkened the skies, stirred up by the hot winds blowing across parched lands to the west.

Weather of another sort took an occasional shot at Kay County. One such instance occurred on the evening of Wednesday, April 18, 1935, as a spring storm blew through the area. The county was hit when strong winds and a small tornado, followed by heavy rains, damaged houses in Blackwell, but caused few injuries. At Ponca City, hailstones, as large as baseballs, bombarded the town, north of Grand Avenue and east of Second Street. One man picked up a hailstone that measured 14 inches around and weighed 1 pound 3 ounces. The hailstones pulverized roofs, both old and new; smashed windows; and stripped trees and shrubs. Cars were especially vulnerable. Some hailstones fell straight through their roofs. Ponca City's globed street lights, known as the "White Way" on some of the streets in Acre Homes, no longer reflected on the 23.9 miles of bricks paving many streets of Ponca City.[1] These globes were demolished, as were the lights in the base ball park. Greenhouses were not only left roofless, but lost their inventory of plants. To compound the destruction, hailstones filled gutters and drains, causing street flooding when torrents of rain followed. In the aftermath, telephone and electrical wires hung in tangles from the poles. Many families temporarily lacked shelter when their homes were badly damaged. They slept in the schools, while insurance adjusters were kept busy trying to assess losses, later estimated a $500,000. Building suppliers and repairmen were swamped with work as they began to repair the numerous homes and buildings that bore the brunt of the storm.[2]

Much less dramatic was the long term effects of the 1930's unemployment. Low farm prices, despair, and dislocation caused people to move from place to place in search of work. None of these problems were completely new to Kay County. After all , the Run of 1893 took place in the midst of one of the nation's worst national financial depression, followed by a second one in 1907, the year Oklahoma became a state. Kay County was fortunate that the oil industry helped buffer their area. Even with the oil, times were still hard, with businesses closing their doors causing unemployment and foreclosures on mortgages.[3]

The population in Kay County, as of the 1930 census, stood at 50,166, double the 1907 county population of 24,757. The Blackwell population in 1930 was 9,521; Kaw City, 1001; Newkirk, 2,135; Ponca City, 16,136; Tonkawa, 3,311; and a county-wide rural population of 17,235.[4]

The Depression was not just a matter of statistics, as unemployment and falling prices affected people individually. E.W. Marland, once a multimillionaire, could sympathize with victims of hard times, having experienced them himself, when he lost Marland Oil Company in 1928. He became a New Dealer in the 1930's and a follower of President Franklin D. Roosevelt. In 1932, Marland ran for congress from the Eighth district, defeating the incumbent from Enid. Marland served two years in the House as an opponent of the big-money interests. In 1934, he became a candidate for governor of Oklahoma, promising to bring the New Deal to his home state. Oklahomans were ready for this economic relief. Marland was inaugurated January 14, 1935.[5]

Moving vigorously to carry out his promise, Marland called in experts from the Brookings Institute to study Oklahoma's state financial problems. Marland set up several boards to research specific problem areas, utilizing his excellent administrative methods on behalf of state government. As a humanitarian, he attempted to lighten the burden of the hard-pressed citizens of the state. After calling for increased taxes and a shift of the tax burden to big business, he ran into opposition from the state legislature. Action on his programs came slowly, if at all. Many of Marland's programs were hamstrung for lack of funds, but he was still able to expand prisons, and to improve orphanages, mental health systems and conservation and reforestation measures. His most outstanding accomplishment was the creation of the Department of Public Safety and the Oklahoma Highway Patrol. Marland's term as governor ended in 1939. He ran for another term in Congress in 1940, but with failing health, he lost the election. He returned to Ponca City and began rebuilding Marland Oil Company, still firmly expecting to strike an oil field as rich as those of the teens and 1920's. However, Marland's time was past. He died on October 3, 1941.[6]

New Deal Plans Help Citizens

E.W. Marland had not accomplished all of his plans to bring economic relief to Oklahoma, but he had succeeded in ushering in many aspects of the New Deal. A Public Works Administration project began in 1936, when a 750-foot long dam was built across the Chikaskia River near historic Rock Falls. Construction also began on Lake Blackwell, and the city of Blackwell profited from its construction.

Ponca City received $100,000 in Public Works Ad-ministration funds to build a new city library. Around $15,000 was spent to buy a site on Grand Avenue; the remaining $85.000 went into the construction of an attractive building with the latest equipment. The new building housed a children's department, club room and museum.[7]Kay County benefited from the National Youth Administration, which provided jobs and vocational training for young people, often excluded from other programs. One of the training centers, for boys, was at Tonkawa, where young men learned the basics of radio. This included

199

mathematics, science, blueprint-reading and construction of radio systems. The boys built systems eventually used by city, state and federal agencies. Other young men were enrolled in a residence center at the 101 Ranch. The Farm Security Administration conveyed a part of the former ranch lands and 50 buildings, in various states of deterioration, to the NYA. The boys at the center rebuilt or remodeled the buildings; built a dormitory, recreation center, barns, a slaughterhouse and several shops. When these were completed they began raising chickens, pigs and cattle.[8]

Later, in 1942, after the NYA was transferred to the War Manpower Commission, a War Production Training Center was established in Tonkawa. It trained young people in sheet-metal work, radio repair, welding, auto mechanics, sewing and other trades that would be useful in the war effort.[9]

Youth oriented government activities centered in Tonkawa because of the University Preparatory School. It was closed in 1917, due to World War I, but reopened in 1919. Tonkawa citizens never gave up on the school, with several Tonkawa men working relentlessly to persuade the legislature to reopen U.P.S. They included G.M. Cassity, T.O. Williams, Logan Hawkins and Dr. J.A. Jones. These men were on hand when the bill to reestablish the school was signed on March 29, 1919. The sum of $209,900 was appropriated, with $83,000 designated to rebuild and reequip Wilkin Hall. Newly appointed President, Richard M. Caldwell, presided over the reconstruction of the school. Classes began September 2, 1919, with 20 faculty members and 300 students in residence. The school name was changed by the legislature to the University Preparatory School and Oklahoma State Business Academy.[10]

The reconstruction of Wilkin Hall proceeded at a slow pace, since much of the school's equipment had to be reassembled or replaced. Despite the fact that this was the "roaring20's," enrollment grew slowly, hampered by other economic conditions. Students from farm families found it difficult to accumulate tuition money, since crop prices had fallen after World War I. The price of wheat, in 1920, was two dollars and 50 cents per bushel, but in 1921, it dropped to one dollar per bushel. To make matters worse, housing became scarce, resulting in more expensive rental rates. Even though Tonkawa began to feel the effects of the oil boom, U.P.S. made progress.[11]

The school was swept with excitement in July, 1921, when Governor J.B.A. Robertson announced that plans were under way to make U.P.A. a two-year junior vocational college. Within two months, a two-year course of standard college work was added to the curriculum. Vocational branches consisted of domestic science, manual training, art, and printing classes. New courses in shop work, masonry, as well as automobile and tractor repair were added. Response from prospective students to the new University Preparatory and Junior Vocational College was enthusiastic.[12] That enthusiasm lasted through the 1920's, as members of the Tonkawa Chamber of Commerce continued to recruit students. In 1928, Dr. Roscoe R. Robinson replaced R.M. Caldwell as president, and in 1939, the last year of Robinson's tenure, enrollment reached 550.[13]

Works Progress Administration funds financed a general rebuilding. The board of regents donated a site, west of the football field, for a new Tonkawa Armory, which was then built by the W.P.A. It was designed to house the second battalion of the 189th field artillery. The University Junior College survived the end of the oil boom in the Tonkawa area; the years of the Great Depression; and the coming of World War II. In 1941, the school was again renamed Northern Oklahoma Junior College.[14]

The 101 Ranch was the site of another New Deal project. Around 1937, the Farm Security Administration controlled much of the former 101 Ranch lands. They organized the 101 Ranch Resettlement Project, supervised by Rex LaCamp. Small "subsistence" tracts were established on a portion of the former 101 Ranch lands. The land was to be divided into 26 farms for landless farmers. They would be allowed to lease the land for a three-year trial period, pay crop rental and if proved satisfactory, they would be allowed to purchase the land over a 40 year period at three percent interest.[15]

Farmers, displaced by the creation of Lake Carl Blackwell, near Stillwater, had first choice of the farms in the 101 Ranch resettlement program. One family came with a horse, a set of harness, a cow, 50 leghorn hens, a wood cook stove, table, four chairs, bed, icebox, 300 quarts of home-canned food and a 1931 Chevy coupe. The farmers could not borrow money, since they did not have collateral; thus, they were encouraged to operate with horsepower alone. To provide these men with extra cash, the government allowed them to tear down old 101 Ranch buildings for materials. The buildings included the hotel, cider mill, grain elevator, packing plant, refinery and some of the barns. One of the buildings demolished was the dilapidated White House. Unfortunately, the soft cottonwood used in its construction was already past saving.[16]

Each family had a house, pole barn, chicken house, well, pump and outdoor toilet. Everyone, including the children, worked hard, raising large gardens, and canning fruits and vegetables. They did not have much money, but plenty to eat. The families became close neighbors and depended on each other, all grateful for the chance to work during the Depression years. The farmers cooperated and shared machinery in order to get the work done faster.[17]

A nondenominational church and Sunday school was organized. Each family donated one dollar towards the purchase of a five-gallon ice cream freezer for summer picnics and get-togethers. The church functioned until the area consolidated into the Marland and Ponca City school districts. The families then became more interested in the area where their children attended school. The community church was dissolved and most attended churches in Marland or Ponca City.[18]

In 1942, farmers in the project formed the 101 Ranch Truck Growers Association. They grew cucumbers and watermelons and shipped over 100 train carloads of watermelons a year. They marketed their produce in Oklahoma City, Chicago, and to wholesalers in many parts of the country. The association disbanded late in the 1950's.[19] Only three families failed to qualify to purchase their land. The success of the 101 Ranch Resettlement Project was due to the fortitude of the individuals who settled the area and their willingness to help each other.[20]

World War II Changes Kay County's Life-styles

World War II began in Europe in 1939. Though the war was still far away, the economy of Kay County and the United States began to revitalize, with ever increasing demands for oil and agricultural products. Although Americans hoped the war would pass them by, after the attack on Pearl Harbor, the nation unified behind the war effort. The first Kay County victim, Lieutenant Robert H. Markley, of Nardin, died in the Japanese attack on December 7, 1941. He was a graduate of Blackwell High School and a former Northern Oklahoma College student.[21]

Although Americans hoped to avoid the war, the country had planned for possible involvement. As early as December, 1939, when the European war was only three months old, the Ponca City Chamber of Commerce made plans for the best utilization of the town's air facilities in the event of war. Ponca City's air facilities dated back to 1919, when E.W. Marland dreamed of making Ponca City an aeronautical center. Speedy air transportation was important to the early oil industry. In 1927, an airport replaced the primitive landing strip. By the late 1930's, there were not only air facilities, but several flight schools in the county. The Ponca City Chamber of Commerce committee promoted the Ponca City School of Aeronautics, one of the first non-college primary flight training programs in the southwest. Fifty students enrolled in the 1939 class, with 10 chosen for further training at government expense.[22]

In early August, 1941, the program went a step further. Harold S. Darr, of the Darr School of Aeronautics; the city of Ponca City; The Royal Air Force of Great Britain; and the

American Army Air Corps agreed to open a training school for British and American pilots. It was located at the Ponca City airport. Within a few days, construction of the first of 17 buildings began on the Royal Air Force Flight Training School No. 6. On August 26, the first 50 British students arrived to begin instruction. Their barracks, not yet completed, caused the pilots to temporarily be housed in the Ponca Military Academy. Even without complete facilities, the first class graduated in January of 1942, followed by more British trainees. In November of 1942, American trainees began arriving as well.[23]

The school was large, capable of handling 400 students, with a support staff of 400 to 500 people and 98 airplanes. Though the school was largely self-contained (a city in itself), students used Conoco's recreational facilities and were welcomed into Ponca City homes. Many lifelong friendships developed. The school trained a total of 1,113 British and 125 American pilots, with 16 fatalities. The school, itself, spent $1,112,744 in Ponca City during its 33 months of operation, not including the salaries of the air cadets and those who worked at the school.[24]

Northern Oklahoma Junior College, in Tonkawa, also provided facilities for training pilots. The civilian aviation training course, approved by the C.A.A., was initiated at the college in 1939. Ground school, consisting of the theory of engines, navigation and meteorology, was taught on the campus. Flight training was carried out at the Ponca City Airport. The second year, the beginning and advanced pilot training courses graduating 48 pilots. Shortly after the attack on Pearl Harbor, the school initiated a one-semester course to prepare high school graduates, without college training, for acceptance into the Army Air Corps. Earlier pilot training courses greatly aided the national defense effort. The school was also approved for naval reserve training. Because a deferment could be obtained by taking a prescribed curriculum authorized by the U.S. Navy, many enlistees between the ages of 17 to 19 years of age took advantage of the plan. Many young enlistees at N.O.J.C. participated with civilian students in the sale of war stamps, scrap drives and many fund raising activities. Tonkawa's civilians actively supported the USO, the American Red Cross, and war bond drives.[25]

Many Tonkawa men were members of the 189th field artillery unit of the National Guard. The unit, stationed in Tonkawa, was organized in 1925 with 60 members, increasing in September, 1940, to 138 members. When called to active duty, they were sent to Fort Sill, Oklahoma, to join the 45th Division. The division took part in the North African campaign invasion of Sicily; the capture of Palermo; and the invasion of Italy at Anzio.[26]

The government chose Tonkawa as the site for a German prisoner of war camp. Section 28, Township 26 North, Range 1 West was purchased and the southeast quarter converted into the prison camp. Prisoners began arriving August 17, 1943. Most were German enlisted men captured in North Africa. The camp consisted of three compounds, designed to hold 1,000 men each. Keeping supplies and feeding these men occupied numerous army and civilian personnel. The camp operated until July 20, 1945, when it was officially closed.[20] One prisoner of war, H.J. Jaenisch, was a talented artist. Nearly 50 years after his return to Germany, two of his paintings were discovered in a small antique shop near Stillwater, Oklahoma. Mary Kelly, who discovered the paintings, launched a search for the German artist in the late 1980's and succeeded in locating him at his home on the North Frisian Island of Amrum. Jaenisch disclosed that one of the paintings was painted from memories of his days in service in Tunisia, where he served with the "Desert Fox", Rommel. His works can be found in studios all over the world. He described himself as a "prisoner in paradise" during his confinement.[27]

Kay County continued to solidly support the war effort. By 1940, 5,491 men had registered for the draft. Men and Women from the county served in all branches of the military. By V-E Day in May 1945, Kay County had one of the three best bond-buying records in the United States, purchasing almost one and three/fourth million dollars worth of bonds. Ponca City raised more than $250,000 for the purchase of a B-17 Flying Fortress, aptly named "Miss Ponca City.".[28]

Those not in service were equally involved in the war effort. Kay County farmers produced wheat and beef to feed the fighting forces and civilian populations of the United States and its allies. Oil-industry workers in the Cities Service and Conoco refineries at Ponca City did their share. Workers walked, rode bicycles or motorcycles, and car-pooled to work to conserve use of precious gasoline. Cities Service (originally Empire Oil and Gas Company) manufactured fuels, oil and lubricants, needed to keep a mechanized army and navy in action. Conoco produced aviation gasoline in huge quantities and set up a large army storage depot at its facility in Ponca City. One local citizen, J.C. Carmack, who retired as a grease maker after 40 years with Continental Oil Company, recalls that although he was of eligible age to be called up to active duly, the government deferred him because he was needed in the refinery.[29]

As men left for military service, women, many for the first time, began working jobs previously considered for men only. Most jobs in the petroleum industry were carefully chosen to fit the concepts of the feminine gender, such as laboratory testing, stenciling, and painting. Eventually, they began operating forklifts and loading boxcars. Women invaded the machine shops, went to work on tank farms as gaugers and operated overhead cranes. Without them, the flow of products from refineries could have slowed to a trickle, but with them, it never faltered. When the war was over and veterans returned home, companies handed workers, like Mrs. Helen Pappan, of Ponca City, an "honorable discharge". Women returned to their homes and kitchens.[30]

There were other war related industries in Kay County besides the refineries which put thousands to work which boosted the economy and helped to end the Great Depression for this part of the state.

Where Did Our Towns Go?

Autwine, Hardy, Eddy, Sumpter, Nardin, Braman and Peckham

After World War II, Kay Countians tried to return to a normal life. The refineries and rich agricultural base helped the county remain one of the most prosperous areas of Oklahoma. The depression of the 1930's brought an end to many towns established either at the time of the Run of 1893 or during the oil boom. The last businesses in Autwine closed in 1930. Mrs. Jerri Boyer, who now owns the land where Autwine once flourished, stated she had elected her husband, Lyn, as "...the mayor of her own little town." Fields of mung beans and milo are now all that can be seen at the site.[31] Hardy's post office closed about 1939; Eddy's post office closed in 1957; and Sumpter faded away about the same time.

Nardin hung on until 1941. Fire destroyed the barbershop; the service station and garage closed and Nardin Produce went out of business. The blacksmith shop was sold and torn down; brick buildings on the south side of Main Street were torn down and the Nardin school was consolidated with surrounding rural schools in 1964. In 1972, the school closed permanently. By 1976, only the Nardin post office, the Kelle Service Station, operated by Vernon and Ruth McGrew: the Johnston Grain Elevator, managed by Robert and Kerry Crow; and the Clyde Co-op elevator, managed by Buck Hoemann, remained in business in what had once been a busy town.

L.V. Crow, in interviewing Nardin old-timers, decided to establish an organization called the "Friends of Nardin". Membership grew to 800 nationwide. Their goals were to find and preserve Nardin's heritage and to seek ways to assist Nardin's growth. A small house on Main Street, donated by Peg Brennan, became the first Heritage House Museum. In 1982, when the Baptist Church closed, the building was purchased by the Friends of Nardin for an expansion of the Heritage House. Many improvements were made in the park: a cook shack, picnic tables, charcoal grill, playground equipment and the Christian Church Bell memorial were added. A reunion was planned to help celebrate Nardin's 80th birthday. It was known as "Nardin Heritage Day", featured Lt. Governor George Nigh and famed Indian artist, Blackbear Bosin. An old-time wheat threshing, complete with an antique vehicle parade; steam engines; music; and entertainment in Pioneer Park ended the festivities. Every year, since 1978, the Nardin Heritage Celebration has been held on Memorial Day weekend. In spite of the ravages of time on its buildings and the effects of advancing technology on its business district, the people of Nardin and the surrounding area are dedicated to working together to preserve their heritage and to make Nardin a better place in which to live, work and play.".[32]

Ox Bow Bend Communities "Bend" With The Times

Kaw City

In the eastern part of the county, Kaw City, Uncas, and Washunga remained quiet, small towns. In Kaw City, the 1930's had been fraught with difficulties. Many of the town's people left for other parts of the country in an attempt to meet everyday problems of earning a living. With many businesses closing their doors, and the two banks combining their operations, there simply was not enough work. In the early 1940's and the beginning of World War II. Kaw City again faced the loss of its citizens to the armed forces and the high paying jobs in the defense industry. The grand old town never regained its place as the center of the farming community it once enjoyed. The Clubb Hotel closed its doors in 1952, after the deaths of both Laura and Ike Clubb.[33]

Another blow was yet to come to the quiet little town in the Ox Bow Bend. In 1957, a move began to construct a dam across the Arkansas River, about eight miles east of Ponca City. Not like the previous floods the town endured, which had come quickly and flowed away as fast as they came, the Arkansas River would inundate Kaw City for the final time with the flooding of the reservoir. The community, consisting mostly of retirees, were faced with the prospect of abandoning their City or relocating. The citizens of Kaw City chose to move their town to higher ground. Construction began on the dam in 1966, and the tedious task of moving the city began, "Old pioneers", as well as "new pioneers", began building their new town overlooking Kaw Lake, on a site west of old Kaw City. Kaw City's Farmer's National Bank moved to Ponca City, where it is now known as the Pioneer Bank and Trust. Water surrounds the "New Kaw City" on three sides. Kaw City is still located in the Ox Bow Bend of the Arkansas River, as it has been since its birth. A positive effect of the move to higher ground has been the beautiful view the citizens enjoy of the large lake which lies beneath Kaw City's feet. Each year, many activities, such as the "Christmas In July" boat flotilla, are celebrated, as well as a homecoming each May. A part of the town's past was moved with them in the form of the old Santa Fe depot. It now is the home of the Kaw City Museum, a beautiful reminder of the past, which displays historical artifacts of the bygone era. In 1995, an expansion of the Kaw City Museum was dedicated, with a large turnout of Kaw City residents, both past and present. Bricks, engraved with the names of those who chose to be remembered, lead the way from the old depot to the new addition. The old town, now in a watery grave, may be gone, but its memory and spirit will live on forever, due to the efforts of the citizens and the Kaw City Museum.[34]

Washunga and Uncas

Little was left of Washunga in the 1960's. Uncas fought a rear guard battle to keep from being flooded by Kaw Lake. Rumors had existed since the 1920's, when the federal government first talked about damming the Arkansas. In the 1960's, the plan became a reality. Uncas residents objected and tried to fight the Corps of Engineers by incorporating as a town in 1967. One resident, Mrs. Paul Jensen, wrote to President Richard Nixon in protest. The Corps won, and Uncas disappeared forever.[29]

Tonkawa, "They All Stay Together"

Tonkawa's Northern Oklahoma Junior College became Northern Oklahoma College on July 1, 1965. This gave the town and school, so much a part of Tonkawa's prosperity, added prestige. Today, in Tonkawa, three area museums are dedicated to preserving local history: the Tonkawa Historical Museum, housed in an old depot in downtown Tonkawa; the A.D. Buck Museum of Science and History, on the Northern Oklahoma College Campus; and the Tonkawa Tribal Museum, at Fort Oakland, two miles east of town. A home from the oil-boom era is listed on the National Register of Historic Places. It is located at 302 North Main Street. Built about 1928 for the Timothy Mahoney family, all the building materials for the house, the most ornate in town, arrived on a railroad car. The home was built with money from the oil boom. Tonkawa's First Presbyterian Church, 4th and N.O.C. Drive, is also on the National Register of Historic Places. The little white church, with cross-gabled roof, side bell tower and steeple, and unique stained-glass windows, acquired from a church in the east, was dedicated in 1905. It is the only original church building in Tonkawa still used as a place of worship.

Tonkawa celebrated the Cherokee Strip Centennial in 1993 and the Centennial of the founding of Tonkawa in 1994, with the creation of a Centennial Park in downtown Tonkawa. From the ashes of a fatal fire, the site, dotted with old foundations, weeds and rubble, has risen a tasteful tribute to the pioneers who homesteaded the land and those who created a town on the barren prairie. A monument dedicated to the early settlers, including 1500 granite pavers engraved with the names of residents, past and present; and a large gazebo with Victorian-era park benches and lamp posts, grace the professionally landscaped park. A Tonkawa pictorial history book has been published to commemorate its 100th birthday. The book title, *Tonkawa, They All Stay Together,* was derived from the meaning of the Tonkawa Indian's tribal name. Aware of their unique heritage, the Tonkawa community looks with pride to the past and with promise towards the future.[36]

Blackwell Survives and Grows

In the northwest area of Kay County, Blackwell suffered what could have been a major blow in 1974. Blackwell Zinc Company announced it was closing its smelter after 58 years of operation. A major employer in Blackwell since 1916, Blackwell Zinc had helped insure the welfare of the town at a time when much of the nation was suffering from unemployment. When it closed, the smelter employed 800 people, accounting for over half of the manufacturing jobs in town. Local commerce relied on the annual $5.5 million payroll. Amax Inc., the parent company of Blackwell Zinc, phased the plant out over a 30 month period, giving Blackwell the opportunity to find new manufacturing businesses to take its place. Amax also gave the city of Blackwell the smelter site and the 130 acres of land it was on. Luck entered into Blackwell's ability to stave off disaster, when the town's rural economy received a sudden boost from the first big Russian grain sale. In a short time, the town changed from a one company town to one with several industries, making its economical base more sound.[37] Reminded of their humble beginnings, after months of planning, Blackwell's Centennial activities began in January of 1993, with activities planned for each month of the Centennial year. The greatest emphasis was directed to activities in September, the month of the Run into the Cherokee Outlet and Blackwell's birthday. All of downtown Blackwell was decorated in a pioneer days theme for the entire month. Blackwell enthusiasts experienced the excitement of the original Land Run at White's Factory Outlet Mall on Thursday, September 9th 1993, with the reenactment of the land Run. Dressed in period clothing, the citizens captured the spirit of the Centennial as they listened to storytellers and enjoyed music and food. Later in the week a Centennial Fun Run/Walk began at the Pavilion, followed by an outdoor pancake breakfast at Main and Blackwell. There was lots of enthusiastic "hollering" while watching the Centennial Parade on Main Street. All day long there were old-fashioned food booths, square dancing, old-time craft-makers, musical entertainment, long forgotten movies, antique displays, clowns, and gunfighter shootouts to keep the crowds in a festive spirit. A beard growing contest and an A.J. Blackwell family look-alike contest drew many contestants and children enjoyed games from the past, along with trolley car rides. Postal stamps were brought to the Pavilion for stamp cancellation, commemorating the date of the Centennial.

Blackwell Regional Hospital sponsored a Historical Homes Tour in the afternoon. At 5:00 P.M., events centered at Blackwell High School with a chuck wagon feed, followed by a Centennial fashion show, a pre-show on Blackwell history and a performance of the play, "Oklahoma". Later, a dance, with music provided by Gene Ellis at the American Legion, finished the night on a pleasant note.

Just as the guns sounded at noon on September 16, 1893, marking the start of the Cherokee Strip Land Run, so the guns sounded once again at noon on September 16, 1993. To mark the start of the next 100 years in Blackwell, citizens dedicated the Centennial Plaza and Monument, located on the south lawn of the pavilion. "Top of Oklahoma" Historical Society's time capsule was also dedicated. After the capsule was embedded at the foot of the monument, a marble marker, bearing the September 16, 1993 date, was laid in the new cement walkway to the Pioneer Monument. It is scheduled for opening at noon, September 16, 2093. Those attending the celebration shared an enormous cake, decorated with the Centennial logo, and ice cream. There were many other events and activities which made the 1993 Centennial a year to remember for a lifetime.[38]

Braman and Peckham Remember The Run

Braman grew in the 1920's with the discovery of oil. The population stretched from 400 to 5,000 in 40 days. By June 19, 1925, Braman newspaper reported that more than $1,000,000 had been spent on drilling in the area. More oil was found in 1937, but the boom did not return with it. However, many years later, wells in the area are still pumping. In 1932, Ed Johnston became mayor of Braman, serving until his death in 1972. Aubery Kelle served twelve years and then Ed's son, Jerry Johnston, became mayor in 1984. He still serves Braman in that capacity eleven years later.

The day of July 4th, 1993, Braman residents honored the Pioneers who were the participants in the Cherokee Outlet Run and those arriving shortly thereafter. Some of the honorees riding in the parade were: Parade Marshall Maurita Day, (daughter of William Orr); and descendants of Jim Smith, Lila Smith Wilson, her daughters, and many others. The Braman Museum was opened to the public and the day found everyone participating in games, contests and enjoying homemade ice cream. In addition, special observance was noted at the annual Memorial Day festivities at Braman Cemetery east of Braman.[39]

Like all other towns in the area, Peckham, established in 1893, found the residents struggling after the end of the oil boom. During its heyday, 400 residents inhabited the small town. Lack of oil and related jobs saw its population dwindle to around 60 residents by 1993. No longer recognized as an incorporated city, Peckham still retains a school, with attendance averaging 70 students. On the second Sunday of each October, the community hosts a homecoming for past and present residents.[40]

Newkirk Weathers A Hundred Years

Judged by the appearance of its commercial building, Newkirk is no exception. The merchants and business men who settled there had dreams that Newkirk would emerge as a great urban center. Because of their foresight, the buildings, still present today, could actually be considered as personal monuments, as many of the buildings contain stones hearing the name of the owner. The territorial period of growth in Newkirk, as in all communities throughout Oklahoma, utilized the building material close at hand. At Newkirk, this was native limestone.

Because Newkirk has the most intact streetscape in the State of Oklahoma, Newkirk's entire commercial district in downtown was added to the National Register as a historic district in 1963. Newkirk possesses the largest collection of territorial limestone buildings in the state. The preservation of these buildings led Newkirk to became one of the first small towns in the state included in the Oklahoma Department of Commerce's Main Street program in 1992. Today, Newkirk is a graduate town of this progressive program.

Growth has continued in Newkirk, still the county seat. In 1984, a million dollar jail facility was constructed by Kay County. In 1990, the City of Newkirk completely revamped the downtown area with new sidewalks, six inch water lines, pocket parks, curb and gutter, trees, benches and decorative lights. The Kay County War Memorial, dedicated to all service men and women who lost their lives in World War I, World War II, the Korean War, and Viet Nam was designed by local resident, Clyde Otipoby, and completed on the Kay County Courthouse lawn in 1992. The "Land of Hope" statue, sculpted by Newkirk Alumni, B. Carman, was dedicated in 1994. This statue is also located on the courthouse lawn."[41]

Four miles east of Newkirk stands a historic Kay County site, the farm home of Jeptha P. Tipton. Tipton built the stone farm home in 1898 from stone quarried nearby. The farm, owned by Dorys I. Peters, Catherine H. Kennedy, Bertha F. Smith and Vineta L. Peters, four descendants of the homestead settled by their grandfather, still stands today with the distinction of an Oklahoma Historical Society Award. The farm in now under consideration for listing in the National Register of Historic Places.[42]

A "Prairie Light" is Extinguished

North of Newkirk stood an institution which first came into existence in 1884. Chilocco Indian School played a major role in the history of Kay County. Thousands of Native American students from across the nation graduated from Chilocco. They took their places in communities, many still leading productive lives. Changing times took its toll on Chilocco, as enrollment

214

began to decline by 1978. In October, 1979, a Senate appropriation sub-committee recommended the closing of Chilocco School, and on May 9, 1980, Chilocco handed out diplomas to eleven graduating seniors for the last time. No longer would the "Prairie Light" shine.[43]

Ponca City Remembers Its Past

Perhaps this letter, originally written at Ponca, Oklahoma (Territory), on September 24, 1893, best sums up the historical beginnings of Ponca City. What the letter says could have referred to each of the new towns and communities which sprang up on that date so long ago.

Ponca, Oklahoma
Sep 24 (1893)

Dear Dug (C.C.) Dutton

Would like to see you spinning over (our) streets and sidewalks with your whirly gig wheels. There isn't one in town but then down here we have towns without houses, streets, or anything but people. Just think of three thousand people coming together in the center of nowhere. Coming from all directions by all sorts of conveyances and afoot, most all in a hurry and not one with a double set of underclothing, a sheet of paper or a pine box to sit on. Some with tents, many with absolutely nothing but themselves, let all these come together and squat down for four days and you have Ponca.

Here we are, no well in town yet, although one is nearly completed: nearest water is one and a half miles away, no wood, a big rain on hand, water running under the tents and everybody happy.

Papers talk about the hardships incident to the opening but there is one thing sure with all of it, the people who are here now have enjoyed it and everybody seems well and hearty. The canteen has been the principal article of furniture and wearing apparel all through the race. A man can go bare-footed, lose his hat, tear off his shirt, loan his pants and have his team and outfit stolen, but if he's got his canteen left, he's alright.

Jack and Milt Welch have just driven up with a load of brush tied on behind the buggy so I guess we will have supper. Milt Welch and Frank West have been building a bedstead this afternoon. It is five by seven and so far as I know it is the only bedstead in town. Many have cots but most all of us sleep on the ground.

Have been pretty well over this country and have found lots of good farm land and some awful poor. They are digging a public well here in town and at a depth of 30 feet are still spading out the dirt which is very red. No timers of any consequence, and as the grass was all burned before and during the opening, it keeps the "stripper" busy rustling to hold down his claim.

There are a few women here but they look lost. Most everybody is a man with three weeks beard on his face and 20 years accumulation of dirt on his body. Since the rain, however I think most of them will invest in a bar of soap, and a pail of water and relinquish their title to the only homestead most of them have gotten. Kind regards to the boys,

Very truly
Frank H. Greene"[44]

In direct contrast to what is mentioned in the letter, you now have Ponca City, 102 years later. Yes, many of the brick streets paid for by the city in 1922 are still enjoyed, but the automobiles which travel along them are much faster and sleeker than those used so long ago. Almost every driveway in town sports several "whirly gig wheels". School children wear designer clothes while learning the 3-R's on their home PC's (personal computers), and most communication between individuals comes through the airways, and not in the mailbox.

Ponca City has enjoyed a prosperous first century. Despite recent economic setbacks due to downsizing by several of the major employers in the area, commerce is booming, as can be seen by many beautiful homes, both old and new, which grace the landscape of an ever-growing city. Historic homes such as the Niemann home of South 8th Street, and the Marland Mansion, located north of the Pioneer Woman Statue, are included on the National Register of Historic Places. Elegant new homes, such as the Harpster and Avery homes on North 14th Street, replace the vast open prairie that was Ponca City in 1893. Bedsteads can now easily be purchased at Smiths' Home Furnishings or any of the many other furniture stores in the area, and meals are served at a multitude of fine area restaurants. Many buildings in the downtown area of Ponca City have been restored into attractive restaurants, bed and breakfasts, and entertainment theaters, such as Bravo's Restaurant, Rose Stone Inn, and the Poncan Theater.

Instead of sleeping on the ground or in a tent, a room at one of the city's many lodging facilities can be found, as new residents find their way into the community. Many other well designed buildings have withstood the test of time. The Ponca City Library still graces the corner of Fifth and Grand, and from its front steps, citizens have the pleasure of looking across at Centennial Plaza, where the water fountain, first built by the Ponca City Chapter of the DAR, still puts on a watery show of lights on occasion. Approximately 7000 bricks, bearing the names of residents of the city, pave the plaza, which is the home of a large statue designed by Jo Saylors for the 100th birthday of the town. The statue features a horse and rider, cast in bronze. On the corner, E.W. Marland's statue is seen by all who pass by.

Women in Ponca City rarely walk around with lost looks on their faces anymore. With a multitude of talented, educated and creative women living in the city, many projects are accomplished which benefit their hometown. Taking lessons from their sister organizations, which sprang up quickly after the Run of 1893, women's groups address a variety of issues concerning the welfare of Ponca City. Some, like the late Laura McDonaugh Streich, have spent much of their adult lives in service to the community, preserving the history of the town so that others may remember what it was like in another by-gone era.

Men are not forgotten in the saga. Drawn by business corporations such as Conoco, Inc., the men of Ponca City have contributed to the welfare of the economy by providing excellence in their job performances, as well as in their civic duties. Everywhere, in and around the city, evidence of the work contributed by men devoted to improvement abounds. Surrounding farms and ranches are well cared for, with the most up-to-date equipment aiding in the survival of the rural economy of Kay County. Because the settlers 100 years ago had the foresight to require sound educations for their children, men and women of every walk of life now use these educations to produce a better environment for their children, by maintaining schools and other opportunities for learning.

After 100 years, Chautauqua, a series of tent programs featuring writers of the gilded age, are presented on the grounds of the Marland Mansion, sponsored by the Ponca City Arts and Humanities Council. In addition, community Concerts fill the air with melodic strains, and Ponca Playhouse provides a variety of professionally directed plays. Youth of the community also provide many hours of volunteer work, such as the Volunteens, who help at the local hospital each year. In the fringe areas surrounding the community, 4-H is still producing state winners. In August, 1995, Michelle Overman, a member of the Kildare 4-H club, was named state winner for her ability in baking breads. As a state winner, she received a $500 scholarship during the State 4-H Congress.[45]

The Great Land Run Is Celebrated

Several years before the Centennial birthday of the city occurred, many citizens joined together to plan a week of special events, so that all citizens could enjoy participating in the celebration. As a result of their dedicated work, there were so many activities that no one person could have attended every event. The program, "The Gift of Willie Cry", was performed at the Poncan Theater, as a remembrance of the oil-boom era. It was written by Earl Sutton and the music was composed by Leslie Rardin. Sold-out crowds enjoyed the performances of local actors and actresses.

The "Parade of the Century" swept down Grand Avenue, past crowds of spectators, estimated to be up to 50,000 people.

There was a beautiful dedication of the Centennial Plaza Statue, designed by Jo Saylors, and the Ponca City Cultural Center Indian Museum was on display for the occasion.

There were trail rides to Kaw Lake; living pioneer history displays on the grounds of the Pioneer Woman Museum; tours of historic downtown buildings and local homes; displays of many beautiful quilts at the Marland Mansion, as well as a street dance and historical reenactments. All these contributed to the festivities in honor of the birthday celebration. Local citizens could almost see a smile of enjoyment cross the face of the Pioneer Woman Statue, as events unfolded throughout the city.

Two years after the Centennial Celebration, Ponca City still thrives on nurturing the history of its past. The 101 Wild West Rodeo celebrated its 36th year in 1995, starting with the Pickett Memorial Event. In August, 101 Ranch old-timers congregated for a weekend of festivities preceding the rodeo.

Just as the movie industry came to Ponca City and the 101 Ranch in the 1920's, 1995 saw the cast and crew of a major Hollywood movie production perform "magic", all over North Central Oklahoma, as it prepared for the movie, *Twister,* a multi-million dollar film scheduled to be released across the nation in

1996. Many local people took part in the movie, which helped to contribute to a sound economic base for Ponca City residents.

Sadly, 1995 also saw the disappearance of many of the last remains of the 101 Ranch, which were swallowed up by the swollen waters of the Salt Fork branch of the Arkansas River. All that remains is a small segment of the blacksmith shop.

Ongoing activities in Ponca City area which continue to foster a sense of community include Octoberfest, the Iris and Fine Arts Festivals, 101 Wild West Rodeo and Parade, Festival of the Angels, Ponca Indian Powwow, and the Cherokee Strip Golf Classic, as well as Kawfest celebrations, 4th of July fireworks, and craft and antique show, such as the "Land of Country".

Looking forward, Ponca City projects include the expansion of the Pioneer Woman Museum and the building of the Standing Bear Monument to the Native Americans. Standing Bear will be honored with a memorial garden park and library facilities, housing a Native American research collection. Fittingly, the monument, which will be located on the south edge of Ponca City, will look down Highway 177 towards White Eagle, the center of Ponca Indian affairs.

History is not static as long as there are men of action. Some events happen and are recorded; others are never known. Some events are remembered because of the pleasure which is derived from their existence, while other events touch the heart of each and every citizen, causing pain. In the early 1990's, Ponca City saw several of its fine men and women leave to serve in the "Desert Storm" War. They served their country well. Fortunately, most were able to return to their homes and workplaces.

Several years later, on April 19, 1995, not only Oklahoma, but the entire nation and the world, was sent into a state of disbelief as they learned of the bombing of the Alfred Murrah Federal Building in Oklahoma City. Citizens watched television that day, in shock, as the travesty unfolded concerning the terrorist bombing. As television and newspapers across the country focused on the suffering of all Oklahomans, Kay County citizens did something which should not be a surprise to anyone. They responded by offering assistance to the victims and the city of Oklahoma City. In Ponca City, lines formed at the local Red Cross bloodmobile, as citizens offered to donate blood, many for the first time. The Kaw Tribe generously donated a considerable sum of money, but did not stop there. They contributed their time to the Blackwell Red Cross. As in the past, Oklahomans participated in many ways to make a terrible ordeal a little less stressful.

The hard working independent souls who made the difficult but courageous choice to settle a new land, knew the trials they would face. Even after 102 years that spirit, fortitude and shameless desire to better ones life and overcome the obstacles with self directed minds and bodies, remains the best feature in the Oklahoma and Kay County citizen.

The help lent to one another was no sacrifice, but an investment in the futures which have come to pass. The county has undergone many transitions—from French and Spanish explorers, to Indian reservations, to cattle ranges, to a patchwork quilt of homesteads.

The Ponca, Running-After-Arrow, predicted that oil would ruin the beautiful country, but he was wrong. The oil boom days of wooden derricks that seemed to obscure the horizon, country roads churned into bogs and ramshackle towns that sprang up across the prairies gave way to country crossroad towns that became centers of wealth and culture.

As anyone who looks across the miles of emerald green spring wheat, rippling in the breeze, can plainly see, the oil is still there, but so are the grain fields and the cattle; so are the deer and the Scissor-tail Flycatcher; and so are the Ponca, the Tonkawa and the Kaw.

Kay County has become the beautiful country once again, no longer are there …

… towns without houses …

Looking Down Grand Avenue Ponca City 1946

ENDNOTES: CHAPTER ONE

[1] Gibson, Arrell M., *Oklahoma: A History of Five Centuries,* Harlow Publishing Company, Norman, Oklahoma, 1965, p. 14.

[2] Gibson, p. 18.

[3] Wagoner, Jay J., *Oklahoma,* Thunderbird Books, Oklahoma City , Oklahoma, 1969, p. 42.

[4] Gibson, p. 18.

[5] Gibson, p. 18.

[6] Wise, LuCelia, *Indian Cultures of Oklahoma,* Oklahoma State Department of Education, 1978, p. 17.

[7] Wise, p. 25

[8] Gibson, p. 18.

[9] Gibson, p. 18.

[10] Wise, p. 25

[11] Wise, p. 25

[12] Faulk, Odie B., *Oklahoma, land of the Fair God,* Windsor Publishing Co., Northridge, California, 1986, p. 25

[13] Dale, Edward Everette and Morris L. Wardell, *History of Oklahoma,* Prentice Hall Inc., Englewood Cliff, New Jersey. 1948, p. 1 (location just south of Colorado border)

[14] Faulk, p. 12

[15] Gibson, p. 18.

[16] Morris, John W., Charles R. Goins, Edwin C., *Historical Arlas of Oklahoma,* University of Oklahoma Press, Norman, Oklahoma, 1982, p. 12

[17] Wedel, Mildred Mott, "the Deer Creek Site, Oklahoma, A Wichita Village Sometimes Called Fernandina, An Ethohistorians View", Oklahoma Historical Society

Series in *Anthropology* #5,Oklahoma, Oklahoma Historical Society, 1981, p. 61

[18] Wedel, pp. 51-52

[19] Wedel, pp. 51-52

[20] Wedel, pp. 51-52

[21] Gibson, p. 18.

[22] Gibson, p. 18.

[23] Blackburn, Bob L., "First Lt. James B. Wilkinson", edited by Joseph A. Strout Jr., *Frontier Adventures: American Exploration In Oklahoma,* The Oklahoma Series IV, Oklahoma City, Oklahoma, Oklahoma Historical Society, 1976, p. 9.

[24] Blackburn, p. 9.

[25] Hollon, W. Eugene, *The last Pathfinder: Zebulon Montgomery Pike,* University of Oklahoma Press, Norman, Oklahoma, 1949, pp. 94-95.

[26] Hollon, p. 122.

[27] Blackburn, pp. 13-14

[28] Blackburn, pp. 12-13.

[29] Isern, Thomas, "George Champlin Sibley, 1811 and 1825-26", in Joseph Stout, Jr.'s *Frontier Adventures: American Explorers in Oklahoma,* Oklahoma City, Oklahoma, Oklahoma Historical Society, 1976. pp. 20, 21.

[30] Isern, p. 21.

[31] Isern, pp. 21-22.

[32] Isern, p. 25.

[33] Blackburn, p. 25.

[34] Gibson, p. 56. Trappers and traders from the east---Oklahoma's

earliest American settlers.

ENDNOTES: CHAPTER TWO

[1] Gibson, Arrell, Oklahoma, *A History of Five Centuries,* University of Oklahoma Press, Norman, Oklahoma, 1965, p. 60.

[2] Hodge, Fredick Webb, *Handbook of North American Indians of Mexico,* Pageant books, New York 1960, p, 947-950

[3] Gibson, pp. 57-58

[4] Wise, Lu Celia, *Indian Cultures of Oklahoma*, Oklahoma State Department ofEducation, 1978, p. 49

[5] Gittinger, Roy, *Formation of the State of Oklahoma*, University of Oklahoma Press, Norman, Oklahoma, 1939, p. 6.

[6] Bolton, Herbert E., *Spanish Borderland,* United State Publishing Association, Inc., New York, 1921, p. 187.

[7] Gibson, p. 62

[8] Gibson, p. 53-54.

[9] Gibson, p. 54.

[10] Bernard Sheenan discussed this rationalization of Indian removal and the reservation policy in *Seeds of Extinction: Jeffersonian Philanthropy and the American Indian*, Chapel Hill, University of North Carolina Press, 1973.

[11] Faulk, Odie B., *Oklahoma Land Of the Fair God*, Windsor Publishing Co., Northridge, California, 1986, p. 43.

[12] Gibson, p. 79

[13] Gibson, p. 79.

[14] Faulk, p. 141.

[15] Gittinger, p. 70.

[16] Morris, Goins, McReynolds, *Historical Atlas of Oklahoma*,

University of Oklahoma Press, Norman, Oklahoma, 1982, p. 22.

[17] Rainey, George, *The Cherokee Strip*, co-Operative Publishing Company, Guthrie, Oklahoma, 1933, pp. 38-41.

[18] Faulk, p. 141.

[19] Gittinger, p. 70.

[20] Gibson, pp. 210-211

[21] Gibson, p. 217

[22] Rainey, p. 41.

[23] Howard, James Howard, "The Ponca Tribe", United States Government Printing Office, 1965, p. xi.

[24] Howard, p. 15.

[25] Zimmerman, Charles Leroy, *White Eagle, Chief of the Ponca*, Telegraph Press, Harrisburg, PA, 1941, p. 57.

[26] Wright, Muriel H., *Indian Tribes of Oklahoma*, University of Oklahoma Press, Norman, Oklahoma, 1983, p. 190

[27] Mathews, John Joseph, The Osages, Children of the Middle Waters, University of Oklahoma Press, Norman, Oklahoma, 1961, p. 107.

[28] Wright, p. 190

[29] Wright, p. 193

[30] Wright, p. 193

[31] Wright, p. 193

[32] Wright, p. 194

[33] Wright, p. 193

[34] Wright, p. 194-195

[35] Wright, pp. 190,193

[36] Morehouse, George P., *The Kansa or Kaw Indians and Their*

History And The Story of Padilla, State Printing Office, Topeka, Kansas, 1908, p. 5

[37] Finney, Frank F., "The Kaw Indians and Their Indian Territory Agency", *Chronicles of Oklahoma*, V. 35, p. 148

[38] Morehouse, p. 11

[39] Morehouse, p. 10

[40] Morehouse, p. 10

[41] Morehouse, p. 3

[42] Morehouse, p. 4

[43] Morehouse, p. 8

[44] Morehouse, p. 8

[45] Morehouse, p. 8

[46] Morehouse, p. 12

[47] Morehouse, pp. 12-13

[48] Morehouse, p. 15.

[49] Haucke, Frank, "The Kaw or Kansa Indians", *The Kansas Historical Quarterly*, Topeka, Kansas, 1952, p. 37

[50] Haucke, p. 37

[51] Morehouse, pp. 20-22

[52] Morehouse, p. 22

[53] Mardock, Robert W., "Standing Bear and the Reformers" in *Indian Leaders and Oklahoma's First Statesmen*, edited by H. Glen Jordan and Thomas M. Holm, Oklahoma Series X, Oklahoma Historical Society, 1979, pp. 3-11

[54] Morehouse, pp. 29-31

[55] Wright, p. 161

[56] Bellmard, Moses, "My People the Kaw" in *The Last Run*, The Ponca City Chapter of the Daughters of the American

Revolution, The Courier Printing Co., Ponca City, Oklahoma, 1939, p. 339

[57] Morehouse, p. 38

[58] Hodge, 654; Unrua, William E., *The Kansa Indians,* University of   Oklahoma Press, Norman, Oklahoma, 1971, pp. 41, 148-152

[59] Morehouse, p. 34

[60] Haucke, p. 42

[61] Haucke, pp. 49-50

[62] Haucke, p. 50

[63] Unrua, p. 214

[64] Haucke, p. 53

[65] Haucke, p. 53

[66] Haucke, p. 54

[67] Wright, Muriel, p. 163

[68] Haucke, p. 54-55

[69] Gittinger, pp. 153, 156

[70] Howard, p. 5

[71] Mathews, p. 129

[72] Howard, p. 6

[73] Zimmerman, p. 50

[74] Zimmerman, p. 71

[75] Zimmerman, pp. 179-183

[76] Zimmerman, p. 178

[77] Zimmerman, p. 180

[78] Brown, p. 54

[79] Zimmerman, p. 181

[80] Zimmerman, p. 184

[81] Mardock, p. 101

[82] Mardock, p. 102, 346

[83] Mardock, p. 102

[84] Mardock, p. 102

[85] Howard, p. 33

[86] Howard, p. 33

[87] Zimmerman, p. 72

[88] Zimmerman, p. 207

[89] Zimmerman, p. 216

[90] Zimmerman, p. 218

[91] Brown, p. 55

[92] Brown, p. 56

[93] Mardock, p. 103-104

[94] Brown, p. 57

[95] Gittinger, p. 13

[96] Brown, p. 58

[97] Brown, p. 58

[98] Howard, p. 36

[99] Mardock, pp. 105-106

[100] Clark, J. Standley, "The Killing of Big Snake", *The Chronicles of Oklahoma*, V. 69, 1971, p. 305

[101] Clark, p. 305

[102] Clark, p. 305

[103] Zimmerman, p. 222

[104] Mardock, p. 105

[105] Mardock, p. 105

[106] Mardock, p. 106

[107] Mardock, p. 106

[108] Mardock, p. 107

[109] Mardock p. 107

[110] Brown, p. 59

[112] Clark, p. 307

[113] Clark, p. 307-308

[114] Clark, p. 308

[115] Clark, p. 308-309

[116] Clark, p. 309-310

[117] Clark, p. 310

[118] Clark, p. 302

[119] Clark, p. 311

[120] Clark, p. 312

[121] Clark, p. 312-313

[122] Howard, p. 5

[123] Zimmerman, p. 226-227

[124] Wright, p. 212

[125] Zimmerman, p. 74

[126] Tate, David, "The Nez Perces In Eastern Indian Territory: The Quapaw Agency Experience" in *Oklahoma's Forgotten Indians*, edited by Robert E. Smith, Oklahoma Historical Society, Oklahoma City, 1981, p. 8

[127] Tate, P. 10

[128] Hodges, p. 634

[129] Osborne, Alan, "The Exile of the Nez Perce in Indian

Territory", *The Chronicles of Oklahoma*, p. 450

[130] Osborn, p. 452

[131] Tate, p. 11

[132] Tate, p. 14-15

[133] Tate, p. 17

[134] Tate, p. 20

[135] Nieberding, Velma, "The Nez Perce In The Quapaw Agency", *The Chronicles of Oklahoma,* V.64, p. 30

[136] Tate, p. 21

[137] Tate, p. 23

[138] Osborn, p. 457

[139] Osborn, p. 464

[140] Osborn, p. 469

[141] Osborn, p. 451

[142] Nieberding, p. 24

[143] Osborn, p. 470

[144] Wright, p. 180-181

[145] Wright, p. 181

[146] Wright, p. 181

[147] Wright, p. 32

[148] Wright, p. 249-250

[149] Wright, p. 250

[150] Wright, p. 32-34

[151] Wright, p. 250-251

[152] Whinery, Mrs. R.C. , "Tonkawa Indians", *The Last Run*, p. 346

[153] Green, Donald, *Rural Oklahoma*, Oklahoma Historical Society, Stillwater, Oklahoma, 1977, p. 63

[154] Whinery, p. 346

[155] Whinery, p. 346

[156] Pioneer Genealogy Society, *Cemetery Inscriptions of Kay County, Oklahoma, The-Go-Ye Mission Inc., Tahlequah, Oklahoma*, 1978, p. 504. The Tonkawa tribe Indian Cemetery is located two miles east and two and one-half miles south of Highways 177 and 60.

ENDNOTES: CHAPTER THREE

[1] Carroll, L.F. Manuscript, June 1, 1938, Newkirk, Oklahoma

[2] Rhinehart, Mrs. Bennett, Blase Marks on the Border: The Story of Arkansas City, Kansas, Mennonite Press, North Newton, Kansas, 1970. p. 168

[3] Hoig, Stan, #1, "The Old Payne Trail and The Boomer Colony Sites", *The Chronicles of Oklahoma*, V. 58, p. 197, Henderson, James C., "The Reminiscence of a Range Rider", *The Oklahoma Chronicles*, v.3, p. 256

[4] Niemann, George H., " Doctor Rides The Buffalo Trails", *The Last Run*, Ponca City, Chapter of DAR, Courier Printing Co., Ponca City, OK, 1939, p. 14

[5] *The Ponca City News*, "Historic Rock Falls Lived and Died Twice as a Town", September 19, 1976, p. 8C

[6] Hoig, #1, p. 150

[7] Savage, William W., Jr., The Cherokee Livestock Association: Federal Regulation and the Cattlemen's Last Frontier, University of Missouri Press, Columbia, Missouri, 1973 p. 33

[8] Rainey, George, *The Cherokee Strip,* Cooperative Publishing Company, Guthrie, Oklahoma, 1933, p. 50

[9] Marriott, Alice Lee and Carol K. Rachlin, *Oklahoma: The 46th Star,* Doubleday, Garden City, New York, 1973, p. 41

[10] Gibson, Arrell, *Oklahoma- A History of Five Centuries*, University of Oklahoma Press, Norman, Oklahoma, 1965, p. 279

[11] Skaggs, Jimmy, "Cattle Trails in Oklahoma", *Ranch and Range in Oklahoma*, Volume 8, The Oklahoma Series, Oklahoma Historical Society, Oklahoma City, Oklahoma, 1978, pp. 7-8

[12] Skaggs, p. 9

[13] Inscription on the Cherokee Outlet historical marker located in front of the Pioneer Woman Museum, Ponca City, Oklahoma

[14] Savage, p. 16

[15] Savage, p. 18

[16] Savage, p. 19

[17] Savage, p. 19-20

[18] Savage, p. 25-26

[19] Savage, p. 34-35

[20] Savage, p. 47-48

[21] Savage, p. 51-54

[22] Savage, p. 51-54

[23] Savage, p. 54-63

[24] Savage, William, #2, "Indian Ranchers", *Ranch and Range in Oklahoma*, pp. 32-33

[25] Woodruff, Burton G., *Stories of Tonkawa Area Settlers as told by their Descendants*, compiled by Marilu Helton, Eleanor Hays, and Velva Rence, 1993, no page number.

[26] Woodruff, no page number

[27] Woodruff, no page number

[28] Rainey, pp. 192-193

[29] Montgomery, T.T., Lotta Mosier, Imogene Bethel, *The Growth of Oklahoma,* The Economy Co. Publishers, Oklahoma City, 1935, p. 122

[30] Rainey, p. 173

[31] Rainey, pp. 174-175

[32] Hoig, Stan, #2, *David L. Payne: The Oklahoma Boomer*, Western Heritage Books, Oklahoma, 1980, p. 75

[33] Hoig, #2   pp. ii-xiii

[34] Hoig, #2   pp, 60-66

[35] Hoig, #2   p, 71

[36] Hoig, #2   p, 192

[37] Hoig, #2   pp, 187-190

[38] Hoig, #2   p, 191

[39] Hoig, #2   pp, 191-192

[40] Hoig, #2   pp, 192-194

[41] Hoig, #2   pp, 194-196

[42] Hoig, #2   pp, 191, 197

[43] Hoig, #2   p, 198

[44] Hoig, #2   pp, 199-200

[45] Hoig, #2   p, 214

[46] Hoig, #2   pp, 216-217; Montgomery, p. 139

[47] Rainey, pp. 167-168

[48] Rainey, pp. 169-171

[49] Wright, Mutiel, *Indian Tribes of Oklahoma*, University of Oklahoma Press, Norman, Oklahoma, 1983, pp. 251-252

[50] Wright, p. 163

ENDNOTES: CHAPTER FOUR

[1] Gibson, Arrell, *Oklahoma – A History of the Five Centuries*, University of Oklahoma Press, Norman, 1964, p. 289

[2] Milam, Joe B., #1, "The Opening of the Cherokee Outlet", *The Chronicles of Oklahoma*, V. 9, p. 277

[3] Milam, #1, p. 277

[4] Milam, #1, pp. 277-278

[5] Milam, #1, pp. 281-282

[6] Gillespie, Mrs. G.W., " G.W. Gillespie, G.C. Smith, and M.L. Smith" in *The Last Run*, Ponca City Chapter   DAR, Courier   Printing, Ponca City, p. 231

[7] Rainey, George, *The Cherokee Strip*, Co-operative Publishing Co.,   Guthrie, Oklahoma, 1933, p. 276-277

[8] Rainey, p. 275

[9] Milam, #1, p. 284

[10] Rainey, p. 276

[11] The Cherokee Outlet had been surveyed between 1871 and 1874   by the United States Government,   and   divided   into counties May 20, 1890, three years   before the Cherokee ceded it to the United States.

[12] Milam, #1, p. 285

[13] Milam, #1, pp. 454-455

[14] Milam, #1, pp. 457-458

[15] Milam, #1, pp. 455-457

[16] Rainey, pp. 268, 275

[17]   Boone, Marijane R., *Newkirk and Kay County Diamond Jubilee,*   no publisher, no date or page.

[18] Milam, #1, pp. 465-466

[19] Milam, #1, pp. 465,467

[20] Milam, #1, pp. 467,470

[21] Rainey, p. 269

[22] Rainey, pp. 273-275

[23] Milam, #1, pp. 458-459

[24] Rainey, p. 262. These fees were eventually eliminated by Dennis Flynn's "Free Homes Bill'.

[25] Milam, #1, p. 457

[26] Inscription on the historical marker erected by Cher-Ok-Kan Gateway Association.

[27] Milam, #1, p. 464

[28] Milam, #2, p. 115

[29] Cunningham, Robert E., *Indian Territory: A Frontier Record* by W.S. Prettyman, University of Oklahoma Press, Norman, Oklahoma, 1957, p. 147; Burger, John S., "Early History of Kay County", *The Last Run*; Little Standing Buffalo, Obie, "Mun-zah-ska Nu-Puha", The Last Run, p. 347

[30] Milam, #2, p. 117

[31] Rainey, pp. 283-284

[32] Hackney, Frank B., "Young Man, You Better Get On", *The Last Run*, p.254

[33] Milam, #2, pp. 117-119

[34] Milam, #2, p. 124

[35] Milam, #2, pp. 122-123

[36] Milam, #2, p. 130

[37] Milam, #2, p. 125

[38] Rainey, pp. 306-307

ENDNOTES: CHAPTER FIVE

[1] Wade, J.S., "Uncle Sam's Horse-Race for Land: The Opening of the Cherokee Strip", *Chronicles of Oklahoma*, V. 35, p. 151

[2] Thomas, A.M., "Notes and Documents", *Chronicles of Oklahoma*, V. 21, p. 423

[3] Thomas, p. 423

[4] Milam, Joe B., "The Opening of the Cherokee Outlet", *Chronicles of Oklahoma*, V. 9, p. 454

[5] Crawford, G.C., "My Race", *The Last Run*, p. 65

[6] Nix, Margaret, "The Romantic Days of the Run are Over", *The Last Run*, p. 35

[7] Kygar, Dan W., "Dan W. and John B. Kygar", *The Last Run*, p. 21

[8] Kygar, *The Last Run*, p. 21

[9] *Ponca City News*, NCOHA files

[10] Nieman, George H., "A Doctor Rides the Buffalo Trails", *The Last Run*, p. 14

[11] Johnson, Bobby H., in "Rural Oklahoma", Edited by Donald E. Greene, Oklahoma Historical Society, Stillwater, 1977, p. 9

[12] Smith, Patricia A., unpublished manuscript, North Central Oklahoma Historical Association file.

[13] Johnson, p. 10

[14] Boone, Marijane, *Newkirk and Kay County Diamond Jubilee*, no publisher, no date, no page

[15] Thomas, A.M., "Early Day County Organization", *The Last Run, Kay County Oklahoma, 1893,* Ponca City Chapter Daughters of The American Revolution, Courier Printing Company, Ponca City, Oklahoma, 1939, p. 304

[16] Thomas, p. 304

[17] Rainey, George, *The Cherokee Strip,* Cooperative Publishing Co., Guthrie, Oklahoma,933, pp. 322-323

[18] Rainey, pp. 338-341

[19] Rainey, pp. 483-484

[20] Nix, p. 36

[21] Dye, Karen, "Socio-Economic Development of Newkirk, Oklahoma", an unpublished thesis, Norman, Oklahoma, 1992, p. 35

[22] Constant, Clella May (Wimer), in *Keepsakes and Yesteryears,* compiled and published by Bethel and Crescent Extension Homemakers of Kay County, V. 1 1981, p. 180

[23] Constant, p. 8

[24] Gasaway, Ruth, in *Keepsakes and Yesteryears, p. 11*

[25] Hadley, Mrs. A.D., "Corn-Bread College", *The Last Run, p. 176*

[26] Bellinghausen, Mrs. L.L., in *Keepsakes and Yesteryears, pp. 29-30* **********

[27] Riggs, Mamie Bissell, "Edgar and Aldia Bissell", *Rooted In The Past-Growing For The Future*, North Central Oklahoma Historical Association, Jostens, Topeka, 1995, p 48

[28] Means, Frances H., "History of the Dale School and the Chilocco Area In Northern Kay County", as told to Nancy Hope Sober

- -

[59] Dye, Karen, "Kildare", unpublished manuscript, 1990 p. 1

[60] Dye, p. 1-2

[61] Littlefield, pp. 31-32

[62] Littlefield, pp. 35-37

[63] Owen, Sena B., "Hugh B. Owen, A Pioneer Democrat", in *The Last Run, p. 110*

[64] Dye, p. 14

[65] Dye, p. 12

[66] Dye, p. 5

[67] Dye, p. 19

[68] *Ponca City News*, September 12, 1993, p. 9KK

[69] Carroll, L.F., unpublished manuscript. NCOHA files

[70] Dye, p. 8

[71] Littlefield, pp. 34-39

[72] *Ponca City News*, 1976

[73] Morris, John, *Ghost Towns of Oklahoma*, Oklahoma University Press, Norman, Oklahoma,1977 p. 61C

[74] Morris, p. 61C

[75] *Ponca City News*, NCOHA files

[76] Morris, p. 60C

[77] Barnes, Louis Seymour, "The Founding of Ponca City", *The Chronicles of Oklahoma*, V. 34, p. 154

[78] Barnes, p. 162

[79] Barnes, pp. 154-155

[80] Barnes, p. 155

[81] Barnes, p. 158

[82] Barnes, L.S., #1, "The Beginning of Ponca City", in *The Last Run, p. 4*

[83] Barnes, pp. 157-158 and 161

[84] Newsome, Earl D., *The Cherokee Strip: Its History and Grand Opening,* New Forum Press Inc., Stillwater, Oklahoma, 1992 p. 101

[85] Barnes, p. 161

[86] Barnes, p. 155

[87] Barnes, L.S.., #2 "Cross Moves To Ponca City", in *The Last Run, p. 51*

[88] Newsome, p. 100

[89] Barnes, p. 160

[90] Newsome, p. 99

[91] Morris, p. 63C

[92] Newsome, p. 101

[93] Barnes, p. 161

[94] Newsome, p. 101

[95] Barnes, L.S.., #1, p. 5

[96] no author, "The Ponca City Schools", in *The Last Run, p. 46*

[97] no author, in *The Last Run, p. 46-48*

[98] no author, n *The Last Run, p. 46*

[99] Jamieson, Bob, "Made Two Runs", in *The Last Run, p. 175*

[100] Van Winkle, Mrs. Marvin K., in *The Last Run, pp. 107-108*

[101] Robinson, Luke, *Made Out of Mud*, Western History Collections, University of Oklahoma, Norman, Oklahoma, 1980,
p. 169

[102] Chambers, #1, p, 25

[103] Chambers, #1, pp. 25-26

[104] Chambers, #1, pp. 25-26 and 28

[105] Blackwell Centennial Board, *Blackwell, Jewel of the Chikaskia*, 1993, no page

[106] Blackwell Centennial Board, no page

[107] Chambers, #1, p. 32

[108] *Ponca City News*, September 19, 1976, p. 12C

[109] *Ponca City News*, p. 12C

[110] Bickford, Warren, "The Blackwell Story: 1893 to 1953", in the *Blackwell Journal,* September 2, 1953, no page, NCOHA files

[111] Blackwell Centennial Historical Committee, no page number

[112] Bickford, no page

[113] Chambers, #1, p. 75

[114] Chambers, #1, pp. 78-79

[115] Chambers, #1, p. 97

[116] Chambers, #1, pp. 105-107

[117] Chambers, Homer S., #2, "Early Railroad Building Operations In Western Oklahoma", in *The Chronicles of Oklahoma*, V. 21, p. 162

[118] Chambers, #1, p. 108

[119] Chambers, #2, p. 162

[120] Chambers, #2, pp. 162-164

[121] Chambers, #1, p. 40

[122] Chambers, #2, pp. 164-167

[123] Chambers, #1, pp. 85-86

[124] Chambers, #1, pp. 89-92

[125] Bickford, no page

[126] Watts, Fred G., "A Brief History of Higher Education Among the Baptists of Oklahoma", *Chronicles of Oklahoma*, V. 27, p. 28

[127] Tannehill, Opal (Harris), "Charlie Wimer's Ryland Fox's Bethel School", in *Keepsakes and Yesteryears*, p. 182

128 Bickford, no page

129 Bickford, no page

130 Bickford, no page

ENDNOTES: CHAPTER SIX

[1] Corbett, William P., "Peerless Princess of the Best Country: The Early Years of Tonkawa", *Chronicles of Oklahoma,* V. 62 pp. 388-390

[2] Corbett, pp. 390-391

[3] Corbett, pp. 392-394; Chamber, Homer S., *The Enduring Rock: History and Reminiscences of Blackwell, Oklahoma, and the Cherokee Strip,* Blackwell Publications, Black, Oklahoma, 1954, p. 118

[4] Corbett, pp. 394-395, 398

[5] Corbett, pp. 395-396

[6] Corbett, pp. 399-400

[7] Corbett, pp. 397-399

[8] Corbett, pp. 402-403

[9] Corbett, p. 403

[10] Corbett, p. 404

[11] Bradley, Mac Hefton., *From U.P.S. To N.O.C.., 1901-1976: The First Seventy- Five Years of Northern Oklahoma College,* Northern Oklahoma College, Tonkawa, Oklahoma, 1976, pp. 2-4

[12] Bradley, p. 4

[13] Bradley, pp. 13-15

[14] Bradley, pp. 16-19

[15] Bradley, p. 37

[16] Bradley, pp. 35,42

[17] Bradley, pp. 42-43

[18] Bradley, p. 45

[19] Bradley, pp. 46-47

[20] Bradley, p. 53

[21] *Ponca City News,* September 19, 1976, p. 8C

[22] *Blackwell Journal-Tribune,* Blackwell, Oklahoma, Wednesday, May 29, 1985, no page, NCOHA,Inc. Files

[23] Sober, Hope, "Braman", manuscript at North Central Oklahoma Historical Association, July, 1995, pp. 1-2

[24] Crow, L.V., "The Nardin, Oklahoma Story", unpublished manuscript, 1994, p. 1

[25] Crow, p. 1

[26] Crow, p. 1

[27] Crow, p. 2

[28] Crow, pp. 1-5

[29] *Ponca City News,* September 19, 1976, pp. 3-10

[30] NCOHA files

[31] *Ponca City News,* September 19, 1976, pp. 3C, 6C, 9C, 10C

[32] *Ponca City News,* September 19, 1976, p. 13C

[33] Prather, Paul, "John Wesely Prather" story, *North Central Oklahoma: Rooted in the Past – Growing for the Future,* North Central Central Oklahoma Historical Association Inc., Jostens, Topeka, Kansas, p. 536; George Meece manuscript, "Stories of Tonkawa Area Settlers as told by their Descendants", compiled by Marilu Helton, Eleanor Hays, and Velva Rence, 1993, no page; Dunkin, Kaye, "Charles Meece" story, NCOHA, p. 468

[34] *Ponca City News,* 1976 p. 15C

[35] Lute, Opal, "History of Peckham, Oklahoma", in Fun and

Fundamental Extension Homemakers "Peckham", 1971, no page.

[36] Lute, no page

[37] *Ponca City News,* September 19, 1976, p. 9C

[38] *Ponca City News* p. 15C

[39] *Ponca City News* p. 15C

[40] *Ponca City News* p. 9C

[41] *Ponca City News* p. 14C

[42] Boone, no page

[43] Bacher, Mrs. Lewis E., "History of Uncas", Newkirk Historical Society Meeting, November 30, 1971, p. 1

[44] Bacher, pp. 1-2

[45] Bacher, pp. 2-3

[46] Bacher, p. 3

[47] *Kaw City Star,* V. 1,#2. August 1, 1902, p. 4

[48] George, Mrs. A.E., "The Story of Kaw City", in *The Last Run*, p. 328

[49] Kaw City Townsite brochure, NCOHA files

[50] *Kaw City Star,* V.1, #2 August 1, 1902, p. 4

[51] George, p. 330

[52] Cline, R.W., *Pioneer Bank Diamond Jubilee: 75 Years of Colorful History,* 1977, p. 6

[53] George, pp. 328-329

[54] Boone, Marijane, "Kaw City", *Ponca City News,* September 12, 1993. p. 11KK

[55] George, p. 328

[56] *Ponca City News, "Kaw Lake Covers Indian Town, Washunga",* September 19, 1876, p. 12C

[57] George, p. 329

[58] George, p. 330

[59] Hofsommer, Donovan L., "Kaw and the Railroad", *Chronicles of   Oklahoma,* V. 50, p. 300

[60] George, p. 330

[61] *Ponca City News,* 1976 p. 12C

[62] *Ponca City News,* 1976 p. 12C

[63] *Ponca City News,* 1976 p. 12C

[64] *Ponca City News,* 1976 p. 12C

[65] Cline, Annette, "Charles Curtis" story, *Rooted in the Past – Growing for the Future,* p. 176-177, Finney, Frank, "The Kaw and Their Indian Territory", *Chronicles of Oklahoma,*   V. 35, p. 418

[66] Amos, Howard, "History of Hardy, Oklahoma", Newkirk, Historical Society Meeting, March 14, 1972, p. 1

[67] Amos, p. 1

[68] Amos, pp. 1,3-4

[69] Amos, p. 4

[70] Amos, pp. 1-2

[71] Brett, Ellen P., "History in the Making", Oklahoma Historical Society, pp. 6-7

ENDNOTES: CHAPTER SEVEN

[1] Boone, Marijane, *Newkirk and Kay Country Diamond Jubilee,* no page

[2] Boone, no page

[3] Dye, Karen, Socio-Economic *Development of Newkirk, Oklahoma,* Norman, Oklahoma 1992, p. 51

[4] Boone, no page; Chambers, Homer S., *The Enduring Rock,* pp. 109-111

[5] Calkins, Charles F., "Charles F. Calkins, Pioneer Merchant and Art Collector" in *The Last Run, p. 104*

[6] NCOHO files

[7] *Ponca City News*, September 13, 1963, p. 9B

[8] *Ponca City News*, September 13, 1963, p. 9B

[9] *Ponca City News*, September 13, 1963, p. 9B

[10] *Ponca City News*, September 13, 1963, p. 9B

[11] Collings, Ellsworth and Alma Miller England, *The 101 Ranch,* University of Oklahoma Press, Norman, Oklahoma, 1989 pp. 45-46

[12] Thomas, James H., "The 101: A Matter of Style", in *Ranch and Range in Oklahoma,* edited by Jimmy M. Skaggs, Volume 8, The Oklahoma Series, Oklahoma Historical Society, Oklahoma City, Oklahoma, 1978, p. 81

[13] Thomas, p. 80

[14] Thomas, pp. 84-85; Collins, pp. 89-96

[15] Thomas, pp. 81-84

[16] Thomas, p. 85; Collings, pp. 112-15

[17] Collings, p. 55; Thomas, p. 84

[18] Collings, p. 142; Thomas, p. 85

[19] Collings, pp. 143-144

[20] Thomas, p. 86

[21] Collings, pp. xii and 182

[22] Collings, pp. Xv and 185

[23] Thomas, p. 87; Collings, p. 186

[24] Collings, pp. Xvi-xvii and 216

[25] Collings, pp. 155-157

[26] Collings, pp. 115-117

[27] England, George Miller, "The Millers and the 101", in *The Last Run, pp. 265- 266;* Collings, pp. 201-202

[28] Pioneer Genealogy Society, *Cemetery Inscriptions of Kay County, Oklahoma,* The-Go-Ye Mission Inc., Tahlequah, Oklahoma, 1978, p. 153; O'Brien, Essie Forrester, *Circus, Cinder To Sawdust,* Naylor Company, San Antonio, Texas, 1959, p. 83

[29] Matthews, Jon Joseph, *The Life and Death of an Oilman, The Careet of E,W, Marland, University of Oklahoma Press,* Norman, Oklahoma, 1989, pp. 74 and 79

[30] *Ponca City News,* September 19, 1976

[31] *Ponca City News,* September 19, 1976

[32] NCOHA files

[33] Matthew, p. 65; Fischer, Leroy, *olahoma Governors: 1929-1955,* Oklahoma Historical Society, Oklahoma City, Oklahoma, 1983, p. 50

[34] Collings, p. 103

[35] Collings, p. 104

[36] Collings, pp. 105 and 212

[37] Van Winkle, Mrs. Marvin K., in *The Last Run,* pp. 107, 108; "The story of Ernest W. Marland", *in The Last Run* pp. 220-222; Fischer, p. 80

[38] No author, Conoco: The First One Hundred Years, published by Special Marketing Division, Dell Publishing Co. Inc, New York, 1975, p. 80;   Mathews, p. 158; Matthews, p. 158

[39] Sachet, Corb, "The Story of Lewis Haines Wentz", in *The Last Run,* p. 212;   Glasscock, C.B., *Then Came Oil: The Story of the Last Frontier,* the Bobbs-Merrill Company, New York, 1938, p. 280

[40] Gilbert, James Leslie, *Three Sands: Oklahoma Oil Field and Community of the 1920's,* published thesis, Norman, Oklahoma, 1967, pp. 47-48

[41] *Ponca City News*, May 16, 1976, p.13G

[42] Bradfield, Joyce, "Social Development of Kay County, Oklahoma, University of Colorado Masters Thesis, 1941, pp. 81, 85

[43] *Ponca City News*, September 19, 1976, p. 14C

[44] Dye, Karen, unpublished manuscript, pp. 1-3, NCOHA files

[45] *Ponca City News*, "Business Good In Dilworth – While Boom Lasted", September 19, 1976, p. 5C

[46] Dye, p. 8: *Ponca City News*, p. 5C

[47] *Ponca City News*, September 19, 1976, pp. 13C and 16C

[48] Gilbert, pp. 10-11, 50 and 79

[49] Gilbert, pp. 50, 78, 80-81

[50] Gilbert, pp. 81-82

[51] Gilbert, pp. 82-86; 104-105

[52] Gilbert, pp. 92-94

[53] Gilbert, pp. 91-97

[54] Gilbert, pp. 97-100

[55] Gilbert, pp. 106-111

[56] Gilbert, pp. 112-113

[57] Gilbert, pp. 113 and 122

[58] Gilbert, pp. 114-115

[59] O'Mealey, LaFreda, North Central Oklahoma Historical Association, Inc. "Elmer Wallace O'Mealey", in *North Central Oklahoma: Rooted and the Past – Growing for the Future,* Jostens, Topeka, 1995, p. 502

[60] Gilbert, pp. 115-118

[61] Gilbert, pp. 121-122

[62] Gilbert, pp. 118-120

[63] Gilbert, pp. 123

[64] Kaw City Museum files

[65] Kaw City Museum files

[66] *Ponca City News*, September 19, 1976, p. 12C

[67] Matthews, pp. 100-101

[68] Matthews, p. 105

[69] Matthews, pp. 169-170

[70] Matthews, p. 177

[71] Matthews, pp. 180-181

[72] NCOHA files

[73] *Harlow's Weekly*, September 20, 1930, p. 3

[74] NCOHA files

[75] *Ponca City News*, September 14, 1949, NCOHA files

[76] NCOHA files

[77] *The Last Run, pp. 102-105*

[78] Ponca City Library, "Richard Gordon Matzene Art Collection Directory", no publisher, back cover.

[79] Matthews,

[80] Sarchet, Corb, "The Story of Lewis Haines Wentz (Oil Man and Philanthropist", in *The Last Run, pp. 214-215; Ponca City News, September12, 1993, p. 7MM*

[81] Muchmore, Gareth, "McFadden Oil Industry Giant", in *Ponca City New*, September 12, 1993, p. 9MM: Matthews, p. 179

[82] "Early Day Baseball Teams", in *The Last Run, p. 173*

[83] *Ponca City News*, "Ponca City Minor League Baseball Reunion", June 22,1994, p.1B

[84] Boone, no page

[85] Matthews, pp. 197-198

[86] Collings, p. 207

ENDNOTES: CHAPTER 8

[1] No author, "Brick Street Study", Historic Preservation Advisory Panel, 1992. NCOHA files

[2] *Ponca City News*, "Storm Damage Estimated at $500,000", April 18, 1935, p. 1

[3] Everman, Michael, in Leroy Fisher's, *Oklahoma Governors 1925- 1955: Depression and Prosperity,* Volumn 19, Oklahoma Historical Society, Oklahoma City, Oklahoma, 1983 pp. 79-85

[4] Bradfield, Joyce, "Social Development of Kay County, Oklahoma", University of Colorado, Master Thesis, 1941, pp. 81, 85

[5] Everman, pp. 83-85

[6] Everman, pp. 86, 89, 98

[7] Oates, Mrs. W.T., "History of the Ponca City Library", in *The Last Running- Aft,* Courier Printing Company, Ponca City, Oklahoma, 1939, p. 60

[8] Hendrickson, Kenneth E., Jr., "Jobs for Students: The National Youth Administration in Oklahoma", in Kenneth E. Hendrickson Jr., ed., *Hard Times in Oklahoma: The Depression Years,* Oklahoma Historical Society, Oklahoma City, Oklahoma, 1983, pp. 122-133

[9] Hendrickson, p. 133

[10] Bradley, Mac Hefton, *A History of 75 Years from U.P.S. To N.O.C..,* *Northern Oklahoma College,* Tonkawa, Oklahoma, 1976, pp. 55-56

[11] Bradley, p. 56

[12] Bradley, p. 60

[13] Bradley, pp. 69,89

[14] Bradley, p. 81

[15] Blumer, Elizabeth, unpublished manuscript of taped interviews with the Dent, Blumer and Bonfy families, N.C.O.H.A. files

[16] Blumer, N.C.O.H.A. files

[17] Blumer, N.C.O.H.A. files

[18] Blumer, N.C.O.H.A. files

[19] Blumer, N.C.O.H.A. files

[20] Blumer, N.C.O.H.A. files

[21] Bradley, N.C.O.H.A. files

[22] *Ponca City News*, May 7, 1945

[23] *Ponca City News*, May 7, 1945

[24] *Ponca City News*, May 7, 1945

[25] Bradley, pp. 88, 95

[26] NCOHA files

[27] Zehr, Kathy, "Tonkawa Prisoner of War Camp Officially Closed   50 Years Ago", *Ponca City News*, August 23, 1995, p. 3C;   and September 27,1995, p. 6C

[28] *Ponca City News*, August 22, 1990, p. 2C

[29] Personal interview of J.C. Carmack by Paula Carmack Denson, August 28, 1994, NCOHA file

[30] Honorable discharge papers of Helen Pappan, NCOHA files

[31]   Personal interview with Lyn Boyer, September 28,1995;

NCOHA files

[32] Crow, L.V., manuscript, NCOHA files

[33] Pioneer Genealogy Society, *Cemetery Inscriptions of Kay County, Oklahoma,* The-Go-Yeh Missions, Inc., Tahlequah, Oklahoma, 1978, p. 159

[34] NCOHA files

[35] *Ponca City News*, September 19, 1976, p.10C

[36] Tonkawa Historical Society, NCOHA files

[37] Seubert, Helen, Blackwell Journal Tribune, September 15, 1993, p. 2C-3C

[38] Reutter, Madelien, NCOHA files

[39] Johnston, Jerry, NCOHA files

[40] Seubert, Helen, *Blackwell Journal Tribune,* September 15, 1993, p. 5D, 8D

[41] Dye, Karen, NCOHA files

[42] *Ponca City News*,"Kay County Farm Recognized With Historical Society Award", October 27, 1993, p. 1C

[43] *Ponca City News*, "Chilocco Established in 1884", September 12, 1993, pp. 4, 11

[44] Courtesy of D. (Dutton) Barrington (1985), NCOHA files

[45] *Ponca City News*, August 21, 1995, p. 5A

[46] NCOHA files

MAPS

Indian Territory

Cattle Trails

Railroads

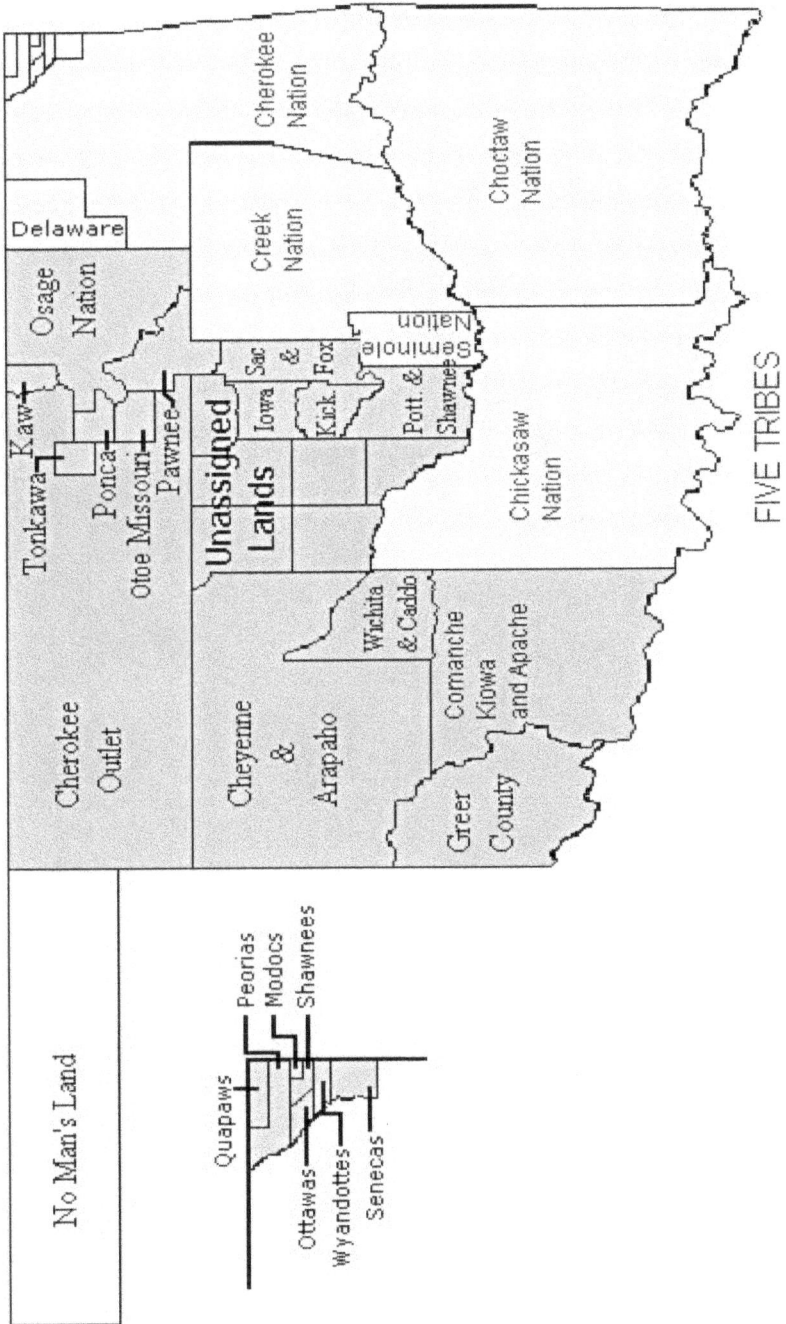

See Cutout

Cherokee Nation

Choctaw Nation

Delaware

Creek Nation

Osage Nation

Seminole Nation

Sac & Fox

Kaw

Iowa

Kick.

Pott. & Shawnee

Tonkawa

Ponca

Otoe Missouri

Pawnee

Unassigned Lands

Chickasaw Nation

Cherokee Outlet

Wichita & Caddo

Cheyenne & Arapaho

Comanche Kiowa and Apache

Greer County

No Man's Land

Peorias

Modocs

Shawnees

Quapaws

Ottawas

Wyandottes

Senecas

FIVE TRIBES

261

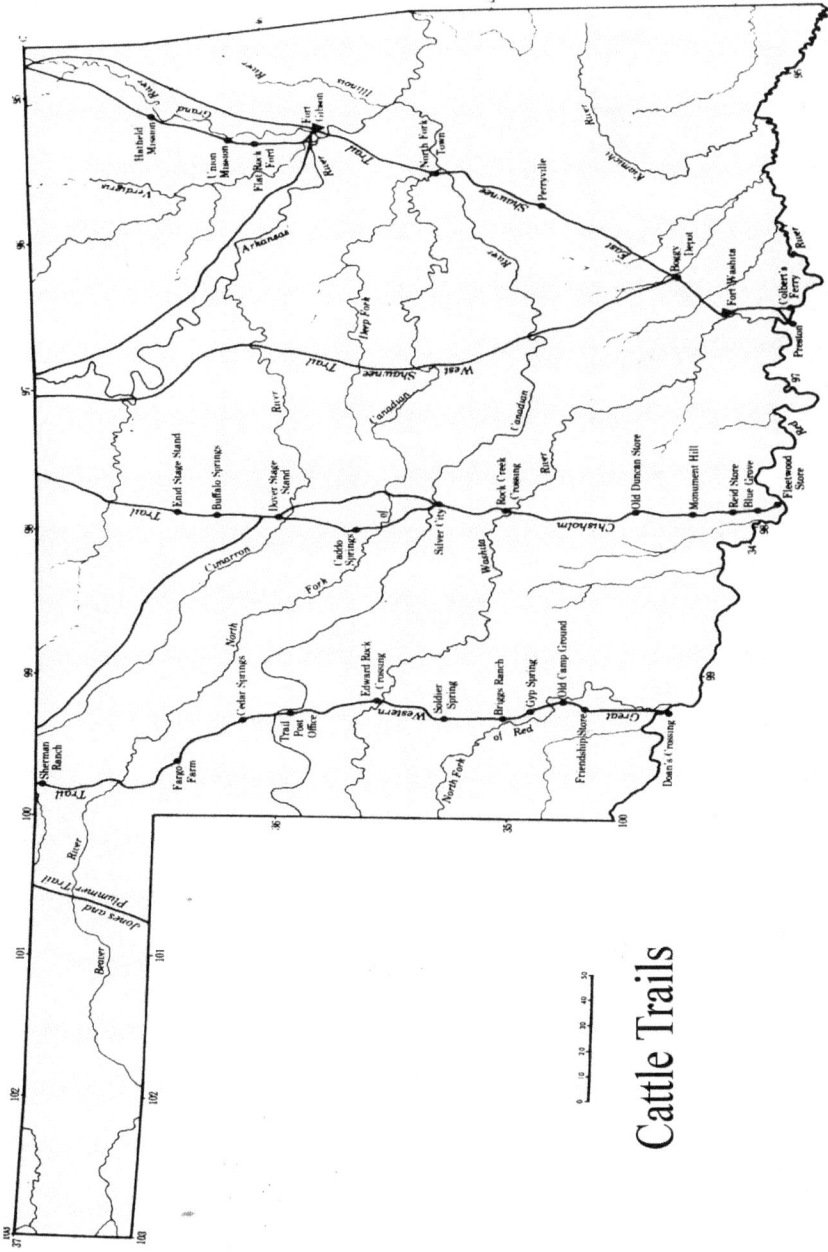

Cattle Trails

0 10 20 30 40 50

263

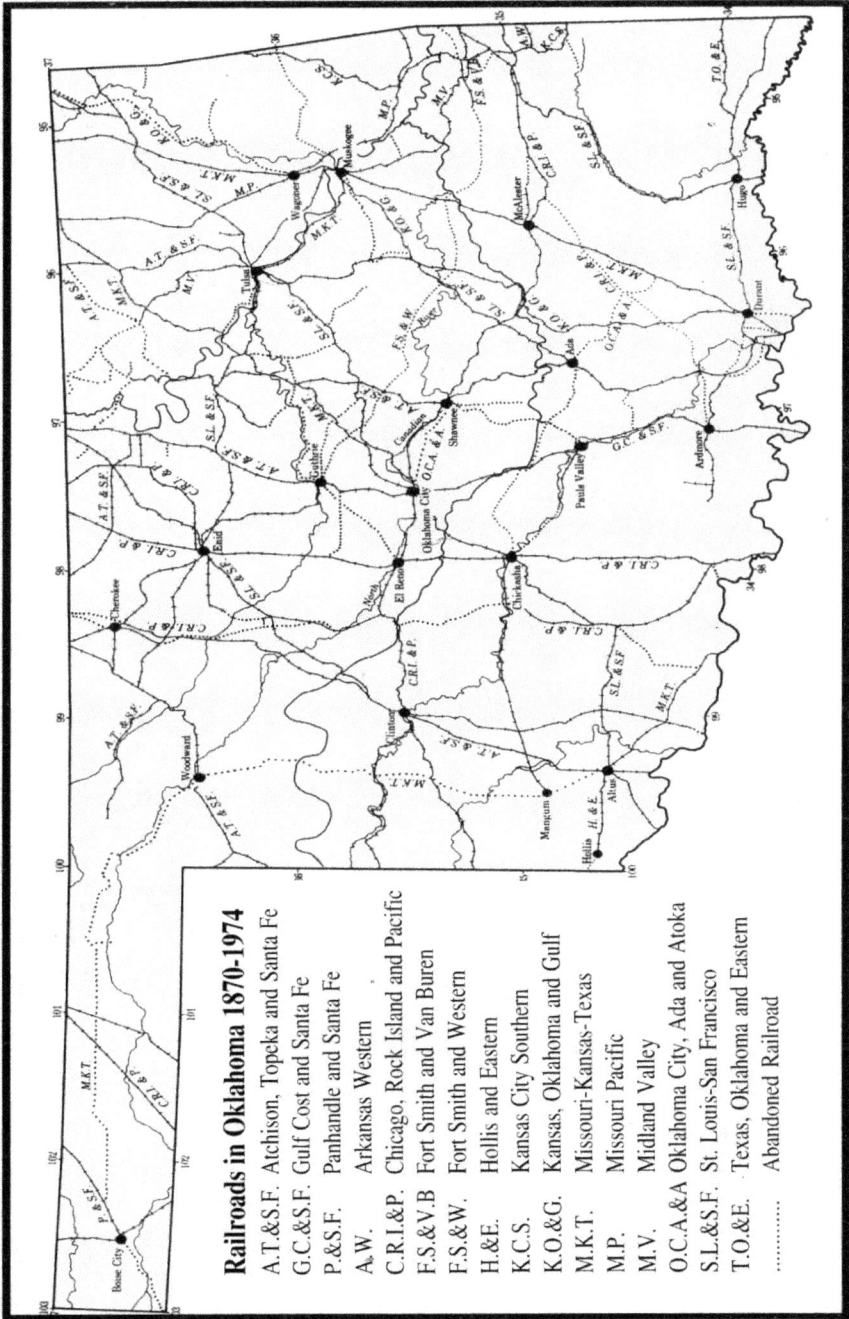

Railroads in Oklahoma 1870-1974

A.T.&S.F.	Atchison, Topeka and Santa Fe
G.C.&S.F.	Gulf Cost and Santa Fe
P.&S.F.	Panhandle and Santa Fe
A.W.	Arkansas Western
C.R.I.&P.	Chicago, Rock Island and Pacific
F.S.&V.B	Fort Smith and Van Buren
F.S.&W.	Fort Smith and Western
H.&E.	Hollis and Eastern
K.C.S.	Kansas City Southern
K.O.&G.	Kansas, Oklahoma and Gulf
M.K.T.	Missouri-Kansas-Texas
M.P.	Missouri Pacific
M.V.	Midland Valley
O.C.A.&A	Oklahoma City, Ada and Atoka
S.L.&S.F.	St. Louis-San Francisco
T.O.&E.	Texas, Oklahoma and Eastern
....	Abandoned Railroad

**If you would like to
recommend our book to others,
you can send them to our
website to find purchase links:**

http://PoncaCityOkla.com/

www.ingramcontent.com/pod-product-compliance
Lightning Source LLC
Chambersburg PA
CBHW072033090426
42733CB00032B/1287